this day with the master

365 daily meditations

this day with the master

365 daily meditations

dennis f. kinlaw
with christiane a. albertson

GRAND RAPIDS, MICHIGAN 49530 USA

This Day with the Master
Copyright © 2002 by the Francis Asbury Society

Requests for information should be addressed to:
Zondervan, *Grand Rapids, Michigan 49530*

Library of Congress Cataloging-in-Publication Data

Kinlaw, Dennis F., 1922–
     This day with the master : 365 daily meditations / Dennis F. Kinlaw.—
  1st ed.
       p. cm.
     Includes index.
     ISBN 0-310-25570-8 (hardcover)
     1. Devotional calendars   I. Title.
  BV4811.K456 2004
  242'.2—dc22

                                        2004013478

This edition printed on acid-free paper.

Interior design by Michelle Espinoza

Printed in the United States of America

---

05 06 07 08 09 /❖ DC/ 10 9 8 7 6 5 4 3 2

To Elsie,
whom, next to God the Father,
God the Son, and God the Holy Spirit,
I have enjoyed most
and to whom I am most indebted

acknowledgments

God's greatest gift to any of us is himself. He came to Moses in a burning bush. He came to Saul on the road to Damascus. He has always come to me through persons who, in giving him, always gave themselves. And persons, like God, always come in families. It is in our physical, spiritual, and intellectual families that we find our life, our identity, and our treasures. If there is anything of value in the pages that follow, you can be sure that its origin is in someone else. All that I have, I have learned through one of the families that God has given me.

Families are made up of persons. Therefore it seems appropriate that I should mention some of the ones who have given the most. It was Sally and Wade that gave me life and put me in a context where I could not escape Christ.

From Anna and Sam came Elsie and the support that made a treasured education possible. Mother Clark was the one who brought me to Jesus in a camp meeting context. Harold Kuhn, Otto Piper, and Cyrus Gordon opened the worlds of philosophy and Scripture. Asbury clarified my calling; OMS exposed me to a world beyond America and the West; and the Francis Asbury Society, through the vision of Harold Burgess, Don Winslow, Paul Blair, John Oswalt, Jess Correll, Winston Handwerker, and others, provided the medium through which I could pay a bit of my debt to God and the world.

This volume could not have been compiled without the encouragement, financially and otherwise, of Albert, Burt, and Joe Luce, among others, and the willingness of Asbury College to provide access to numerous tapes for transcription. The one who actually birthed this work through considerable labor has been my own granddaughter, Cricket Albertson. She is a special joy and a most valued member of my physical, intellectual, and spiritual family. To all of these and the numberless host of others I would indicate my humble gratitude.

Dennis F. Kinlaw
Wilmore, Kentucky

january 1

the new year

isaiah 43:16–21

I will give you every place where you set your foot, as I promised Moses.
Joshua 1:3

The new year brings hope. As we look into the year that opens before us, we would like to think that it could be better than the one behind us. That yearning for something better is a gift from God and a promise that the hope can be realized. God wants the year before you to be the best that you have ever had. The key lies in where you look for fulfillment. It must not be within yourself, for your resources have not suddenly increased. You need resources that are fresh and new and can enable you to claim a measure of effectiveness and fulfillment that you have not yet known.

God is the God who wants to make all things new, and his presence can be recognized by the element of radical promise that confronts us when we come to know him. With God comes the word that the future can be better than the present. When Abraham met God, the experience contained a promise staggeringly large. It was that the barrenness of an old woman and the emptiness of a home would change. In the meeting when God met Moses was the assurance that he was made for more than defeat and shepherding. The promise was given to him that God would use him to set his people free. In fact, Moses was to be God's man to build a nation. In Joshua's relationship to God was the promise that God had a land for his wandering people. In David's communion with God, he learned that God intended to give his people a capital city, a temple, and a throne that would last forever. The Hebrew prophets told of the King who would sit on that throne, one greater than Moses or David, and of a kingdom of people with new hearts where the will of God was not an external command but an inward delight. John the Baptist announced his own role as the messenger who had come to tell the people that the kingdom of heaven was at hand.

The very mark of the people of God in the Old Testament was that their faces were turned toward the future and were marked by confidence and expectation. Can we who live on this side of Bethlehem, Calvary, Easter, and Pentecost do otherwise?

all things new

revelation 21

He who was seated on the throne said, "I am making everything new!" Then
he said, "Write this down, for these words are trustworthy and true."
Revelation 21:5

Yesterday we spoke of the fact that the people of God are marked by the set
of their faces. They look to the future, and they look with anticipation.
Implicit in fellowship with God is the promise that the best is yet to be. Of
course, there are those in the Old Testament who did not see this. One who
seems to be in that class is the writer of Ecclesiastes, who says that there is
nothing new under the sun, that what has been will always be, that all things
are wearisome, more wearisome than one can express (Eccl. 1:8–10). But
this is a minority voice in the Old Testament.

- The psalmist tells us of a new song that the Lord has given him
  (Ps. 42:8).
- Isaiah writes of new things to be learned and a new name (Isa. 42:9;
  62:2) and of a new heaven and a new earth (Isa. 65:17; 66:22).
- Jeremiah proclaims a new covenant and new mercies every morning
  (Jer. 31:31; Lam. 3:22–23).
- Ezekiel tells of a new spirit and a new heart (Ezek. 11:19; 18:31;
  36:26).

The New Testament picks up this theme and promises

- a new birth (1 Peter 1:3),
- a new life (Rom. 6:23),
- a new self (Eph. 4:24; Col. 3:10),
- a new attitude (Eph. 4:23),
- a new commandment (John 13:34),
- a new and living way (Heb. 10:20),
- a new creation (2 Cor. 5:17; Gal. 6:15), and
- a new heaven and a new earth (2 Peter 3:13; Rev. 21:1).

It should be no surprise for us, after we have looked at all the above, to
find the concluding word coming from God himself, "I am making all

things new" (Rev. 21:5). Apparently God never quits making things better because this word comes as the last word in human history. He is the God of eternal renewal.

But what about the author of Ecclesiastes' doleful words? He may be a keener observer than we thought. He says there is nothing new under the sun, and he is right. The true newness never comes from us, from the natural. It comes from beyond us, from the God with whom we have the privilege of walking. Our response has to be: Everything is new under the Son, for it is he who makes all things new.

the holy one

isaiah 63

In all their distress he too was distressed,
and the angel of his presence saved them.
In his love and mercy he redeemed them;
he lifted them up and carried them
all the days of old.
Isaiah 63:9

We have been thinking about the possibilities that come with the presence of God in our lives. The guarantee of that presence, though, can never be assumed. It is conditional. All of the Old Testament illustrates this.

God is God alone and is to have no rival or competitor in our lives. He is offended and grieved when we let anything invade that central place intended for him. He is saddened because we inevitably suffer when we let anything encroach on his rights and place. The psalmist understood this. In Psalm 16:4 he notes that sorrows increase for those who "run after other gods," so he will not participate in offerings or praises given by those with divided hearts. He confesses that Yahweh is Lord and that even the good ceases to be good when God is not in control. That is why Jesus was firm in his insistence that we should seek his rule first (Matt. 6:33).

God is God alone, and he is also the Holy One. He hates all that is unclean and all that defiles. As the Holy One, he is a consuming fire. But his burning character was never intended to be destructive to us. It is his means of purging us as he did Isaiah (Isa. 6:5–7). If we care more about his presence with us than we do about our sins and uncleanness, then he will consume our defilements and make us pure. If we become more committed to our sins than we are to him, then his presence becomes destructive to us because of the corruption to which we are wedded.

Israel had rejected the preaching of Jeremiah, so God permitted Ezekiel to witness the removal of his presence from Jerusalem. Ezekiel watched as the glory of God, his holy presence, rose from above the ark and from between the cherubim in the Holy of Holies. He saw it move to the threshold of the temple and then leave the city and move to a distant mountaintop. God departed from his people (Ezek. 10:1–20). The result was the destruction of the temple and city and the exile of Israel for seventy years in Babylon. God the Holy One could not live with Israel's sin.

The beauty of all this lies in the fact that God's presence is better than the experience or the rewards of our sin. And he has the power to make us clean. Charles Wesley understood this and sang about it:

He breaks the power of canceled sin,
he sets the prisoner free;
his blood can make the foulest clean,
*his blood availed for me.**

If we let the Holy One purge us, we will have reason to sing as well.

*Charles Wesley, "O for a Thousand Tongues," *Hymns for Praise and Worship* (Nappanee, Ind.: Evangel Press, 1984), no. 81.

face to race

revelation 22:1 – 5

And I—in righteousness I will see your face;
when I awake, I will be satisfied with seeing your likeness.
Psalm 17:15

I have always been enamored with the work of Michelangelo. I remember having the chance to spend a few moments in the Sistine Chapel in Rome. Longing to carry some of the splendor with me, I bought some tremendous photographs. One of them was the famous scene of God creating man. Michelangelo was an absolute master of painting the human form, and in this painting Adam is strong, muscular, and vigorous, but he is also lifeless. God's finger is extended, and the spark of life goes into Adam. Adam's face is positioned so that when the spark of life comes into his being from the finger of God and consciousness breaks into his soul, his eyes open, and he sees his first sight. The first image Adam beholds with his eyes is the face of God. This is the way human creatures are to live, gaining life from the finger of God and gazing into his face.

For it is the God who commanded light to shine out of darkness, who has shone in our hearts to give the light of the knowledge of the glory of God in the face of Jesus Christ (2 Cor. 4:6).

my face will go with you

exodus 33

My Presence will go with you, and I will give you rest.
Exodus 33:14

Moses was perhaps the greatest man who ever lived besides the Lord Jesus. He walked and talked with God in intimate ways and knew God as a man knows his friend. All throughout the exodus and the wilderness wanderings, God spoke directly to Moses, and Moses spent time in God's personal presence. It was to Moses that God revealed his name, and it was to Moses that God gave his Law. Through Moses, God led the people of Israel and provided for them.

The relationship between Moses and God was one of intimacy and reciprocity. Exodus 32–34 tells the sorrowful story of the Israelites' betrayal of Yahweh with the golden calf and Yahweh's desire to bring destruction on them. Moses interceded for the people, and God relented. Then he instructed Moses where to lead the people next: "Go up to the land flowing with milk and honey. But I will not go with you, because you are a stiff-necked people and I might destroy you on the way" (Exod. 33:3).

Moses was not about to continue the journey without God's presence. He knew the necessity, the value, the delight of God's company, and he refused to move or to lead without his presence. "If your Presence does not go with us, do not send us up from here" (v. 15).

So God agreed, "My Presence will go with you." The Hebrew actually says, "My face will go with you."

As you journey into a new year, does the face of God indeed go with you? Or are you traveling without the face of God? A face is an incredible thing. It can speak louder than a voice, more tenderly than a touch. God desires a face-to-face relationship with his people so we can see in his face what he wills for us, what pleases him, and what brings him sorrow.

In Jesus Christ we can see the face of God, revealed by the Holy Spirit. We are to live every day in such a way that we can sense his face and know his presence. Do not begin this year alone when you could be face-to-face with God himself.

his presence, not his signs

exodus 33

Teach me your ways so I may know you.
Exodus 33:13

In Exodus 33 God tells the Israelites to pack their bags and move forward. He is ready to take them to the land of promise. Moses listens attentively to Yahweh's directions and then responds to God directly. He wants to know exactly who God plans to send along to help him shoulder the burden of leadership. Moses is overwhelmed with all the people, whose complaints, sin, and criticism seem continual. Moses recognizes his strong need and feels an intense desire for God's presence.

God reassures Moses. "My face will go with you," he says.

In grateful desperation, Moses cries out to Yahweh, "Teach me your ways so I may know you."

Think of Moses' situation for a moment. He had watched a bush burn without the leaves even turning brown. He had heard a disembodied voice coming out of that bush. He had been instructed to throw down his staff, and when he did it became a snake. He had watched a succession of plagues. He had seen the powerful Pharaoh broken and humbled. He had stood in front of the sea and watched it part for the safety of his people. He had drunk water that came out of a rock because he had spoken to the rock. He had been sustained by the amazing provision of manna and quail. He had stood on the top of a smoking, flaming mountain without perspiring, and he had been given the laws of God directly from God's hands. He had watched all of this, and yet he asked to know more of God himself. He wanted to know the source of all the miracles. He wanted to know God personally.

Most of us enjoy God's fireworks, but Moses had seen all of that, and his heart still hungered for something more—for God himself. Does your heart hunger for God's signs or for God himself?

january 7

stumbling into the future

isaiah 30:18–21

For this God is our God for ever and ever;
he will be our guide even to the end.
Psalm 48:14

In the Hebrew language, the future is behind a person and not out in front. Instead of striding confidently into the future, the Hebrews talked about stumbling backward into it. We can see the past, but we cannot see the future, and we can never tell exactly where our foot will land. Isn't this an accurate description of life's uncertainties? Christ asks us to put our hand in his because he can see the future as well as the past. He is the one who transcends time's boundaries. He is the Lord of tomorrow as much as he is the Lord of today and yesterday. He can see exactly where each footstep will go. It is never irrational for us to put our hand in the hand of God. In fact, it is the only rational choice for us, considering our vantage point in life. If we choose to go alone, we will most certainly back into something destructive.

As a Christian you do not know what the future holds, but you do know who holds your hand. If you get ready to put your foot down in the wrong place, he will stop you and nudge you in another direction. He will shift your direction often, and as you look back on the way he has led, you will find that he has never guided you into a dead-end street or into a destructive situation. When your hand is in his and you come to the end of the way, you will be able to say, "I never lost a day."

The essence of being a Christian is putting your hand in the hand of Christ and turning your back on any rights to the direction of your life. Your future becomes his, and he leads you.

jobs for all

exodus 38:22 – 23

Then the LORD said to Moses, "See, I have chosen Bezalel son of Uri, the son of Hur, of the tribe of Judah, and I have filled him with the Spirit of God, with skill, ability and knowledge in all kinds of crafts."
Exodus 31:1–3

Be careful how you value a person who is different from you. It is easy for us to judge other people by our own interests and strengths. The very one you esteem the least may have exactly the gift that one day you will need.

When I was in college, I developed a friendship with a student who was not at home in academic circles. He felt sure that God had called him into the ministry, but he had trouble with his Greek requirement. Getting through college had been difficult, but meeting seminary requirements was too much. He had a gift, though, when it came to mechanics. He kept the philosophy professor's car running for him.

My friend became a pastor in a small town. When I was with him, I found that his people loved him. As we talked, though, he said, "You know we have a car garage in our town. I stop by to visit with the mechanic and find an almost insatiable urge to just crawl under one of those cars and get good and greasy."

I was not surprised when I heard that he was applying to serve on the mission field. Later his field superintendent said to me, "We could not operate without him. He keeps all the machines functioning that are so necessary for our work, machines that none of our seminary graduates could ever fix. And he is our pilot. In any emergency he is the most valuable person in our operation. His spirit is such too that the nationals all love him."

God knows what he is doing when he puts us here, and there is a place for everyone. If your gifts are different from those of others, don't despair. Find the place where you fit. If another person's gifts are different from yours, don't scorn. You may not have needed that person yet, but you will. We must approach every individual with a bit of anticipation, expectation, and delight. Think of Bezalel. Who would ever have thought God could use a man who was an artist, a designer, and an architect in the wilderness (Exod. 31:1–11)?

my identity

acts 26:1 – 18

Paul, a servant of Christ Jesus, called to be an
apostle and set apart for the gospel of God.
Romans 1:1

When we meet Christ, two revelations occur. The first is of Jesus. We discover that he is Lord and Savior. We recognize who he is and what he has come to do for us. But a second revelation also comes to us. We discover our own identity. This second revelation is twofold. We know we are sinners whom Christ has loved and redeemed, and we understand that our reason for existence is to serve him.

Paul saw and understood both of these revelations. On the Damascus road he met Jesus. What he learned in that moment was a shock. The one whom he hated as a blasphemer was actually the Lord and Messiah, who had come in love to save him. Paul also saw himself: he was a sinner. From his own point of view, he was the worst of sinners (1 Tim. 1:15) because of his persecution of Christ's church. Paul also discovered what he was to be: an apostle. This understanding became the defining characteristic of his life. In nine of the thirteen letters attributed to him, Paul begins by identifying himself as an apostle, and in another he calls himself Christ's servant. In yet another, he says that he is Christ's prisoner. When Paul found Christ, he found out who Christ is, what Christ came to do, who he himself was, and what he was supposed to do in this world.

When you think of yourself and your role in the world, or when someone wants to know who you are, do you identify yourself in terms of what you learned when you met Jesus? Paul, I think, would say that you should.

i am available

jeremiah 20

Before I formed you in the womb I knew you,
before you were born I set you apart;
I appointed you as a prophet to the nations.
Jeremiah 1:5

The prophet Jeremiah was a timid man living in a time that called for courage. When God called him to be his voice, Jeremiah tried to excuse himself because of his youth. At times during Jeremiah's ministry he wished to flee the pressures of God's call. Once he decided to keep quiet and speak no more about the voice of God within him, yet the message burned inside his heart. He could not keep silent; he had to proclaim the word of truth. Sometimes Jeremiah wished that he had never been born, for his mission was not an easy one, and he seemed poorly suited for it. In a wonderful way God chooses weak instruments to do his bidding. Jeremiah was a man with human frailties, but he was a chosen instrument of God. In the first chapter of Jeremiah, we read about his divine mission:

To uproot and to tear down,
To destroy and to overthrow,
To build and to plant (Jer. 1:10).

To this tender, sensitive, shrinking soul was given the task of proclaiming the judgment of God upon the existing order in Israel and preparing the way for a new kingdom. He was to stand alone; he was opposed, suspected, and scorned throughout his entire ministry. Jeremiah had to deliver his message in the most public places and on the most public occasions. He was mistreated, imprisoned, and finally (according to tradition) martyred for proclaiming that message, but when Jesus came, some people thought he was Jeremiah come back to life (Matt. 16:14).

The beauty of the story of Jeremiah is that his suffering was not wasted. More than any other prophet in Israel, Jeremiah gave to God's people the spiritual and intellectual categories they needed in order to understand Jesus and the Cross. Isaiah pictured Christ in word, especially in Isaiah 53. Jeremiah pictured Christ by his life. His very weaknesses and frailties made him a key to help Israel understand Christ.

Do not scorn your frailties, your weaknesses. They may prove to be your greatest assets when they are submitted totally to Christ. No suffering is ever lost when it is an offering to him.

before and after

titus 3

And we, who with unveiled faces all reflect the Lord's glory,
are being transformed into his likeness with ever-increasing glory,
which comes from the Lord, who is the Spirit.
2 Corinthians 3:18

God not only wants to forgive us; he also wants to regenerate us, make us new creatures. Forgiveness is the first step. It removes the things that alienate us from each other. God forgives our offenses against him and forgets them. Therefore, when he sees us he is not offended. We accept that forgiveness. Then when we turn to God, we are not afraid or loaded with guilt. The personal relationship between us and God is wholesome, good, and free. But he wants to do more. He wants to transform us to fit us for a future very different from our past.

Forgiveness and regeneration are like two sides of the same coin. They cannot be separated. Salvation is more than a change of record. It is a change of us. It deals with our sin, the bent within our nature that causes us to commit our sins. It affects who we are as well as what we do. Paul makes this clear as he writes to his understudy Titus. Notice his language: "At one time we too were foolish, disobedient, deceived and enslaved by all kinds of pleasures" (Titus 3:3). Christians have a past of which they cannot boast, but it does not determine their future. Paul is clear: "But when the kindness and love of God our Savior appeared, he saved us" (Titus 3:4–5). The change is a washing of rebirth and renewal by the Holy Spirit. We now have a new life as well as a new relationship to God. And that new life is God's life within us.

My present, therefore, is different from my past. It is as different as the sources from which the before and after come. The before had its source in a "me" empty of him. The after has its source in the very life of God that now lives within me. Small wonder that there is a difference.

january 12

believing in one another

philippians 1

*Being confident of this, that he who began a good work in you
will carry it on to completion until the day of Christ Jesus.*
Philippians 1:6

One of the marks of the early church, evidenced by Paul's relationship with
the Philippian believers, is the confidence they had in Paul, and he in them.
This belief in each other came out of their trust in God. It is a dangerous
thing for me to believe in a person because of that person's value, and it is a
dangerous thing for a person to believe in me because of my value. People
are broken reeds and will fail each other. Any hope that people will not fail
each other must be based on the goodness, faith, and power of God.

Paul's message in Philippians 1:6 is clear: "Being confident of this, that
he who began a good work in you will carry it on to completion until the
day of Christ Jesus." Paul is saying that his belief in the Philippian church
is based on the Lord Jesus.

Take heart! The Father's belief in each person comes out of the atoning
blood of Jesus. He has begun something precious in you, and he will complete it. He has chased you, and he has brought you to himself. He has
placed within your heart a yes, and now the work that he has started in you
he is going to finish.

What we find of joy in each other will be enhanced because of what
God is doing in our lives. I believe in you because I believe in him!

paul's prayer

philippians 1

God can testify how I long for all of you with the affection of Christ Jesus.
And this is my prayer: that your love may abound more
and more in knowledge and depth of insight.
Philippians 1:8–9

Paul prays for his beloved people, asking that they will receive three characteristics essential to a Christlike life: love, knowledge, and discernment.

John Wesley writes, "If anybody preaches . . . about anything more than love, he is aside from the mark, because the thing which you need is to be perfected in love and filled with all the fullness of divine love; and, if that is so, that will be fulfilling of all the law of God." The apostle Paul says that the Philippians have known divine love, but he is anxious that they know more. He prays that they will overflow with love; or rather, that divine love will overflow from their lives. What is divine love? Love for God and love for others; love that encompasses and love that enables us to care more for others than for ourselves.

Paul continues by saying that divine love is not all the Philippians need. Their love must be accompanied by knowledge. Love without knowledge can be damaging. Knowledge comes from being exposed to information and experiencing the meaning of that information by assimilating it into our own lives. Paul did not want the Philippians to simply have love; he knew they needed knowledgeable love.

The third thing Paul wanted for his people was discernment. He realized that they needed to know how to use knowledge wisely. The key to discernment lies in a close relationship to the Holy Spirit. There is no substitute for divine love, knowledge, or discernment. Only God can give divine love; knowledge comes as we live and learn about life in that love; discernment comes when we put love and knowledge together by opening ourselves to the Spirit of truth. Then love can be wise, and life will be creative and fruitful.

outside our expectations

mark 8:27 – 38

[This grace] has now been revealed through the appearing of our Savior,
Christ Jesus, who has destroyed death and has brought life and
immortality to light through the gospel. And of this gospel I was
appointed a herald and an apostle and a teacher.
2 Timothy 1:10–11

In Jesus' day, Israel did not think the way that God thought, and so when God came they crucified him. They rejected him because he did not fit their pattern. They thought they knew how the Messiah was supposed to come. When Jesus did not meet their expectations, they determined that he was a dangerous heretic, and they killed him. Jesus also did not meet the disciples' expectations. They did not crucify him; they simply forsook him. When the battle was being fought, they turned and ran.

The major reason they forsook him was that they did not think the way he thought. They did not understand him. He was not performing the way they knew the Messiah was supposed to perform, and it threw them into confusion and chaos.

One of the things they could not understand was the greatness of God's love, the amazing lengths to which God was willing to go to redeem humanity. They did not expect him to make the sacrifices he made. He went farther than their expectations, and so they missed the greatness of his love.

How far was he willing to go to redeem us for himself? He was willing to take on human form so we could visualize him in our human minds. He enabled us to see God as a human being, so we could understand him when he speaks to us. God's love and willingness to change form for the sake of humanity was absolutely beyond the expectations of all the disciples. They did not know what to do with this sacrificial love.

a creator who redeems

john 1:1 – 5

The LORD reigns forever,
your God, O Zion, for all generations.
Psalm 146:10

In the Psalms, we frequently find two themes woven together, God as the Redeemer and God as the Creator. The God of the Old Testament is the Redeemer not only of humanity, but of all things because he is the Creator of all things. There is not anything God did not make. And he not only made all things, but he also sustains all things. He is the only God, and all that exists is dependent upon him. It is his own creation that he is redeeming, and history is the place in which he will bring about this redemption. He is God alone without rival or competitor. He is the ultimate one and the only one. Therefore, he is the inescapable one. He will ultimately rule whether I want him to or not.

What is this Creator/Redeemer God like? Psalm 146 tells us of his righteousness and his goodness. He has concern for the orphans, the oppressed, the hungry, the prisoners, the blind, the broken, the strangers, and the widows. He loves the righteous and will turn upside down the way of the wicked, for he is the eternal guardian of truth. He is God alone, and he will reign forever. This God is the God of the psalmist and his people. Little wonder that the psalmist is lost in adoration. This is a God who is supremely good.

the existing chasm

genesis 5

*The LORD God formed the man from the dust of the ground and breathed
into his nostrils the breath of life, and the man became a living being.*
Genesis 2:7

Other ancient religions have genealogies similar to the ones found in our
Scripture. However, those of our Scripture have one key difference. When
the other ancient near-Eastern genealogies are pushed back to the very beginning, we find that the first leaders were always parented by at least one god.
The chasm between divinity and humanity was bridged, so they were
extremely compatible and continuous. The gods were merely superhuman
beings, so the gods suffered from and were captive to all the same vices that
troubled humanity.

The Hebrews believed differently. Scripture records that at the absolute
beginning of the human race there was a man who was not God. History
starts with a man who was a created object, made from the dust.

One would think that the people who believed humanity had the divine
in it would be greater respecters of life. This is not true! It is when one recognizes one's weakness that one can realize the amazing love of God that
condescends to relate to people completely different from himself. When
we begin to understand God's incredible and unsurpassable love for human
persons, we want to love other people in the way that he does.

Do we acknowledge God's goodness in loving us, and are we sharing
that goodness with others whom he loves?

choose for yourselves this day

joshua 24

Choose for yourselves this day whom you will serve, whether the gods your forefathers served . . . or the gods of the Amorites, in whose land you are living. But as for me and my household, we will serve the LORD.
Joshua 24:15

The closing chapters of the book of Joshua are Joshua's final words to the people of Israel. Israel is in the promised land, and Joshua wishes to renew the covenant between Israel and Yahweh before he dies. He reviews the history of the covenant and speaks about God's faithfulness to his people. He calls them to choose whether or not they will serve Yahweh. Joshua is very aware that after his death the temptation for compromise with the Canaanites will be strong, and a compromise would mean death for Israel's culture and faith. Joshua is anxious for the people of God to reaffirm their loyalty to the God of Abraham, Moses, Sinai, and the conquest, and so he calls them to do so. The people acknowledge God's actions for them, and they pledge their allegiance to Yahweh.

Joshua's appeal to the people is based on God's actions for Israel and not on Israel's actions for God. God has chosen and blessed Israel, and their motive for serving him must be his great mercy and grace to them. The same is true today. The important thing is not what we have done for God but what God has done for us. The deliverance from Egypt, the provision in the wilderness, the crossing of the Jordan, and the conquest of the land are historical pictures of the redemption provided for us in Christ. He will provide for those who trust in him and will give them grace to overcome all foes.

The effectiveness of Joshua's plea is indicated in the closing verses of his book. "Israel served the LORD throughout the lifetime of Joshua and of the elders who outlived him and who had experienced everything the LORD had done for Israel" (Josh. 24:31). It is necessary for every individual in every successive generation to see the work of God personally. Each of us must come to a meeting with God in which we enter into a covenant relationship with Yahweh. Therefore the word to us is still: "Choose for yourselves this day whom you will serve."

closed doors

luke 18:1 – 8

These are the words of him who is holy and true, who holds the key of David.
What he opens no one can shut, and what he shuts no one can open.
Revelation 3:7

Presidents of small colleges find themselves in many unusual situations. I sat in my family room one night surrounded by a room full of young women whose dorm was being renovated. My wife had invited them over, thinking they needed a little extra attention. Because I was the only male there and desperate to steer the attention away from myself, I asked the students to share how they came to Asbury College.

One of them had very fascinating story. She told about how she had been on drugs and into so many other harmful things that she had flunked out of another college. After that, she had found Christ, and when she found him, he said to her "I want you to go to Asbury College." So she applied, and the admissions office turned her down. She called the director of admissions and said to him, "I am coming to Asbury."

He responded, "Oh no, you can't come. Your application has been rejected."

"Well," she said, "God has called me to come, so I must come." The director of admissions called the dean of women, and the dean called the young woman and told her that she had not been accepted and therefore could not come.

The young woman's response was, "Yes, I understand that, but I have to come because God has called me, and I already have my car packed, and I am on my way."

Asbury accepted her because of her persistence and her faithfulness to the call of Jesus on her life. We had turned her down because of her poor grades, but by the grace of God she brought her grades up. As her life came under the lordship of Jesus Christ, she was able to do things that had been impossible for her.

Sometimes God asks us to do things that look impossible not only to ourselves but also to those around us. Are we as persistent as we need to be? Are we as faithful to the calling that he puts on our lives as we must be if we are to be faithful to him? He has the capacity to open doors that no person can shut.

deadly treasures

luke 12:13–21

*Do not be afraid, little flock, for your Father has been pleased
to give you the kingdom ... Provide purses for yourselves that
will not wear out, a treasure in heaven that will not be exhausted,
where no thief comes near and no moth destroys.*
Luke 12:32–33

I know an Episcopal minister who served in a rural parish for several years
before pursuing a career in teaching. He lived on a farm while he served in
the pastorate. One Sunday morning he was puttering about the barn before
church when his three-year-old daughter came running in, holding out her
pudgy little hand. She said, "Look what I found, Daddy. Isn't it pretty?"

My friend saw the morning sunlight glisten on the object in her hand.
It was a double-edged razor blade. He thought to himself, *How do I get that
blade out of her hand? If I try to take it away from her, she will clutch it tighter,
and if she does that, she may cut herself badly enough to scar her hand for life.*

So he said, "Honey, that is very dangerous. It will cut you. You must
not close your hand. You must give it to Daddy."

"But it is mine," she squealed. "I found it!"

"Yes, I know, but it is dangerous. You must let me take it." He stepped
closer, and she began to close her tiny hand. "Don't do that, Honey," he
said. "It will cut you, and then I will have to take you to Dr. Jones."

"I like Dr. Jones," she answered, smiling. "He gives me suckers when I go."

It is not easy for a theologian to reason with a three-year-old!

Finally, my friend assumed a curious attitude about his daughter's new-
found treasure. "It certainly is pretty," he said. "May I take a look at it?" He
cupped her little palm in his, and while he shared her pleasure in the find,
he gently pulled back her fingers one by one till he could lift the deadly
instrument from her hand.

When Jesus comes into your life and says, "Let me take over," it is not
because he is trying to steal your treasures or strip away your character. He is
trying to protect you and help you be all you were intended to be without any
unnecessary scars or wounds. He wants to link your wisdom with his wisdom,

your knowledge with his knowledge, and your power with his power. He never attempts to destroy you; he simply brings you to the fulfillment for which you long.

If he is approaching you today, whatever you do, do not close your hand on the things that you hold. Give them all to him.

destructive work

numbers 22

Now all has been heard;
here is the conclusion of the matter:
Fear God and keep his commandments,
for this is the whole duty of man.
For God will bring every deed into judgment,
including every hidden thing,
whether it is good or evil.
Ecclesiastes 12:13–14

There are two elements that can cause work to be destructive. One is if the work serves no worthwhile purpose, and the other is if it produces guilt in the worker. The result of both will inevitably be harmful. People were made to create and to create something good. Millions of people are involved in work that is destructive to other persons. The product of their work not only serves no useful purpose but has a damaging effect on its users. Little wonder that the soul of the worker becomes corroded. No paycheck, no matter how large, and no loud claim to social usefulness can make up for the inner consciousness that the labor of one's mind or hands has defiled or harmed brothers and sisters for whom Christ died.

Many people's use of time is not obviously destructive; it is simply without a worthwhile end. Human persons cannot tolerate meaninglessness. We live for values. Inevitably work that serves no purpose will speed natural forces of dissolution.

What is your work? Are you giving your life for something that is worthwhile? Is your work in any way harmful to fellow persons? If it is, you will never find true fulfillment or true happiness.

the moment of illumination

acts 2

"For my thoughts are not your thoughts,
neither are your ways my ways,"
declares the LORD.
"As the heavens are higher than the earth,
so are my ways higher than your ways
and my thoughts than your thoughts."
Isaiah 55:8–9

When my heart is clean, my head is more perceptive. When my heart is clean, I think more clearly. I can see better, and I can hear better.

Before Pentecost, Peter never understood the Cross; when Jesus told him that he must suffer, Peter rebuked him. For Peter, the Cross seemed wrong. He could not think like Jesus thought. However, on the day of Pentecost, Peter came out of the upper room anointed with the Spirit, looked at the crowd and said, "Let me explain this to you; listen carefully to what I say" (Acts 2:14). Suddenly Peter saw the Cross as the fulfillment of the Scriptures. He knew the Cross was right.

Human minds are always servants. If they are servants of self-interest, then they will seek to justify self-interest. If they are wholly possessed by God, then they become his servants. Then they can understand his ways; they can see his truth.

George Mueller had been a Christian for four years. One evening he came to a place of total surrender. In the next four hours, Mueller explained, he learned and understood more of Scripture than he had in the preceding four years of his Christian life. We must be totally surrendered in order to see God's ways. If our hearts are divided, we will have a divided head. If God possesses our whole hearts, then our minds will become instruments of his Spirit.

jesus' last gift

john 14:15 – 31

And if the Spirit of him who raised Jesus from the dead is living in you,
he who raised Christ from the dead will also give life
to your mortal bodies through his Spirit, who lives in you.
Romans 8:11

The most tender scene in the gospel of John is one that takes place on the night before the Cross. Jesus bids farewell to his friends, who for three years have forsaken home, family, and vocation to follow him. As the months have passed, their affection and attachment to him have deepened. Now they are convinced that he is the King for whom Israel has waited. But Jesus is not under any illusions. He knows that the following day will bring what seems to be tragedy and not triumph, and it is his task to prepare his friends for what awaits him.

The last gift that he seems to want to leave with them is the person of the Holy Spirit. These men have built their lives around him, and to them the prospect of life without him is almost unthinkable. Their memories of life before Jesus are exceedingly misty and gray, and each one knows he could never return to a pre-Jesus existence. Jesus attempts to alleviate their pain by telling them that he will send another to take his place. This one will continue to guide, instruct, and comfort them. In fact, he will live with them forever, finishing in them what Jesus has begun. This one who is coming is the Spirit of Jesus. Each believer in Jesus has the personal privilege of having a life-giving, fruit-producing stream flowing from within through the power of the Holy Spirit.

What a tragedy it would be to live without accepting the last gift that Jesus gave.

the same spirit

john 14:15 – 31

If you love me, you will obey what I command. And I will ask the Father,
and he will give you another Counselor to be with you forever—
the Spirit of truth. The world cannot accept him,
because it neither sees him nor knows him. But you know him,
for he lives with you and will be in you.
I will not leave you as orphans; I will come to you.
John 14:15–18

It took me a long time to realize that the Spirit whom Jesus gave to his disciples was not just the third person of the Trinity; it was the Spirit who had empowered Jesus' own life and ministry. The secret to Jesus' life was the Spirit, and the Spirit is anxious to be the secret of your life and mine.

The Spirit was the one who initiated Christ's conception. It was he who anointed Jesus at his baptism. The word *Christ* means "anointed," so it was the Spirit who made Jesus the Christ. It was the Spirit who led Jesus and sustained him through his temptation in the wilderness. The Spirit was the source of Jesus' power over the demonic, and the Spirit enabled him to endure the Cross. The writer of Hebrews speaks of Christ as the one "who through the eternal Spirit offered himself unblemished to God" (Heb. 9:14). It was the Spirit who, with the Father, raised Jesus from the dead. The Spirit was the key to the earthly life of Jesus.

Now on Jesus' last night before the Cross, he told his disciples that he wanted them to have the same one in their lives who had been in his own. He promised them the Holy Spirit. And that promise is to you and me as well. Have you received him? Do you let him gently lead you? This is your privilege as a believer in Jesus. Read the promise in Luke 11:13: "If you then, though you are evil, know how to give good gifts to your children, how much more will your Father in heaven give the Holy Spirit to those who ask him!"

his way is good

romans 8

Who among you fears the LORD
and obeys the word of his servant?
Let him who walks in the dark,
who has no light,
trust in the name of the LORD
and rely on his God.
Isaiah 50:10

Human beings are creatures who, because of our finitude, are never quite at home. Balanced on a razor's edge called the present, which is gone before it can be named, we can never really relax. We are creatures with a past we cannot shake and a future we do not control. The evanescence of the present and the uncertainty of the future produce anxiety. This is all part of being human.

How do we live with an anxiety that is part of our very existence? The Christian has equipment and resources not available to any other. First, the believer knows the one, the only one, not caught in our transience, the sovereign God who created this finite existence, who rules his creation with a sovereignty greater than that with which a Beethoven arbitrarily corrects a score. The Christian knows the Maker of the future.

The Christian also knows that God is kindly disposed to human beings. God has demonstrated that in nature, in grace, in life's bounty, and in Christ's Cross. He has revealed it in the character of the person of Jesus Christ, his Son. His will toward us is good. It cannot be otherwise because that is his nature. He is love. Love for you.

But his love is conditioned by truth. Jesus never spoke much about his love; rather, he demonstrated it. He spoke about truth and the right way to live. God, in his sovereign goodness, has a way for you into the future, and it is good. Find that way and you will witness his goodness and his love. Make your own way and futility, emptiness, and discontent will force you to call him Judge. Find his way and you will call him Friend and Father.

first or third person?

exodus 3

God said to Moses, "I am who I am. This is what you are to say
to the Israelites: 'I AM has sent me to you.'"
Exodus 3:14

Theology books are always written in the third person. They present God as an object to be studied, and one rarely hears of anyone being converted while reading a theology book. The only way a person can ever be converted is if God is understood not in the third person but in the first person. He must become the subject and we must become the object. Unfortunately, most of Christianity is a massive effort to keep God in the third person. But there is no salvation until he is in the first person and we deal with him face-to-face.

God identifies himself to Moses as I AM WHO I AM. Another way to say it is "I'M I AM." God wanted Moses to tell the people of Israel that I AM had sent him. He wanted to be in the first person, not just to the leader, but to every man, woman, and child of the Israelite people. Regrettably, the scribes who translated the Old Testament into the Greek Septuagint changed "I AM WHO I AM" to "I AM the One Who Is." This shifted the emphasis from the Hebraic first person to the Greek third person.

Is he in the third or the first person for you? Are you talking about him, working for him, reading of him? Or are you talking, working, and reading with him? Is your life a face-to-face communion with the I AM?

completing calvary

2 corinthians 6:1 – 12

As God's fellow workers we urge you not to receive God's grace in vain.
2 Corinthians 6:1

There is no question as to whether God is all powerful or whether salvation is always the work of God alone. Only he can save. However, the reality is that when he moves to save us mortals, he reaches out for one of us to work with him in that redemptive process. Read Isaiah 50:2; 59:16; 63:5; and Ezekiel 22:30. We know that when he wanted to save Israel, he turned to Moses. And when he wanted to reach the Gentile world, he called Paul. He looks for those who will work with him to save their kind.

We must be careful that our business is to work with God, not for him. He alone can save, but he has made human relationships in such a way that those who will surrender to him become his instruments in the salvation of the world.

It is the surgeon who operates, not the scalpel. We are different, though, from the scalpel. It has no choice, but we do. We can refuse to be instruments of God, or we can let ourselves become his fellow workers. What a high privilege to let the saving power of God work through us.

a pledge to truth

john 8:32; 14:6; 18:38

He is the Rock, his works are perfect,
and all his ways are just.
A faithful God who does no wrong,
upright and just is he.
Deuteronomy 32:4

All Christians have an obligation to be students of truth. In fact, we are called to develop a love affair with the truth. It is ultimately truth, not knowledge or skill, that really sets us free and makes us wholly creative. *Truth* is a strong word. There is something almost numinous about it. We should not speak of it lightly or casually.

Knowledge is quite different. It is something we can gain, something we can control, and something we can use. Knowledge, when we gain control of it, becomes ours, and we profit from the acquisition of it. Truth is another matter. Truth should gain and control us instead of being controlled by us. There is an element of unrelenting moral demand in truth; it is other-centered. It matters not whether we have mastered truth and can use it; it matters only whether we have surrendered to truth and are willing to obey it.

Someone has suggested that truth is like a potential spouse who to be known truly demands of us commitment and a pledge of undying fidelity.

returning to danger

genesis 32

*Go back to the land of your fathers and to your relatives,
and I will be with you.*
Genesis 31:3

There is something in all of us that makes us want to run away from our problems. We tend to be escapists, leaving behind the painful things we hope never to face again. In Scripture God has an ironic and wonderful way of making us go back and face the things that we want to bury or ignore. God refuses to allow us to remain unhealed. It is his business to get us to face the problems that are in our lives and to be victorious over them. We are never conquerors when we run away. We are not conquerors in the grace of God until we can face our problems and overcome them.

God told Jacob to return to Canaan, the land from which he had fled, the land where the brother whom he had offended lived. Jacob waited until God specifically called him to go, and I am confident that Jacob's first question in response to God's call was, "Lord, is Esau still living?" Esau was still alive, and God's personal presence was the only promise of protection that God gave to Jacob.

Are you running from hidden fears in your life? God may be asking you to return to the place from which you fled in order to overcome your fear, your hurt, your pain. His promise of protection is the promise of his presence.

god's protection

genesis 3:7 – 24

*The LORD God made garments of skin for
Adam and his wife and clothed them.
Genesis 3:21*

The clothing that Yahweh made for Adam and Eve after they sinned is analogous to the veil in the temple that divided the holy place from the Holy of Holies. Neither was there simply to cover up that which was beautiful; rather, each existed to protect the beautiful from defilement. Adam and Eve needed clothing only when love had turned into lust and they began to see each other as distinct objects to be used. The garments were not to cause separation; they were to protect from the results of the separation caused by sin. The curtain in the temple was not to separate the people from Yahweh, but to protect them from thinking that they had found him and could control him.

The difference between the Israelites and the people around them was not that the Israelites had a God and the Canaanites did not. The latter had many gods. The difference was that the Israelites had the true God, who could redeem, save, and bless. The Canaanites' gods not only were sterile and impotent, but they were also defiling. God wanted the Israelites to know that they had the true God, and he wanted to protect them from defilement.

The things in our lives that seem to be God's restrictions to keep us from what we want are really his loving hedges to protect us from throwing ourselves into the murky, slimy waters of sin. Let us not resist his attempt to protect us and keep us for that which is beautiful, clean, and pure.

a conditional future

deuteronomy 28

This day I call heaven and earth as witnesses against you that I have set
before you life and death, blessings and curses. Now choose life,
so that you and your children may live and that you may love the LORD
your God, listen to his voice, and hold fast to him.
For the LORD is your life, and he will give you many years in the land
he swore to give to your fathers, Abraham, Isaac and Jacob.
Deuteronomy 30:19–20

Are you uneasy about your future? You have a significant role to play in
determining what that future will be. Your role is to relate to the one who
controls every future. Note the word of God to ancient Israel: "Do not let
this Book of the Law depart from your mouth; meditate on it day and night,
so that you may be careful to do everything written in it. Then you will be
prosperous and successful" (Josh. 1:8).

God had given Israel his word so they could know how to order their
lives so as to properly relate to him. If they would center their lives around
his direction, the future would be good. The Israelites were the only ones
who could destroy their own future. The same is true for us; no one can hinder God's future for us except ourselves.

The year before us should be better than the one behind us. If it is so,
it will not be because of what we do in ourselves. It will simply be because
we have established a right relationship with the one who was, who is, and
who is to come and because we have stayed in communion with him.
Rejoice in his hope. He is our future.

january 31

giving myself away

john 19:25 – 27

Father, forgive them, for they do not know what they are doing.
Luke 23:34

One of the greatest witnesses to the faith I ever knew was a lady who decided that her children needed religion, so she began dropping them off at church every Sunday. As her children learned about Jesus, they began to share with her, and a hunger developed in her heart for Christ. She grew so desperate for him that she overcame her fear of attending church enough to slip into the back of a Sunday school class in absolute terror, afraid that she would be asked a question. Instead of humiliation, she found Christ.

She became an amazing church visitor. There was a radiance about her that would get her in any door. Not until several years after I met her did I realize that she was not the most beautiful person in the world. The beauty about her came from her radiant love of the Lord Jesus.

This lady developed cancer. She found herself in the hospital and hooked up to all kinds of machines. One day she asked her doctor how long she would live without the machines, and he replied that it would be about a week.

"Doctor," she said, "How long will I live if I stay on these machines?" He answered that it would be about six weeks. "Take me off," she said. "I would rather spend those last five weeks with Jesus."

Her husband came to visit and she said to him, "I want you to pray with me about when I am to die. If I die during the night, my night nurse will be distraught because we have become very close. But if I die right around the shift change at 2:45, then the day nurse will be here with her, and she will be able to handle it better."

Twenty-four hours later, at 2:45 A.M., she died. She did not know what she was facing, but she knew to whom she was going, and because of that security her last thought was for the well-being and comfort of someone else. Would it not be wonderful if we lived in such a way that when we are ready to die, we would be thinking not of ourselves but of other people? This is true freedom, giving to others until the very end.

This is exactly what Jesus did as he committed his mother to the care of his disciple John. At the very end, he was thinking of others.

faith on a cross

luke 23:39 – 43

Lord, remember me when You come into Your kingdom.
Luke 23:42 NKJV

The greatest example of faith in all of the Scriptures, according to John Calvin, is the faith of the thief dying on the cross next to Jesus, because he said to Jesus, "Lord, remember me when You come into Your kingdom." What do you suppose the people standing under the crosses who heard his plea thought? Surely this criminal's agony had crazed him. He had called Jesus "Lord." Lord of what? Jesus had not even been able to keep his own clothes. The soldiers below had gambled for his cloak. His crown was of thorns. He had no retinue except for a few women and John. All others had forsaken him. He was an object of wrath to state and church. Even God had forsaken him. But the thief spoke of Jesus' lordship and his kingdom. What did he see that no one else saw?

The Scriptures make clear that there is an invisible world as well as a visible one, and that only the invisible world makes sense of the one we can see. But not many have eyes for the invisible world. Moses did, and the writer of Hebrews explains Moses' remarkable life accordingly: "He persevered because he saw him who is invisible" (Heb. 11:27). Moses could see what others could not, and what he saw gave him a different reading on reality. Luke tells us how Cleopas and his friend walked with Jesus on the road from Jerusalem to Emmaus and never knew who he was until "their eyes were opened" (Luke 24:31).

The eyes of the dying thief were opened, and he saw and believed. That is the particular work of the Spirit of God and is the mark of those whom God has touched. Peter speaks of those who have been "called . . . out of darkness into his marvelous light" (1 Peter 2:9).

As the sun hid its face and the darkness settled that noon over Golgotha, a light shone in the heart of a dying thief, and he saw what others could not see.

Can you see?

eternally man

matthew 1:18–23

*"She will give birth to a son, and you are to give him the name Jesus,
because he will save his people from their sins." All this took place
to fulfill what the Lord had said through the prophet: "The virgin
will be with child and will give birth to a son, and they will
call him Immanuel"—which means, "God with us."*
Matthew 1:21–23

What a different picture Jesus gives us of God from that which we naturally
develop. For a long time I understood God to be the sovereign Lord and final
Judge, who sat on his throne watching for my failures so he could chastise me
and remind me of the vast gulf that exists between him and me. But this is not
the biblical picture of God. God is Lord and Judge, but he is also Immanuel,
"God with us"—and the preposition *with* carries remarkable overtones.

The *with* speaks of identification. God, in Christ, became a man. Distance and otherness were bridged by that *with* in Immanuel. He took our
state, and he took our problem. Paul says in 2 Corinthians 5:21 that "God
made him who had no sin to be sin for us." He took our alienation and our
death when he cried, "My God, my God, why have you forsaken me?"
(Matt. 27:46).

But God intended that *with* to be reciprocal. He decided to be one with
us because he wanted us to be one with him. And the astounding thing is
that he wanted us to be with him in more than destiny. The *with* speaks of
more than place. It also speaks of character. That is why God insisted that
Israel be holy. They needed to be holy if they were to fulfill their mission as
a holy nation. They needed even more to be holy if they were to be with
him because he said, "I am holy." That is why one of God's most glorious
promises in Scripture is the reference to every believer in the New Testament as a saint. The Father, through Christ's sacrifice of himself as one of us,
can put his life into us until we, who by nature are sinners, can become companions with God. Yes, and more than companions. We are to be children
of the Father and the very bride of his Son. Jesus is "Immanuel," "God with
us," so we can be with him in a remarkable way.

god's horsemen

zechariah 1:1–17

They are the ones the LORD has sent to go throughout the earth.
Zechariah 1:10

There are times when as Christians we become discouraged with ourselves, and in our despair we wonder if we can ever really be what God created us to be. Most commonly this comes after some failure in our lives in which we know we have not done what God wanted us to do. Then in repentance we come again to God, but there lingers in our heart the despair that comes from knowing that we have failed.

This is exactly where the people of Israel found themselves during the Babylonian captivity. So they began to reconcile themselves to their failure by suggesting that perhaps this was all that God could do for them. They began to wallow in self-pity. They began to say that God had forgotten them. This is a miserable place for any believer to be in, drowning in pity and accusing God of forgetfulness.

Zechariah was the prophet to the people of Judah during the Babylonian captivity, and he had a vision. He saw some horsemen who went out over all the earth, and he asked the Lord about them. The Lord responded that these were his agents; their mission was to cover the earth and report to God what they found. God knew exactly what was happening with his people, and he wanted to reassure them of that.

There is not a single event that takes place in the world of which God is not aware. We may think he has forgotten us, but he has known every moment and every hour of our existence. He knows everything that has happened to us. His eyes are on us, and they have never wavered. He does not forsake us. We are never out of his sight.

february 4

chained lions

zechariah 1:18–21

For this is what the LORD Almighty says: "After he has honored me
and has sent me against the nations that have plundered
you—for whoever touches you touches the apple of his eye . . ."
Zechariah 2:8

The people of Israel had suffered greatly. They had been carried into exile
in Babylon. When they were finally permitted to return to their homeland,
it was a shambles. Their capital and their temple had been destroyed.
Though they were home, they were pawns of the empires that contended for
supremacy in their world. They lived their lives in fear. Then Zechariah came
with a vision to remind Israel that behind the surrounding forces was a
power that was greater than them and was good.

Zechariah's vision was of four horns representing the forces that had
trampled Jerusalem and its people, the kingdoms Israel had feared. But
Zechariah also saw four carpenters, who cut down the four horns that had
ravaged Israel. God used this vision to remind Israel that ultimate power is
in the hands of God and that he would determine the rise and fall of all the
forces that impinged upon them. None could get beyond his control. In the
same way, outside forces touch us only with his permission; they have no
power to destroy us.

There is a priceless scene in John Bunyan's *Pilgrim's Progress.* Christian
and his companion are faced by two ferocious lions that block their way;
the path lies right between the lions. The pilgrims are terrified until they
notice that each lion is chained so he cannot quite reach the narrow path
they must follow. The lions can roar at the travelers all they want, but they
cannot touch them. The pilgrims tremble as they proceed, but they are safe.
The lions in the believer's path are never unchained. And the one who holds
the chains is a carpenter from Nazareth.

god, our wall of protection

zechariah 2

"Jerusalem will be a city without walls ... And I myself will be a wall of fire around it," declares the LORD, "and I will be its glory within."
Zechariah 2:4–5

Christians tend to be on the defensive. They live in an alien world that does not understand the Christian perspective and values. Often that world turns hostile, and Christians seek protection and security. Instead of marching joyously out to claim God's world for him, believers set perimeters and build walls.

Israel had suffered greatly at the hands of her enemies. Jerusalem and the temple had been destroyed. The people had been exiled to Babylon. Now some had returned, and they were beginning to rebuild Jerusalem. In a vision Zechariah saw a man with a measuring line going out to determine the size of the city and decide where the city walls would be. A heavenly messenger appeared and said, "Run, tell that young man, 'Jerusalem will be a city without walls'" (Zech. 2:4). The city of God was not to be for containment. It was to be for overflow. From it the knowledge of God was to flow out to all corners of the earth and to the end of time.

But if Jerusalem had no walls, where was its security? The Lord says, "And I myself will be a wall of fire around it ... and I will be its glory within" (Zech. 2:5). The presence of God himself was to be the city's glory and its security. Jerusalem was to be earth's umbilical cord through which grace could flow to the whole world. It needed openness, not blockage. God's presence would guarantee its safety and his anointing its success.

Are you afraid of living without walls? Hide yourself in his presence and you will find that his presence is your protection.

the fatherhood of god (part 1)

ephesians 3:14–20

*For this reason I kneel before the Father,
from whom his whole family in heaven and on earth derives its name.
Ephesians 3:14–15*

It is surprising to find in Scripture how intimate God wants to be with us. There is much in the Gospels about the kingdom. Jesus told his disciples, "As you go, preach this message: 'The kingdom of heaven is near'" (Matt. 10:7). That God is Lord over his creation is clear. But a prior figure used in Scripture demonstrates the character of God's kingship. Before God was King, he was Father, and his fatherhood is more ultimate than his kingship. Kingship speaks of his relationship to his creation. He reigns and will reign over it all. But fatherhood speaks of a relationship within the very nature of God that was there before he spoke anything into existence. In the bosom of eternity, before there was time or space or humanity, the second person of the triune Godhead called the first person of the Trinity not *Lord,* but *Father.* So the family is a more ultimate social reality than the kingdom. The origin of the family is not in time but in God.

Paul understood this. In 1 Corinthians 15:20–28 he tells us how Christ will destroy "all dominion, authority and power" (15:24). He has put all of his enemies under his feet, and he will hand over the kingdom to the Father from whom it came. In Revelation 21:6–7 John tells us that when all things are finished and the end has come, those who have drunk from "the spring of the water of life" and have overcome will inherit all things, and God will be their God and they will be his children. That is why Jesus said, "When you pray, say: 'Father'" (Luke 11:2), and that is why new believers find within their spirit a voice born of the Holy Spirit crying "Abba, Father" (Gal. 4:6).

The parent-child relationship—the family—is an eternal concept, not merely a temporal or historical one. Everyone you will ever meet has a family. People come in families. Is that because God does too? The early Christians understood that he does when they began their affirmation of faith with the words "I believe in God the Father."

Do you need to allow the Holy Spirit to change your response when you hear the word *Father* or the word *family?* Some of us come from such broken families that we assume that God the Father is not good and that a heavenly family would be the nightmare of our earthly reality. It's not true. Don't let your brokenness keep you from finding healing in the perfect family.

the fatherhood of god (part 2)

john 17:24 – 26

When you pray, say: "Father."
Luke 11:2

The church leaders of the first three centuries emphasized the fatherhood of God. Their personal love for God the Father influenced their work, theologies, and lives profoundly. It determined their prayers, their liturgy, their doxologies, and even their creeds. Note what comes first in the Apostles' Creed: "I believe in God the Father." Before an assertion of God's sovereignty or the recognition of him as the Creator, the Source of all things, comes the affirmation of his fatherhood. The beginning of all things comes from a father.

The family metaphor is primary in the early church. In the Middle Ages and still today the understanding of God as Judge and the language of courtrooms and laws predominate, but this understanding is secondary for the earliest church fathers. For them the concepts of reconciliation and healing were even more important than that of justification. The picture was far more personal and, I think, far more powerful.

Elevating the picture of God as Father so it is the primary image we have of God does not diminish his other roles, but enables us to understand them better. If the Judge is our Father, the judicial process is going to be very different from a process in which he is just an impartial third party. We must remember that before God ever created a creature, he was Father. This is who he is in his essence from all eternity.

the fatherhood of god (part 3)

john 14:9 – 14

"Our Father which art in heaven."
Luke 11:2 KJV

We as Christians often forget how privileged we are. We enjoy many benefits of the gospel that people in other religions never understand. Several years ago I had the honor of hearing a woman from Pakistan tell about her conversion. For many years, her husband had been a major figure in the Pakistani government. She told about reading the New Testament and how impossible it was for her to believe that people could begin a prayer with the words "Our Father." One thing she knew about Allah was that he was not like humans. He was greater than human beings and infinitely different; human categories could never be used to describe him, certainly not one as personal and direct as "father."

She said that when she came to faith in Jesus Christ, her first response was to lift her heart and say, "Father," and the moment she uttered the word, she fell on the floor in absolute terror of being killed for her impertinence. But instead, the heavenly Father came to her in all his love and compassion, and she heard one word: "Daughter." She recalled, "I wept uncontrollably at the reality that God in his sovereignty and greatness could belong to me in that kind of relationship."

He is our Father. Do we need a reminder of the depth of the love and compassion he has for us?

jesus' pain

mark 14:32 – 42; john 18:1 – 2

God made him who had no sin to be sin for us,
so that in him we might become the righteousness of God.
2 Corinthians 5:21

On the night before he died, Jesus left the upper room and led the eleven disciples through the city gate and across the brook Kidron to his retreat on the Mount of Olives. It is not without significance that John mentions the crossing of the Kidron Valley. The sacrificial blood that was poured out on the temple's altars drained into this brook, and it was running red with the blood of the paschal lambs as the Lamb of God passed over it. Within the walls of Jerusalem there was no spare room for gardens, so the wealthy citizens had gardens outside the city. One of these, the property of a friend of Jesus, had been his nightly retreat during Passion Week.

The disciples were greatly fatigued from the events of the week and were ready to sleep, but Jesus asked them to sit and wait while he went by himself to pray. Taking Peter, James, and John with him, he went farther into the garden as untold suffering and sorrow settled upon his soul. "Tarry ye here, and watch" (Mark 14:34 KJV), he pled with them, but though their spirits were willing, their flesh was so weak. They could not watch with him one hour. They were not ready to strengthen him when he, fairest Lord Jesus, Son of God and Son of Man, needed support. They could not, so an angel was sent from heaven to strengthen him in his pain as "he poured out his life unto death" (Isa. 53:12) and as he "who had no sin" prepared to become "sin for us, so that we might become the righteousness of God" (2 Cor. 5:21).

How keenly Jesus must have felt the sin of the world upon him that he needed and asked for support. How dreadful the load must have been that he had to cry out, "Father, . . . take this cup from me" (Mark 14:36). Let us never think that when he gave "his life a ransom" (Matt. 20:28) the price was cheap. Salvation is free to us—we cannot buy it—but it cost him everything. Let us not take our sin lightly; we must realize the exceeding horror of our sin, which pressed down upon him so that his sweat became great drops of blood falling to the ground.

a model in suffering

matthew 26:36–46

Going a little farther, he fell with his face to the ground and prayed,
"My Father, if it is possible, may this cup be taken from me.
Yet not as I will, but as you will."
Matthew 26:39

In Gethsemane, we see two different responses to trouble: Jesus' submission and the disciples' fear. We must learn from Jesus what our attitude should be when life becomes painful—one of earnest prayer to our Father who is in heaven. We must not try to stand in our own strength; rather, we must learn new dependence on him. The person who will depend on God in times of trial and pain is the person whom God will be able to use. Above all, we must submit our will to the will of God: "Yet, not as I will, but as you will." Our greatest problems come not from trouble, but from our resistance to trouble when we close our eyes to the will of God as it is revealed to us in difficulty. Thank God for trouble! It will drive us to him!

The disciples did not follow the model of Jesus; instead, they left him in his time of greatest weakness. They looked at their circumstances instead of to him. They forsook Jesus and fled. How it must have pained him! Peter denied him three times. How that must have pierced his soul! We must watch and pray lest we enter into temptation and forsake him when times are difficult. The Lord will not cast us off when we stumble and fall, and he has given us a way of escape so that we need not falter (1 Cor. 10:13). His is a grace that can keep us even when the opposition is great.

Jesus is looking for men and women, young people and old people who will stand fast for him, who will put him first, and not only when life is pleasant. When life includes misunderstanding, sarcasm, scorn, and persecution, he has grace to keep us faithful.

He will not forsake us. Should we forsake him?

holiness as presence

jeremiah 9:23 – 24

*Sanctify them by the truth; your word is truth. As you sent me
into the world, I have sent them into the world.
For them I sanctify myself, that they too may be truly sanctified.*
John 17:17–19

Jesus uses the word *holy* very sparingly in the Gospels. On one occasion he
quotes a rabbinic proverb, "Do not give what is holy to the dogs" (Matt. 7:6
NKJV), but other than that, until John 17 the only time he uses the word
holy about anyone is when he refers to God the Father, God the Holy Spirit,
or himself, God the Son. Then, on the last night of his life, when he faces
the Cross, knowing all that it means for him, he prays for his disciples, asking the Father to make them holy (John 17:17). For the first time the reader
finds an indication that it is possible for human beings to share in the holiness of God.

When God puts his holiness into a human heart, it does not become a
human possession. Rather, when the presence of God himself comes in and
fills a person's heart, it enables that person to share in God's holy character.
It is possible for the Holy One to come and dwell in us so we begin to look
like him. Does God's presence fill your life?

a pathway of light

isaiah 58:8 – 9

For the LORD will go before you,
the God of Israel will be your rear guard.
Isaiah 52:12

The Lord God says that he will go before us and that he will come behind us as well. He will be our double protection. I suspect that God wants to lead some of us in new directions, and there may be a little panic in your heart at that thought. Perhaps God wants you to go into full-time Christian service, or perhaps he is calling you overseas or is asking you to change careers in some other way. If he is speaking to you about a future that makes you apprehensive, remember that he will go before you. He will never send you without his presence. We never simply go for him; we always follow him. If the eternal Christ is marching out in front of us, what can we possibly fear?

Not only does God lead us, he also protects our back. The person who is not surrounded by the presence of God is following a delusion. You may spend thirty years living out that delusion, but in the end it will produce only sterility, emptiness, and bankruptcy. Only the person who has put a hand in Christ's and said, "Anywhere, anything, I will follow you," has a good and eternal future.

Are you placing your hand firmly in his, without any reluctance or hesitation to go with him wherever he leads? If you choose to travel without his protection, your tomorrow will have darkness and defeat, but if you allow him to surround you completely, your tomorrow will be a pathway of light, truth, and hope.

a well-read christian

1 corinthians 9:24 – 27

*Do you not know that in a race all the runners run,
but only one gets the prize? Run in such a way as to get the prize.*
1 Corinthians 9:24

One day when my son was home during his medical training, we had a conversation about his work. I said to him, "In medicine you have found what you want to do. You are going to give your life to it, and you will love it. You are going to give everything you have, and you are going to give it night and day. But you must be careful. The first thing you know, you will wake up and be fifty years old, and the only thing you will have between your ears will be human anatomy and how to cut on it. That is a pretty thin ration on which to live intellectually, emotionally, and spiritually. You need to start forcing yourself every day to read something that is not medical so that when you are fifty, you will be a human person as well as a surgeon. You ought to read your Bible from beginning to end every year for ten years. If you read three chapters a day and five chapters on Sunday, you can work your way through it in a year, and in ten years you will be a halfway intelligent Christian layman."

This principle is true even if your vocation is not as demanding as the medical profession. Every Christian person ought to read things outside their immediate field of interest so they will have a well-rounded and well-informed body of knowledge, and every Christian person needs to spend time every day in God's Word. As the years pass, the time studying God's Word will become the most valuable time you have spent, and you will be more of a real person and more of a true person because of your time with God.

hearing the message

acts 10

*Therefore I want you to know that God's salvation has been
sent to the Gentiles, and they will listen!*
Acts 28:28

Our witness to the gospel message should never be parochial. We are not presenting an American or European gospel. The gospel comes from the living God, who made all people. He knows all human needs and has made preparation for each individual. Our communication of the good news must differentiate it from our eccentricities, our differences, and our particularities. It needs to be presented in such a way that each hearer can identify the message as personally, poignantly, and practically applicable.

When I was a pastor I found that a typical congregation was a bit like an orchestra. Each of my sermons needed to include aspects that would appeal to different people or groups of people in the audience. An illustration about music would capture the imagination of some in my audience and draw them into the service. A historical story or allusion would delight and surprise the history buffs in the crowd, and suddenly they would become active listeners.

Wise is the one who can speak in such a way that identification takes place between the people listening and the one speaking. That is what language is all about. It helps us to know one another; it helps us to understand each other; it means that we value one another. Most of all, it enables us to effectively communicate the message of salvation.

buried in your work

matthew 25:14 – 23

Then I heard the voice of the Lord saying, "Whom shall I send?
And who will go for us?"
Isaiah 6:8

There is plenty of worthwhile work to do. As long as one human being made in the image of God is suffering and you have the capacity to help, there is work for you. God wills that we be like him, and his work is for others. Our work is to please and glorify him by working for other people.

A young American student was looking for the church of John Berridge, who was a preacher friend of John Wesley. An Anglican pastor took him to Berridge's grave. The tombstone had this inscription:

Here lie the earthly remains of John Berridge, late Vicar of Everton,
an itinerant servant of Jesus Christ who loved his Master and His Work,
and after running on His errands for many
years was called to wait upon Him above.

Reader, art thou born again?
No salvation without a new birth.
I was born in sin February 1716.
Remained ignorant of my fallen state until 1730.
Lived proudly in faith and works for salvation till 1754.
Admitted to Everton vicarage 1755.
Fled to Jesus alone for refuge 1756.
Fell asleep in Christ January 22, 1793.

When the student had finished reading, the vicar said, "You will note on which side of the church Mr. Berridge is buried. You see, this is the side where the unbaptized and suicides are buried. He lived for sinners in his life. He did not want to be parted from them in his death."

Dare I urge you today to find work of such worth that when your remains are laid in the ground to await God's call, you will want him to find you buried in your work?

Westminster Shorter Catechism (1647), Question 1.

finding joy in commitment

deuteronomy 6

I am the LORD your God, who brought you out of Egypt,
out of the land of slavery. You shall have no other gods before me.
Deuteronomy 5:6–7

It is fantasy to believe that there can be any true joy in life without obligation. On occasion we may enjoy freedom from obligation, but to take our wishes seriously—as if they were possibilities for real life—is illusion, and illusion is deadly. True joys are always and only rooted in reality. Life's greatest ecstasies are found within life's most binding and sacred commitments. Run from the commitments, and life's deepest joys will be tragically diminished or defiled.

The dream of removing responsibilities and duties in order to relax and enjoy ourselves is false and fleeting. There is little to enjoy in a self that lacks a sense of duty and a commitment to it. Our dreams are often insubstantial and devoid of enduring existence. They are an illusion.

I urge you to look closely at your commitments. Your joys in life will be as meaningful and extensive as your commitments are. The reason should be obvious. Human persons are finite; we are creatures. Therefore, our purpose and fulfillment will never be found in ourselves. We are made to look out, to look beyond, and to look to. We are made for God. There is no higher word of wisdom than the old catechetical instruction "Glorify God and enjoy Him forever."* Part of the beauty of that word is that forever includes today.

kingdom greatness

john 13:1 – 20

Jesus knew that . . . he had come from God and was returning to God;
so he got up from the meal, took off his outer clothing,
and wrapped a towel around his waist. After that,
he poured water into a basin and began to wash his disciples' feet.
John 13:3–5

One of the most difficult things for the disciples to grasp in Jesus' teaching about the Cross was the fact that he must suffer for them. He was the Christ, their Messiah-King. Even if they had expected to suffer for him, the idea that he should suffer for them seemed contrary to reason. Indeed, it was contrary to human wisdom. God's ways are not natural according to our fleshly understanding. Paul declares, "Very rarely will anyone die for a righteous man, though for a good man someone might possibly dare to die" (Rom. 5:7); no one dies for the unrighteous. But Jesus told the disciples that God was commending his love to them because Christ was going to die for sinners, the just for the unjust. It hardly seemed right, but it is God's way of redemption.

On the night before the Cross, Jesus gave the disciples a lesson on their relationships to each other. The ways of kingdom service are contrary to natural instinct. The disciples had been filled with pride and a false sense of self-importance. They had been arguing about who should be the greatest among them. James and John had even asked for the seats at Christ's right and left in his kingdom. Now Jesus showed them the way of kingdom greatness. It is the way of service. He took the towel, basin, and water and knelt to wash their feet. It is proper for the worshiper to kneel before the One who is worshiped, but now the One worshiped was kneeling to wash the feet of the worshiper. Needless to say, this was a shock to them, but it was a good lesson. Jesus showed them that true greatness is through humility and service. If he was not too good to serve them, they should not be hesitant to serve one another. The point is not who can be first in honor, but who can be first in service. The Eleven must never have forgotten the lesson. It is one that we must never forget either.

knowing jesus

john 17:1 – 5

I want to know Christ.
Philippians 3:10

In the third chapter of Paul's letter to the Philippians, he opens his soul and reveals to the church the one passion of his life: "I want to know Christ and the power of his resurrection and the fellowship of sharing in his sufferings" (Phil. 3:10). Paul was a Jew, so there is no question but that he spoke Hebrew very well and understood the Hebrew Scripture. In the Old Testament knowledge tends first of all to be personal.

Most people focus on knowledge *about* something, and there is objectivity, detachment, and separation in this type of knowledge. The word *know* is used in another way in the Old Testament. Genesis 1–3 tells the story of Adam and Eve and the Tree of Knowledge of Good and Evil. In order to understand that word *knowledge,* one must read Genesis 4:1: "Now Adam knew Eve his wife, and she conceived and bore Cain" (NKJV). The kind of knowledge indicated here is deeply personal and reciprocal. It is easy to understand why God did not want his people to have this intimate understanding of evil. A man's knowledge of his wife is infinitely different from his knowledge of physics or history. Knowledge of those things is to be used, but the knowledge of another person is a knowledge of identification and reciprocity. In that relationship your life becomes mingled with another's, and the two become one.

Paul's desire to know Christ is a desire to have his life merged with Christ's in such a way that he cannot be separated from Jesus and Jesus cannot be separated from him. The two have become one—not in essence, but in relationship.

pentecostal language

acts 2

Each one heard them speaking in his own language.
Acts 2:6

The most important language for communicating the gospel is not the language of culture or of common experience. The true language of the soul is the language of the Spirit. It is no accident that all the people present for Pentecost heard the message in their own tongue. We will never be ready to reach all people until each of us has had a personal Pentecost. The baptism of the Holy Spirit with its cleansing, transforming, enlightening, and educating power produces an identification point with other people. Suddenly we are able to build bridges to people we never expected or hoped to reach. This is the power of Pentecost. When a formerly ineffective preacher or lay witness comes under the anointing of God, that one speaks a language that every person can understand and with which everyone can identify. The speaker suddenly sounds like power itself.

We must believe this because we are living in a day when many Christians ask, "How can we communicate the gospel to people who are not like us—to people who have been conditioned differently from us?" Frankly, people's conditioning is not of ultimate importance. Because every human being is made in the image of God, his Word can be brought into each person's language, and one has not really heard the message of the gospel until one has heard it in one's own language. Notice the respect that God paid to all the people on the day of Pentecost. He did not say to the Parthian, "Now I know you don't understand Aramaic very well, but the gospel is in Aramaic, and if you listen very closely you will probably understand it." Instead, a man stood up and spoke, and suddenly the Parthian came roaring out of the crowd and said, "Wait a minute! This is for me!"

God declares that every person deserves the chance to hear the message in his or her own tongue with the familiar idioms, overtones, and connotations. How often we forget this and insist that people hear the gospel in English. God, forgive us.

lavish love

mark 14:1 – 9

*While he was in Bethany, reclining at the table in the home of a man
known as Simon the Leper, a woman came with an alabaster jar
of very expensive perfume, made of pure nard.
She broke the jar and poured the perfume on his head.*
Mark 14:3

The seventh chapter of Luke's gospel records the story of a dinner given for
Jesus at Simon's house. In the middle of the feast a woman comes and
breaks a jar of ointment and pours it over Jesus. She also wets his feet with
her tears and dries them with her hair. Matthew and Mark speak about the
Passover being held at Simon's house, and they record a similar incident
that took place at that time. John wanted to show the lavish affection that
Mary of Bethany poured out on Jesus because of what he had done for her
and her family. She washed his feet with her tears and anointed him with
an expensive perfume. Interestingly, John tells us that it would have taken
eight months' wages to feed the five thousand, and twelve months' wages
to buy the perfume Mary poured on the feet of Jesus. This is what we call
lavish love.

Another indication of Mary's lavish love came when she dried his feet
with her hair. A fascinating story appears in rabbinic literature about a
woman whose sons all became high priests. She stood quite high in the Jewish community because she had six sons who went into the Holy of Holies.
This was a remarkable thing in the history of Israel. When people asked her
about her holiness, she said, "God has favored me because the rafters in my
bedroom have never seen my hair unloosed." A Jewish woman did not
loosen her hair except in the presence of her husband.

Mary loosened her hair and dried the feet of Jesus. She gave herself
totally, completely, and lavishly to him. John records that a fragrance filled
the air. Such love is a fragrant offering to God.

the light of the world

isaiah 58:9 – 12

*Let your light shine before men, that they may see your good deeds
and praise your Father in heaven.*
Matthew 5:16

In the tabernacle of Yahweh, inside the Holy Place, there was a lamp stand that had six branches of solid gold and supported seven lamps. The lamp stand stood on the south side of the sanctuary. Pure olive oil was used in the lamps, and they burned from evening to morning. The continual burning symbolized the uninterrupted worship and the unceasing emission of light by the people of God.

This light was to remind them of two things. First, it was the only light in that tabernacle. Revelation 21 pictures the new Jerusalem in which there is neither temple nor light. The Lord God Almighty and the Lamb are the temple and the light of that new city. The light in the tabernacle points us to him who is the Light of the world. Christ himself is our light.

Second, the light reminds us of our mission: Jesus said his followers were to be lights to the dark world. It is the business of believers to shine as lights in the midst of a dark and shadowy society. All light has its source in God, so any light we possess will be derived from his presence. We shine not by our own might or power, but by the Holy Spirit.

In the same way that he is our light, we ought also to be the light of the world around us.

losing the spirit

1 samuel 15; 16:14 – 23

Now the Spirit of the LORD had departed from Saul,
and an evil spirit from the LORD tormented him.
1 Samuel 16:14

It is possible for a person to know the Spirit and then lose the Spirit from his or her life. This thought is biblical, although we do not enjoy entertaining it. One person that Scripture mentions as being filled with the Spirit was the first king of Israel, Saul. Significantly, there was little that was royal about him until the Spirit came upon him. He was timid and afraid, but when he was anointed, the Spirit came upon him, and he was a good and righteous king. Then in his own self-will he decided to go his own way instead of going the Spirit's way, and the Spirit was taken away from him. In the same hour that David was anointed king in Saul's place, the Spirit departed from Saul and rested upon David.

Saul wandered for the rest of his days. He sat on a throne, but he was stripped of his true royalty. He had all the external trappings, but none of the internal realities. The thing that had made him a king before God and the people had been taken away. There is no question but that Saul was on David's mind when David wrote the cry in Psalm 51:11, "Take not thy holy spirit from me" (KJV). David had seen a man from whom the Holy Spirit had been taken, and he recoiled from the thought of it.

A person who has known intimacy with the Holy Spirit can lose that intimacy. This is why it is never safe to find security in merely talking about the Holy Spirit without obeying him.

first time, all the way

1 samuel 15 and 18

*Does the LORD delight in burnt offerings and sacrifices
as much as in obeying the voice of the LORD?
To obey is better than sacrifice,
and to heed is better than the fat of rams.*
1 Samuel 15:22

The story of King Saul is a tragic and gripping tale about the failure of a man to be all that God had called him to be. At one point in his life we particularly see the selfish nature of his heart. A young lad named David had killed Goliath, and the Hebrews had a great victory over their enemies. When they came back into the city, the women began to sing: "Saul has slain his thousands, and David his tens of thousands" (1 Sam. 18:7).

In reality, David had killed one enemy, and Saul had led the entire army, but selfishness distorts our picture of ourselves and others, and there sprang into Saul's heart an uncontrollable jealousy and bitterness. He determined in his heart that David would have to be eliminated. Interestingly enough, when Saul first met David, he had loved him, but as soon as David became a threat to Saul's reputation, Saul saw him as the enemy. That is the problem with the self; if a person lets it remain uncrucified, uncleansed, and unpurged, it will ultimately produce the worst kind of evil inside the heart. If our lives are ever going to count, we are going to have to belong to God in a way that Saul was unwilling to do. Our hearts must be surrendered to him so fully and completely that other people are not a threat to us but a blessing, God's provision for us.

Saul not only had a selfish heart; he also was a man who had learned to settle for partial obedience. When God told him to destroy the Amalekites, he assented with his mouth but not with his heart. His army killed the worthless and despised creatures that were not valuable as a sacrifice to Yahweh, but they kept alive the healthy livestock. They gave the lesser things to God, and God will never be content with that. He wants all and he wants the best. Saul was willing to give the dregs and the margins of his life, the things that were not particularly pleasing to him, but he was not willing to give God that for which God asked. And so he settled for partial obedience.

Our family has a motto that we teach our toddlers when they are learning to obey: "First time, all the way." If you do not obey the Lord Jesus the first time he asks something of you, and if you do not obey him completely, you are endangering yourself and the people around you.

willing to wait

1 samuel 24

He said to his men, "The LORD forbid that I should do such a thing
to my master, the LORD's anointed, or lift my hand against him;
for he is the anointed of the LORD." With these words David
rebuked his men and did not allow them to attack Saul.
1 Samuel 24:6–7

The key to David's character may be seen in his reaction to Saul. Samuel had anointed him, so David knew that he was destined to be king. He knew that he was called of God to that role. In fact, the Spirit of God had already departed from Saul and had come to him, making him qualified to be king. He had all of the kingly authority, and it was all gone from Saul. Moreover, the people of God were suffering under Saul's tragic leadership. It seemed an ideal time for David to make his move.

One day David was hiding from Saul in a cave, and Saul came into the cave to relieve himself, not knowing that David and his men were lurking in the shadows. One of David's men turned to him and said, "The Lord has delivered Israel. God has given him into our hands." The temptation for David was to think, *Now I have a chance to fulfill God's will and save Israel.* But David said, "Don't you touch him." It was God's business to put David on the throne, and David was not about to put himself there. He believed that when God wanted to make him king, he would do it.

We can never rush the will of God. David could wait because he knew he could trust God. Our efforts profit nothing; only the Spirit of Jesus gives life and direction. During these days, do you have a spiritual need in your heart? Are you pushing him? Today is the day to meet God. Do not be content until you are free to let the Spirit of God order your life.

marks of a christian

mark 10:17 – 30

Jesus looked at him and loved him. "One thing you lack," he said.
"Go, sell everything you have and give to the poor, and
you will have treasure in heaven. Then come, follow me."
Mark 10:21

The story of the rich young ruler helps us understand which characteristics of an individual do *not* make that person a Christian. The story concludes with Jesus' demands for discipleship.

The sincerity of the rich ruler did not make him a Christian. One can tell that he was sincere because he ran to Jesus and knelt before him. He was not ashamed of his desire or need. He honestly sought eternal life. In fact, he was a good man, but this did not make him a Christian.

The righteousness of the rich ruler did not make him a Christian. He was remarkably upright, keeping all the commandments. He was clean and faithful. He did not steal or deceive, and he did not kill by murder, ill will, or resentment. He did not lie or defraud people. He even honored his parents. And yet, all these righteous actions did not make him a disciple of Christ.

The love of the Lord Jesus did not make the rich ruler a Christian. Christ loved him, but that love was not enough to make him a follower of Christ.

If sincerity and righteousness and the love of God are not enough to make a person a Christian, what is necessary? Here again, the story of the rich ruler helps us to understand. Becoming a Christian means believing that Jesus is trustworthy and surrendering our life to his control. A Christian is a person who believes in Jesus enough to follow Jesus.

once and for all

romans 8:35 – 39

I am my beloved's,
And my beloved is mine.
He feeds his flock among the lilies.
Song of Solomon 6:3 NKJV

Some people argue against the possibility of entire sanctification, insisting that we have to settle the question of who our first love is day by day. But when I awaken every morning, I do not have to decide if I am married or not. That decision was made long ago. I am so glad that there is no turning back. My relationship with my wife is a symbol of my relationship with Christ. I have made a permanent covenant with her and am also able to make an eternal commitment to him that will never be broken. I do not have to choose to make that commitment every day. Once I have made that covenant, the only way it can be broken is through treachery on my part.

God will not break his part, and he gives the Holy Spirit to prod and help me to want to keep mine. A person will face occasional questions about that relationship, but there is a difference between having questions and repudiating the covenant.

This is the covenant that God wants between his children and himself. We do not have to face it over and over again. We can make an inner commitment of heart to him. That one-time decision costs our whole heart and our whole life. We must love him more than anything else in existence. If we want to enter into a deeper relationship with God, he must be our first love, and that love must overshadow and control all of the other loves in our life.

sanctification and marriage

isaiah 54:1 – 5

"For this reason a man will leave his father and mother and be united to his wife, and the two will become one flesh." So they are no longer two, but one. Therefore what God has joined together, let man not separate.
Mark 10:7–9

If our relationship with the Lord Jesus is a love relationship, is there anything in the covenant of marriage that could teach us about being entirely sanctified in our relationship to Jesus? Three characteristics of marriage apply to our ultimate love relationship. First of all, marriage is exclusive. It is the counterpart to the first commandment, "You shall have no other gods before me" (Exod. 20:3). A marriage partner demands exclusive love, and so does God.

Second, marriage touches every aspect of our existence. The totality of the commitment is complete. There are no areas of our life that are left unaffected by our relationship to our spouse. The relationship with Jesus is similar. It is meant to be a total relationship, one affecting and determining everything else in our lives.

Finally, marriage is a permanent relationship. It is an unconditional giving of the self to another person forever. Our relationship with Jesus is supposed to be a permanent relationship that we would not violate under any condition.

It is terrifying to think of committing oneself to God exclusively, totally, and permanently unless one understands this commitment in terms of a love relationship. For some people marriage is a bit frightening, but it is a relationship for which the human heart longs. The demands that Jesus makes on us are simply those necessary for any beautiful and loving marriage relationship.

identification with god

john 1:1 – 5, 14

We proclaim to you what we have seen and heard,
so that you also may have fellowship with us.
And our fellowship is with the Father and with his Son, Jesus Christ.
1 John 1:3

How is it possible for one to identify with God in such a way that one can share in the fellowship of the Trinity without actually becoming God? How is this closeness compatible with the incredible otherness between human beings and God? In Islam there is no possibility of such fellowship; God is completely other and cannot have close interaction with human beings. On the other hand, in Eastern religions such as Hinduism and in New Age philosophies, human beings can so completely identify with God that they become part of the "divine soul." The distinction between humans and God blurs until humanity is lost in divinity. Neither of these approaches is consistent with biblical thought about humanity's relationship to God, which allows for both fellowship and distinction.

In Christianity a person can be in God but can never be God. Otherness of being is never lost. God can become human, and at one moment of history he did become human, but the process can never take place in the other direction. The basis of this is the Trinity, in which three persons maintain their total distinctiveness and yet have complete unity. It is a unity with otherness. It is a mingling without the formation of a compound. The fellowship and unity between members of the Godhead is ontological—it is part of their essence. The fellowship between human persons is psychological and ethical. The fellowship between human persons and the Trinity is conditional. We can have fellowship with God while he retains his otherness and we retain our personal identity. Our fellowship with God makes us more truly human than we have ever been before. It heals our humanity and completes our personhood.

march 1

---

opportunities missed

numbers 13 – 14

If the LORD is pleased with us, he will lead us into that land, a land
flowing with milk and honey, and will give it to us.
Only do not rebel against the LORD. And do not be afraid of the people
of the land, because we will swallow them up. Their protection is gone,
but the LORD is with us. Do not be afraid of them.
Numbers 14:8–9

One of the most tragic stories in Scripture occurred at Kadesh Barnea when the people of Israel lost the privilege of entering the Promised Land. One man from each tribe was chosen to go and investigate the land of Canaan before the Israelites attacked. They were gone for forty days, and when they returned, they were filled with fear. Giants filled the land, which was walled and heavily guarded. Only Joshua and Caleb urged Israel to arise and enter the land. Numbers 14 is a sad chapter of Scripture because the Israelites turned back from the Promised Land in fear and actually cried out to return to Egypt, the land of their bondage.

It is amazing how quickly we forget what God has done for us. This people had been delivered from Egypt by God's great miracles and mighty power. God's leadership had been completely trustworthy, but they were unwilling to continue to trust him. God had led them safely, and they had built their identity on God's promise that he was going to give them the land of Canaan. They had left Egypt because of that promise, and now they were on the brink of entering the land, but they failed to see God's faithfulness because of the ten spies' negative report. The promise of God's presence, of which Caleb and Joshua reminded them, meant nothing to Israel. They chose not to trust in God.

Unlike Yahweh, who had always been trustworthy, Israel had proven itself unworthy of the opportunity God offered. God pardoned their sin because of Moses' prayer, but as a penalty he refused to allow his people, with the exception of Caleb and Joshua, to see the land of promise. The Israelites were left to wander aimlessly through the wilderness because they refused the great opportunity when it came. As the spies had taken forty days to search out the land, now Israel would wander forty years in the wilderness. When Moses told these things to Israel, the people mourned greatly and begged God for another chance, but it was too late.

The sadness of the story still grips the reader. How true to life it is. There is a "tide in the affairs of men" that if seized leads to greatness. If it is missed, one is left to wander. Opportunities do not stand waiting at the door. Are you among those who wander?

a single attachment

acts 6:8 – 7:60

And surely I am with you always, to the very end of the age.
Matthew 28:20

John Chrysostom was a preacher in the early church. Because of his witness for Christ, he was taken before the emperor, who informed him that he would be put in prison for his faith. Chrysostom answered that the Lord would go with him to prison. Then the emperor threatened to take away all his possessions. Chrysostom was not bothered by this; he simply answered, "There is no way for you to take away all that I possess. My treasures are in heaven, and you cannot reach that far."

Finally, the emperor said in consternation, "Well, I will banish you to the remotest corner of the kingdom." Calmly Chrysostom informed the emperor that the remotest spot in the world was part of his Savior's kingdom and that his Lord would be there too.

God wants us to be people who are free from the necessity of certain places, people, and things so we may be unencumbered. Then he can trust us with more significant assignments. When we do not need anything but him, we truly become available for service.

The gifts of God are merely blessings to be enjoyed; we must have only one necessary attachment, and that is to our Lord Jesus.

opened eyes (part 1)

genesis 21:8 – 21

Then God opened her eyes and she saw a well of water.
So she went and filled the skin with water and gave the boy a drink.
Genesis 21:19

Scripture records many stories of God opening his children's eyes. One example is that of Hagar. This Egyptian servant girl was thrust out of Abraham's camp with her child, Ishmael. Her food ran out, and she was perishing. She cried out to God in her despair, and, as the story says quite simply, "God opened her eyes and she saw a well of water." It was enough water to save their lives.

God opened her eyes and she saw a well. Some people may think that God conjured up a well in the wilderness, and then Hagar saw what God had produced. I believe that there was a well there all along that she had never observed before. When God touched her and opened her eyes, she could see something that was part of her life but that she would never have seen if not for the quickening, illuminating touch of God.

There are incredible resources in your life that you may miss if you do not let Christ touch your eyes. You will find there are things in your natural possession about which you would never have known and that you would never have utilized if it had not been for his quickening touch.

I had the privilege of sitting with a missionary in Korea who was responsible for feeding eighteen thousand widows and orphans a day. We sat on a hilltop overlooking a saltwater lake. At least that's what I saw: a lake formed by the tide. This missionary envisioned rice fields that could feed his orphans and widows. He saw a stone causeway that would hold back the tide. He saw the rain that would fill up the low places and make possible the rice fields that would supply food for the people. God had given this man a burden and a responsibility, and God was opening his eyes to see what he could do to meet those demands. And the missionary did just what God had shown him he could do.

Has God given you a burden? Somewhere there are resources for you to meet that responsibility. You must have his quickening touch on the eyes of your imagination so you can see the resources that are available to you.

opened eyes (part 2)

numbers 22–23

Then the LORD opened Balaam's eyes, and he saw
the angel of the LORD standing in the road with his sword drawn.
So he bowed low and fell facedown.
Numbers 22:31

The second Old Testament story of opened eyes involves a man and his donkey. It is told in Numbers 22.

A pagan king wanted the prophet Balaam to curse Israel. He offered Balaam abundant wealth if he would just curse God's people. As Balaam started off to do the king's bidding, his donkey stopped and would not move in spite of Balaam's beatings and abuse. Finally, God opened Balaam's eyes, and in front of the recalcitrant donkey there stood an angel of the Lord with a flaming sword.

It is interesting that an animal could see better than a person, but that may often be the case. We choose to see what we want to see. Balaam chose to see wealth, and therefore he could not see the angel of God who had come to slay him. God gave us this ludicrous story to tell us that unless he touches our eyes, we may spend our lives pursuing what is wrong, useless, or even evil. Unless he touches us, we may never even know that we are on the path of destruction.

There are many people in today's culture who believe they are giving themselves to noble causes, but some of those causes will ultimately be destructive to human well-being. The people involved may never know that the things to which they gave their lives hurt people instead of helping them. Unless Christ is allowed to open our eyes, we will waste our lives on that which is ultimately meaningless, empty, or even destructive.

"Guard your steps when you go to the house of God. Go near to listen rather than to offer the sacrifice of fools, who do not know that they do wrong" (Eccl. 5:1).

opened eyes (part 3)

2 kings 6:8–23

And Elisha prayed, "O LORD, open his eyes so he may see."
Then the LORD opened the servant's eyes, and he looked
and saw the hills full of horses and chariots of fire all around Elisha.
2 Kings 6:17

The third account of opened eyes is a fascinating little story about the prophet Elisha and his servant. The military plans of the Syrian king had been frustrated time and again because of Elisha, and the king was angry. He suspected there was a spy inside his inner circle because every time he made a military move, the Israelites were expecting it and were prepared for it. Unbeknownst to the Syrian king, God was telling Elisha the plans the Syrian king made, and Elisha would relay those plans to the king of Israel, who would deploy his forces accordingly.

The Syrian king grew so angry that he made a plan to capture Elisha by surrounding the city in which he lived. When Elisha's servant saw the army surrounding their town, he was terrified and went to Elisha in fear. Elisha prayed that the Lord would open the servant's eyes so he could see that the number with them was greater than the number against them. God opened the eyes of that servant, and he saw the skies filled with chariots of fire, the servants of God surrounding the Syrian army.

This did not occur every day in Elisha's life, and it will not occur every day in your life. However, if you let Christ open your eyes, you will find there are days when you have resources available to you that you never knew. Some days there are even supernatural resources that no one around you will be able to see. There will come days when you need those resources and need to see that the resources with you are greater and more numerous than those against you. On such days, let Christ open your eyes.

march 6

opened eyes (part 4)

luke 24:13 – 35

*When he was at the table with them, he took bread, gave thanks,
broke it and began to give it to them. Then their eyes were opened
and they recognized him, and he disappeared from their sight.*
Luke 24:30–31

It was the Sunday after the crucifixion. There were two men, not preachers or apostles, but laymen who were walking from Jerusalem to Emmaus. They were lovers of Jesus, and now the Christ they had known and in whom they had trusted was dead. They were mourning, and they wept as they walked. Suddenly a stranger joined them on the road. When he learned the cause of their grief, he opened up the Old Testament to them and explained the meaning of the Cross. He stopped to eat with the two men, and when he broke the bread, their eyes were opened, and they knew it was Jesus himself.

The living Christ is really present, as literally present in your life as he was with Cleopas and his friend that night. They never knew he was there until he opened their eyes. Whatever your circumstances are today, they are not as hopeless as Cleopas and his friend believed theirs to be. Jesus is present in those situations that seem the most destitute and horrifying. It is his presence that will make sense of your situation. It is his presence that will bring hope and joy into your circumstances. Christ is with you. Have you forgotten that? Let him open your eyes so you can see him.

the high priest

hebrews 7 – 8

Such a high priest meets our need—one who is holy, blameless,
pure, set apart from sinners, exalted above the heavens.
Unlike the other high priests, he does not need to offer sacrifices
day after day, first for his own sins, and then for the sins of the people.
He sacrificed for their sins once for all when he offered himself.
Hebrews 7:26–27

It is essential for us to understand the role of the priests in the Old Testament because it will enable us to understand Christ's role in our redemption. The priests were the mediators between God in his holiness and human beings in their unholiness. Has God's holiness changed? Has the sinfulness of people decreased? Hardly! The same need for mediation exists today, but it is met in a different way. It is no longer met through the ministry of earthly priests. We have a great High Priest who does not need to make atonement for himself as the priests of Israel did. Our High Priest is the sinless Christ Jesus.

A second thing to be learned about the priestly role is that God is not to be approached lightly. In Old Testament times God placed barriers between the people and himself in order to protect the people. Only members of a special tribe could minister in the house of worship, and only members of one family from that tribe could offer sacrifices. Further, only a single member of that family could come into the presence of God behind the veil in the Holy of Holies, and he could go there only once a year. The priest had to make atonement for his own sins before he made atonement for the people. If he did not, the penalty was death.

The holiness of our God remains pure and powerful, but we no longer approach him through an earthly and sinful priest. We have access to the Father through Jesus, who in his death rent the veil of the temple and made access for all persons to come boldly to God. But we do not come alone. We come through Jesus, so our boldness is not presumption. It is based on the atoning work of Christ. In the institution of the priesthood we see a picture of what Christ came to do. He did away with the Old Testament priesthood, but the ministry and reality of that priesthood he took upon himself and performs for us even today.

So "approach the throne of grace with confidence" through Christ (Heb. 4:16).

> *No condemnation now I dread;*
> *Jesus, and all in Him, is mine.*
> *Alive in Him, my living Head,*
> *And clothed in righteousness divine,*
> *Bold I approach th' eternal throne,*
> *And claim the crown, through Christ my own.* *

---

*Charles Wesley, "And Can It Be That I Should Gain," *Hymns for Praise and Worship*, no. 115.

double it!

psalm 4

In the morning, O LORD, you hear my voice;
in the morning I lay my requests before you
and wait in expectation.
Psalm 5:3

It is wonderful sometimes what impact a single sentence from another person can have on you. I was a freshman in college, and the best thing in my Christian life was a hunger to please God and to know him better. A senior student of remarkable maturity befriended me. I decided to ask him how I could grow more quickly in my Christian life. His response was, "How much time do you pray?" I am sure I lied to him. His response was simple: "Double it!" That closed our conversation. Just a simple sentence. "Double it!" I went away with his words ringing in my ears.

I knew that my friend's pattern was to have quiet time first thing in the morning. It was necessary for me to work when I was in college, and I had a bakery job that began quite early. The prospect of following my friend's example was not an easy one for me. I was about as undisciplined as someone my age could be. But I set my alarm clock an hour earlier and began to try to do what my friend suggested. Only God knows how many times I fell asleep on my knees as I tried to begin my day with God. I have no regrets about that. A habit was being formed without which my life would have been tragically empty. Slowly what I did in duty became a delight. I found I could live without other things, but I could not live without time with Christ.

My life has had many significant moments, but as I look back, I must admit that those two simple words spoken by a senior to an undisciplined and struggling freshman were among the most important.

In the morning, O LORD, you hear my voice;
in the morning I lay my requests before you
and wait in expectation (Ps. 5:3).

do what you have to do

luke 23:6 – 12

*Then, dipping the piece of bread, [Jesus] gave it to Judas Iscariot,
son of Simon. As soon as Judas took the bread, Satan entered into him.
"What you are about to do, do quickly," Jesus told him.
John 13:26–28*

It was the last time Jesus would see Judas in this world. They had spent some three years together. Now Judas goes out to his own destruction and Jesus makes no plea for him. His word is simply, "What you do, do quickly."

Scripture is clear that a moment can come in a person's life when God has nothing more to say. It has all been said, and we have rejected it. We see this in Jesus' appearance before Herod. Jesus refused to even acknowledge Herod's presence. It is not often that one ignores a king, especially when one has been hauled before him. Nor is it common for a prisoner to refuse to answer a judge, especially when the prisoner's life is at stake. But Jesus had nothing to say to Herod. It had all been said.

Herod had known John the Baptist. John had talked to Herod about righteousness, truth, and holy things. Herod had responded by having John beheaded to please a dancing girl. Then Herod heard about Jesus. He was delighted that Jesus was coming. He had heard of Jesus' miracles. In his superstition and curiosity, he thought that he could get Jesus to perform one of his miracles before him. However, Jesus did not come to entertain or amuse. He came to save. If a person has no interest in salvation, Jesus has nothing to say, so he refused to play Herod's game and refused even to speak to him.

Who is this Jesus? It is the Savior of infinite love who stretches out his arms to receive a sinful world. But because he is also the God who makes us free, he will not presume on our freedom. When our choice is made, when our face is set, he will respect our decision. There is just nothing more for him to say.

disciples of joy

psalm 100

*So continuing daily with one accord in the temple, and breaking bread
from house to house, they ate their food with gladness and simplicity of heart,
praising God and having favor with all the people. And the Lord
added to the church daily those who were being saved.*
Acts 2:46–47 NKJV

The early Christians were people of joy. The Word says that "with gladness
and simplicity of heart," they ate their meat; they praised God and they
rejoiced (Acts 2:46 NKJV). There is a passage in the Psalms that speaks
about rendering to God "the sacrifices of thanksgiving" (Ps. 107:22 NKJV).
Christian joy is not something that solves all our problems, and it is not
something that comes automatically. Joy is not even necessarily something
that is given to us, but is something that we choose. Joy is not a commod-
ity that God drops as a gift into our hearts. Joy is an option; it is a choice
instead of a gift.

Certainly, this was true in the early church. The first believers chose to
suffer joyously because it was Christ's will for them. The world is dumb-
founded with people who take the difficult in front of them and choose to
see it as a joy. That attitude of joy will make an enormous difference in the
ministry to which you have been assigned, whether it is in a business office,
in a church, or in your home. You will never be as tempted to run away from
your situation when you look at it through eyes of joy and even see it as
God's gift to you. Joy is a choice.

Hear the old Scottish version of Psalm 100:1–3:

All people that on earth do dwell,
Sing to the Lord with cheerful voice.
Him serve with mirth, his praise forth tell
*Come ye before Him and rejoice.**

I like that word, *mirth*. Are you mirthful with him?

---

* *The Psalms of David in Metre* (Dallas, Tex.: Presbyterian Heritage Publishers, 1991).

pioneers by design

psalm 8

*Rule over the fish of the sea and the birds of the air and over every
living creature that moves on the ground.*
Genesis 1:28

Some of the most delightful surprises in my life have come from the portions
of Scripture that seem most objectionable to the world. Out of these con-
troversial passages come the most illuminating insights. For example, the
Creation story, which is normally read through a fog of confusion, has
become the very basis of my intellectual freedom. Genesis 1 and 2 lay the
foundation for all the rest of Scripture and human history.

- Lesson 1: There is only one God. He is the Creator of all things.
- Lesson 2: All that he has made is good.
- Lesson 3: He has made the world not only for my enjoyment, but
  for my mastery, and not just for control, but for stewardship.

These lessons reveal that I am free—or rather, obligated—to explore
and discover all that is part of my world. This offers the most exciting challenges. Anything that gives me a better understanding and control of his
purposes in this world is a valid Christian calling. God has given human
beings a marvelous curiosity and has placed us in a world designed to
encourage our curiosity.

God's people have largely forgotten this command because we are pre-
occupied with ourselves. Our forgetfulness though does not nullify God's
command. Christians, of all people, should feel the most comfortable in
intellectual pursuits. Christians are the people whose basic philosophy jus-
tifies study. We were made to discover the world that God has given to us.
We are pioneers by design. If we choose to see ourselves in that light, our
approach to all of life will be different. We will diligently seek to learn and
grow. We will delight in the world he has given us.

presence: the basis of revelation

john 16:12 – 15

Righteousness goes before him
and prepares the way for his steps.
Psalm 85:13

Only God can make himself known in human experience. Revelation is simply the presence of God in human history through which human persons come to know who he is and what he does. There is a certain kind of knowledge that is knowledge about something. This type of knowledge does not demand personal interaction; it only requires observation and study. Christian theology and divine revelation are more than this. Christian theology is personal knowledge of the three divine persons in one God. We enter into a personal relationship and learn about him through personal interaction. Out of this relationship comes a knowledge that is deeper and truer than any acquired from third-party information.

When I was a pastor I found myself ministering to a young couple who were both doctors intending to go on the mission field. They told me their love story. When they were in medical school, Tom was assigned to study a certain cadaver, and when he looked over that cadaver at his partner, he found himself looking into the eyes of a very beautiful young lady. Somewhat befuddled, he said, "What are you doing here?"

To which she pertly replied, "I am going to be a medical missionary."

"So am I," he responded. When the team of two students studied that cadaver, they gained medical knowledge, but there was another type of studying going on as she watched him and he watched her. Eventually he said, "I'd better start dressing up when I go and study that cadaver." The knowledge they were gaining of each other was very different from and far more influential and life-transforming than the knowledge they were gaining of human anatomy.

When you come to Scripture or when you come to know Christ, do you approach him as something to be studied? Or is he someone who stole your heart before you even knew it. Are you now on a mission to learn more and more about him? Your approach to Christ will determine how well you know him.

do not grieve the spirit

isaiah 63:7 – 19

And do not grieve the Holy Spirit of God, with whom
you were sealed for the day of redemption.
Ephesians 4:30

What makes it possible for someone to be living in intimacy with God and then to lose that intimacy? I believe that it is a matter of inner attitude which determines all personal relationships.

The Scriptures speak of four negative attitudes that one can take toward God's Holy Spirit. The first of these is found in Ephesians 4:30. The King James Version says, "And grieve not the holy Spirit of God." The Good News Bible (Today's English Version) says, "And do not make God's Holy Spirit sad." There is something to be said for the Good News translation because it emphasizes the personal character of our relationship with the Holy Spirit. It is possible for us to hurt the Holy Spirit.

A personal relationship has to be very close in order for grief even to be possible. You can grieve your mother or father, you can grieve your husband or wife, you can grieve a close and intimate friend, but you cannot grieve a casual acquaintance. You can offend him, but not grieve him. You can certainly never grieve an enemy. You can make him mad or hostile, but that is not grief. The word *grieve* indicates a tender, intimate, and loving relationship in which someone who loves deeply is hurt.

Two questions: Are you living in the close, intimate relationship with the Holy Spirit that makes grief a possibility? Second, is he grieved with you? If so, do not wait another minute before you make amends.

do not quench the spirit

acts 2

Do not quench the Spirit.
1 Thessalonians 5:19 NKJV

The second attitude one can take toward the Holy Spirit is described in 1 Thessalonians. "Do not quench the Spirit" (NKJV). Only a fire can be quenched. John the Baptist's words about Jesus were, "He will baptize you with the Holy Spirit and with fire" (Matt. 3:11). On Pentecost, the Spirit came in power and this baptism of fire occurred. The tongues of fire rested on the disciples' heads, and a fire was kindled within their hearts. It was out of this blaze in the hearts of the disciples that the fire began to spread throughout the world. A fire comes to a person's soul when that believer is filled with the Spirit, and there comes a passionate burning to know Christ and to share his gospel. An ignited person with an ignited heart is the one baptized by the Spirit's fire.

However, that raging, beautiful fire of devotion can be extinguished. Paul declares it possible to douse the fire that burns within; to reduce the raging flame that burns brightly in your soul until all that remains is a blackened, cold cinder. Where there was once warmth and light, there is now only coldness and death.

Interestingly, in 1 Thessalonians 5:19, Paul does not give any description of how one quenches the Spirit's fire; he simply commands the Thessalonians not to do so. A fire is quenched when water is poured on it. Sin is the "water" in our lives that grieves the Spirit and puts out the Spirit's flame.

Is your life white-hot with the fire of the Spirit? Or have you let the fire be put out?

do not resist the spirit

acts 7

You stiff-necked people, with uncircumcised hearts and ears!
You are just like your fathers: You always resist the Holy Spirit!
Acts 7:51

The third attitude toward the Holy Spirit was described by Stephen when he was making his defense before he was martyred. He was speaking to the Pharisees who were out to destroy him, and he said they had "uncircumcised hearts," or "unbaptized hearts." The Pharisees had been baptized in the ritual bath of purification *(mikvah)*, but the ceremony was simply the symbol without reality. It did not reflect any internal or eternal change. Let me paraphrase Stephen: "Boys, you are careful about the outside, but you are without the internal reality. You are deaf to God's message and empty of his Spirit. You are just like your ancestors. You too have resisted the Holy Spirit."

A believer's relationship with the Spirit of God can move with remarkable speed from a close, intimate relationship to one in which the love has been extinguished, and finally to one full of opposition and resistance. Once one begins to grieve the Spirit, the next step is to quench the Spirit's voice, and ultimately resistance to the Spirit of Jesus takes up residence in the heart unless one repents. Do not resist the Spirit. The consequences are too dire.

do not insult the spirit

matthew 12:25 – 37

Anyone who rejected the law of Moses died without mercy on the testimony of two or three witnesses. How much more severely do you think a man deserves to be punished who has trampled the Son of God under foot, who has treated as an unholy thing the blood of the covenant that sanctified him, and who has insulted the Spirit of grace?
Hebrews 10:28–29

The fourth attitude toward the Spirit is found in the letter to the Hebrews. It is in a passage where the writer is speaking about people who once knew the truth and then decided to disobey. The writer says that those who disobeyed the Law of Moses were put to death and judged guilty on the basis of a couple of witnesses' testimony. How much more shall we be held accountable for treating lightly the blood of God's covenant, which was shed to cleanse us from sin. The one who rejects God's covenant insults the Spirit of grace.

We have moved from grieving the Spirit to quenching the Spirit to resisting the Spirit. There is a progression in these negative attitudes toward the Holy Spirit that culminates in the insulting of the Holy Spirit. The writer of Hebrews indicates that the punishment for this offense will be much greater than death.

How can we as Christians ensure that we never insult the Spirit? The Pharisees used to have a policy that was called "fencing the Law." Instead of asking, "How far can we go before the Law is broken?" they set a hedge around the Law so they would never risk breaking it. They took this protection to extremes, but the idea was sound.

We must focus our attention on not grieving the Spirit. If we never grieve him, we will not quench him. If we never resist him, we will not insult him. If we do not grieve the Spirit, we will live in a personal, vital, loving, giving, believing relationship with him that will make our lives full of his blessing, his joy, his peace, his power, and his fruitfulness.

jesus alone satisfies

john 6:22 – 52

Jesus answered, "I tell you the truth, you are looking for me, not because you saw miraculous signs but because you ate the loaves and had your fill."
John 6:26

In Scripture, it seems that the miracles are always double-edged swords; the carry a double significance. The first meaning is very simple and obvious: th miracle meets the immediate need of the moment in a way that is impor tant to the purposes of God. Always in these miracles there is another side The miracle is not simply an act of God to meet a need; it also becomes parable with spiritual significance. This was the normal pattern of the mir acles Jesus performed.

The feeding of the five thousand functions on these two levels. Th crowd was hungry, and Christ looked at them with compassion, knowing that some could not make it home without nourishment. They were ther because of him, and he felt responsible for their well-being, so he fed them On a deeper level, Jesus took this miraculous event and made it the basis fo his presentation to them of the sacrament of the Lord's Supper. He taugh them about their own hungers and appetites, which earthly elements woul never meet. If they ever wanted to be truly satisfied, they must participat in that which his body and his blood represents. They must have his very lif within them. Only he could satisfy their souls.

Jesus may be meeting the physical needs of your life, and yet you ma be totally unaware that he wants to meet a much deeper and more burnin need in your heart. He wants to satisfy you with himself. Ultimately, noth ing else will do.

self-transcendence

john 15:1–8

As the Father has loved me, so have I loved you. Now remain in my love.
John 15:9

Through his grace, God has made it possible for me to live in his presence
every moment, so heaven actually begins for me right now in time and space.
Albert Orsborn, the poet-general of the Salvation Army, understood this
freedom of love.

> *Spirit of Eternal Love*
> *Guide me, or I blindly rove*
> *Set my heart on things above*
> *Draw me after thee.*
> *Earthly things are paltry show*
> *Phantom charms that come and go*
> *Give me constantly to know*
> *Fellowship with thee.*
>
> *Come O Spirit, take control*
> *Where the fires of passion roll*
> *Let the yearnings of my soul*
> *Center all in thee.*
> *Call into thy fold of peace*
> *Thoughts that seek forbidden ways*
> *Calm and order all my days*
> *Hide my life in thee.*
>
> *Thus supported, even I,*
> *Knowing thou art ever nigh,*
> *Will attain this highest joy*
> *Living unto thee.*
> *No distracting thoughts within*
> *No surviving hidden sin*
> *Thus indeed will heaven begin*
> *Here and now in me.* *

*Albert Orsborn, "Spirit of Eternal Love," *Songbook of the Salvation Army* (London: Salvationist
Publishing, 1953), no. 538.

in his image

psalm 104

*Whether you turn to the right or to the left, your ears will hear a voice
behind you, saying, "This is the way; walk in it."*
Isaiah 30:21

Work is the common lot of humankind. This is one of God's greatest gifts:
something to do. One does not need to worry about the dignity of one's
work. God set the pattern, and his work was manual labor; for we are the
work of his hands. God wills that persons should work, not as a punishment, but that they might share the divine lot, that he might bring fulfillment to them. Creatures made in the image of the Creator have a creative
tendency that needs expression. It will find its fulfillment in the work he
gives them to do.

Each person must find a place of service. All persons were made to work.
The unhappy person is the one who has no job or is in the wrong job. God
has a place for you, and he will direct your steps to that place. The Lord can
order the steps of every person, but if he is not in control, then there is no
order. Open yourself to the leadership of the Spirit, and your steps will be
directed by him. There may be moments of questioning and wondering, but
there will be no dead-end streets. The psalmist says that if we love the Lord,
none of our steps shall slide, and our future will be peace (Ps. 37:31, 37).

march 20

the courageous spirit

acts 13:44 – 14:28

*They returned to Lystra . . . strengthening the disciples and
encouraging them to remain true to the faith. "We must go through
many hardships to enter the kingdom of God," they said.
Acts 14:21–22*

One of the characteristics of the early church was courage. The Twelve crept
fearfully into the upper room to protect themselves from the authorities,
but they came out on Pentecost boldly proclaiming the risen Christ to everyone they could reach. Your knees may knock together for a time as you go
out into ministry, but that's all right. Keep on going. Do the thing Christ
asks you to do, and he will fill you with his Spirit and therefore with courage.
The courage comes only when you act.

The first Christians became unstoppable. The world had no categories
to deal with people like these. They did not fear prison, and they did not fear
death. The world had no weapons to use against them that could succeed
(Isa. 54:17).

On Paul's first missionary journey the citizens of Lystra stoned him so
badly that the Christians there believed him to be dead. However, he was
revived and continued on to preach in Derbe. Then, instead of returning to
safety, he went back to Lystra to check on the believers. He was anxious to
go back to where he had been stoned and beaten and encourage them by
telling them what a marvelous thing it is to be a Christian. He returned to
Lystra to strengthen the believers and encourage them to continue in the
faith. Then he went on his way from Lystra, rejoicing.

Do we know anything about that kind of courage? The same Spirit who
was in Paul can be in you and me.

superintendent of construction

2 corinthians 3:16 – 4:1

And we, who with unveiled faces all reflect the Lord's glory,
are being transformed into his likeness with ever-increasing glory,
which comes from the Lord, who is the Spirit.
2 Corinthians 3:18

There are some things that cause pain to the Spirit of the Lord Jesus that we never think about. One of them is laziness. Do you know that we can grieve the Spirit of Jesus by loafing our time away? Laziness always makes us feel defiled because it separates us from Christ's presence. Another grief to the Spirit of God is when Christians treat other people inconsiderately. A discourteous attitude insists on exact retribution, on making other people feel exactly how they made us feel. This desire for revenge, even in small things, always stems from self-absorption, and this is sin. A third grief to the Spirit occurs when a believer becomes despondent and lives in that despair. Continual discouragement never comes from Christ; it always comes from another source.

God started a process in our hearts when he won us to himself, and that process is to make us like himself. The Spirit of God is the superintendent of construction on the project that is our lives. It is his business to bring us to the place where we look holy like him. The aspects in me that cause the Spirit pain are the things I hold on to, resisting his surgery, his cleansing, and his chastening. He desires to make my life conform to the image of Christ, in whom is found no laziness, no discourtesy, and no despondency.

sweet-smelling fragrance

philippians 4:14–20

*And my God will meet all your needs according to his
glorious riches in Christ Jesus.*
Philippians 4:19

When Paul wrote to the people in Philippi whom he loved so deeply, he was facing death, so his manner was very tender. This church had taken a missionary offering and sent it to Paul. He wrote to thank them and declare their gift to be a "a fragrant offering, an acceptable sacrifice, pleasing to God" (Phil. 4:18). Paul was overjoyed that the church wanted to be a part of his mission to the Gentiles. They were giving so the world could be redeemed. He assured them, "My God will meet all your needs according to his glorious riches in Christ Jesus."

We have the unfortunate habit of taking single verses and pulling them out of their context. Have you ever quoted that verse about God supplying what is needed? That promise was not declared in a generic fashion. It was spoken to people who had contributed to the work of God. The promise is that if one shares willingly in God's work, God will share in that one's life. A reciprocity emerges between God and his people.

I once led a Holy Week series at a formal Presbyterian church in the South. This church radiated incredible power and life, and it had one of the largest groups of university students I have ever seen in any church. As I glanced at the bulletin, I found the reason for its dynamism: 51 percent of its budget was set aside to send for overseas missions.

When we care about what God cares about and show that care in sacrificial giving, he is free to bless us and honor us because we are honoring him. Our giving is a fragrant offering to God. Do you want to please God? Be a part of spreading the gospel across the earth through your offerings, your prayers, and yourself.

a promise of jesus

john 2:13 – 25

To those who sold doves he said, "Get these out of here!
How dare you turn my Father's house into a market!"
Then the Jews demanded of him, "What miraculous sign can
you show us to prove your authority to do all this?"
Jesus answered them, "Destroy this temple,
and I will raise it again in three days."
John 2:16, 18–19

Scripture has some interesting things to say about symbols. The temple is the primary symbol in God's Word. Remember when Jesus cleansed the temple, and the authorities there asked him what right he had to do it? He responded that if they pulled the temple down, he could rebuild it in three days. The symbol of the temple was not the important thing; it was the reality behind the symbol that was crucial. The temple was a promise that God wanted to live among his people. He had told Moses that his house was to be the center of Hebrew life. But even that was not close enough. God wanted to be closer than in a house, so he decided to become one of us. The temple was a promise of Bethlehem—a promise of the Incarnation itself. When the Reality to whom the temple pointed walked into that symbol, the authorities did not recognize him for who he was. Their love for the symbol had become idolatrous. They treasured stones and mortar more than God himself.

Symbols that no longer point to their true meaning are a lie, and God refuses to allow them to remain. Forty years after the temple authorities tortured and killed Jesus, the Reality behind the symbol, God allowed Roman soldiers to tear down the temple, the symbol, stone by stone. However, Jesus was destroyed for only three days; the symbol of Jesus—the temple—was destroyed forever. It was no longer needed.

What are the symbols in your life? Are you holding on to the symbol and rejecting the reality? Is the symbol pointing the way to Jesus himself?

the temple of the spirit

matthew 13:10 – 23

*But the Counselor, the Holy Spirit, whom the Father will send in my name,
will teach you all things and will remind you of everything I have said to you.*
John 14:26

Samuel Logan Brengle told the story of a friend of his who was reading one
day when the Holy Spirit said to him very clearly, "This book is not for you."

The man replied, "Oh?" and continued reading.

The Spirit replied, "No, I wish you would not read this. I do not want
it in your mind."

The man put the book down and said, "Thank you, Lord."

I have never forgotten this illustration. The Spirit of God wants control of our mind. That means there are certain things that do not belong
there. He says to us, "Don't you know that you yourselves are God's temple
and that God's Spirit lives in you?" (1 Cor. 3:16). There are some things that
may be all right for other people, but the Spirit of Jesus has checked our
spirit regarding them. These things may seem unimportant, but some of the
most determinative choices of my life have involved the little things that
seemed insignificant.

Are you walking closely enough to the Spirit of Jesus that he is free to
speak to you about your attitude, your words, your books, your thought life,
your friendships, your finances, your entertainment? When he asks you to
change your behavior, do you listen? If you do, you will enjoy a remarkable
inner freedom that releases you to be more creative.

in the holy of holies

matthew 27:51; hebrews 10:19 – 25

*Therefore, brothers, since we have confidence to enter the Most Holy Place
by the blood of Jesus, . . . let us draw near to God with a sincere heart
in full assurance of faith, having our hearts sprinkled to cleanse us from
a guilty conscience and having our bodies washed with pure water.*
Hebrews 10:19, 22

When a Jewish man entered the outer court of the temple, he confronted an altar designed for animal sacrifices. There blood was shed, life was taken, and carcasses were consumed as atonement for sin. Afterward the man washed in the laver (or basin) that was also there as a symbol of cleansing. These things had to be completed before he moved on: the sacrifice for the forgiveness of sins, and the washing of regeneration.

If a man came that far, he could enter the Holy Place and there find the bread of the Presence, which symbolized life. Similarly, when we arrive on the other side of conversion and the forgiveness of sin, we begin to walk in the light of God's truth, and Jesus begins to feed us with himself.

A man could go even deeper into the temple, to a place called the Holy of Holies. When the high priest went beyond that which separated the Holy Place from the Holy of Holies, he found himself in the very presence of God. Under the old covenant the high priest was admitted there only once a year. Christ, in his death, opened that way for all of us. The immediate presence of the holy God is our privilege.

If you have tasted God's holy immediate presence, you will not have much use for life without that intimacy. If you have ever reached the point where he has glorified himself in you, you will never want to leave that place of his holy presence.

Are you still living in the outer courts? Let God push you farther and farther into his presence. Jesus became the sacrifice so you and I could lay down our lives as sacrifices as well. Once we have laid down ourselves, we can go inside the veil, and Jesus himself will become our life, our joy, our glory.

When Jesus has become that, you don't need anything else. It doesn't matter whether the way is easy or rough. He is enough. It doesn't matter whether he fills your hands or empties them. He is enough. It doesn't matter whether you are sick or well. He is enough. It doesn't matter whether you are living or dying. He is enough. When you enter the Holy of Holies, you do not need anything because Jesus is enough.

march 26

the beatitudes

matthew 5:1 – 12

Blessed are the poor in spirit,
for theirs is the kingdom of heaven.
Matthew 5:3

The Beatitudes are some of the most well-known of Jesus' sayings. In them Jesus speaks of the character of those who will inhabit his kingdom and of their role in the world. The character portrayed in the Beatitudes is vastly different from that which the world applauds. Human ideas of a king and a kingdom are ideas of pomp, wealth, and ceremony. How different are these ideals of poverty of spirit, meekness, mercy, purity, peacefulness, and hunger for righteousness. How different is this kingdom from the kingdom the disciples expected. And how different from what we naturally prefer! But these are the characteristics that should be in our lives if we profess to be members of Christ's kingdom.

Blessed can be translated "happy," although it means much more than transient happiness. It means enjoying all of the riches of grace that come when God's face shines about you. If you sense your spiritual poverty and mourn over it and meekly submit yourself to God, you will certainly hunger and thirst for God's righteousness. And you will not go unsatisfied; God will fill your life with his fullness. The citizens of God's kingdom are merciful because they hope to obtain mercy from God. Other attributes that bring happiness are purity and peaceableness. Those who are in the kingdom now have the nature of the King. The world often misunderstands and opposes them, but the reward will be great for those who are persecuted and misunderstood because of the gospel of Jesus. In fact, the inheritance of the prophets and of Christ will be theirs.

Note the exhortation to manifest the virtues listed here. Is there a hunger in your heart for God to bring them into your life? You are really not ready to begin a day unless you have an appetite and a hunger for him and his character. If you want him, he will meet you somewhere today. May you find him!

"i rest my soul on jesus"

mark 15:21 – 40

Come to me, all you who are weary and burdened, and I will give you rest.
Take my yoke upon you and learn from me, for I am gentle and
humble in heart, and you will find rest for your souls.
Matthew 11:28–29

I lay my sins on Jesus
The spotless lamb of God;
He bears them all, and frees us
From the accursed load:
I bring my guilt to Jesus,
To wash my crimson stains
White in His blood most precious
Til not a spot remains.

I lay my wants on Jesus:
All fullness dwells in Him;
He heals all my diseases,
He does my soul redeem:
I lay my griefs on Jesus,
My burdens and my cares;
He from them all releases
He all my sorrow shares.

I rest my soul on Jesus,
This weary soul of mine;
His right hand me embraces,
I on His breast recline.
I love the name of Jesus,
Emmanuel, Christ, the Lord;
Like fragrance on the breezes
His name abroad is poured.

I long to be like Jesus,
Meek, loving, lowly, mild
I long to be like Jesus,
The Father's holy Child.
I long to be with Jesus
Amid the heavenly throng
To sing with saints His praises
To learn the angels' song. *

This hymn was written for children by Horatius Bonar, the Scottish pastor-saint. It speaks to little ones and to older ones alike of the deep need of the human heart and the remarkable richness to be found in the Lord Jesus. What a way to begin a day!

march 28

song of salvation

psalm 100

You will receive power when the Holy Spirit comes on you;
and you will be my witnesses in Jerusalem, and in all Judea and Samaria,
and to the ends of the earth.
Acts 1:8

Samuel Chadwick reported that in the early hours of a Sunday morning after he had wrestled all night over the text, "You will receive power when the Holy Spirit comes on you," he realized that he knew the power of the Spirit theoretically, but not empirically. It was in those predawn hours of a Sabbath morning that the Holy Spirit came to him while he was on his face in his study. Later that morning when he preached, there were more conversions during one service than he had previously seen in months of ministry.

When the truth becomes radiant life within us, people are attracted to the light. Do you know the fullness of the Holy Spirit in your heart as well as in your head? Do you know the consciousness of the forgiveness of sins? Do you know freedom from sin itself?

My sin—O the bliss of this glorious thought—
My sin, not in part but the whole
Is nailed to his cross and I bear it no more,
Praise the Lord, praise the Lord, O my soul!*

When full salvation becomes personal and real, it breaks forth into a song. It is not merely a staid proposition, but beautiful music. It is not intended to be mechanically repeated, but to overflow in joyous exclamation. When the people of God sing of full salvation, people without Christ begin to listen. They are longing for music to fill their empty and silent hearts.

---

*Horatio G. Spafford, "It Is Well with My Soul," *Hymns for Praise and Worship*, no. 418.

the key to life

2 timothy 3:10 – 17

All Scripture is God-breathed and is useful for teaching, rebuking,
correcting and training in righteousness, so that the man of God
may be thoroughly equipped for every good work.
2 Timothy 3:16–17

As you pore over Scripture, you should keep seeking to understand those great biblical clues that will enable you to interpret life as a Christian. How much happier and how much more effective all of our lives would be if we were thoroughly biblical in our outlook and orientation. Scripture is where the key to the interpretation of reality really is. There are so many of us who do not understand life. There are so many of us who live in confusion and uncertainty. God wants his children to see, to discern, to perceive, and to know, and therefore to be able to lead and to help others. We will never be ready to do that until we have come to the place where the Bible is not simply a book of magic or merely a religious book, but rather the key to life. It is the clue to reality given to us by the One who created reality.

I doubt that one can understand the basic realities of life—whether the nature of God, the nature of persons, the nature of marriage, the nature of the state, or the nature of one's vocation—until one knows Scripture very well. The thing that now commends Scripture to me is the fact that it is the most realistic of all books; it is safe for me to plumb its depths and then to base my life on it.

Jeremiah 10:23 tells us that our way is not in us. Jesus informs us that our way is in him (John 14:6). And we find Jesus best in his Word.

last instructions

john 13 – 14

*Jesus knew that the time had come for him to leave this world
and go to the Father. Having loved his own who were in the world,
he now showed them the full extent of his love.*
John 13:1

On the last night Jesus had with his disciples, he spoke about many things,
but perhaps three of these are the most important for us. First, he spoke
about the sacrifice of himself. The Lord's Supper, which Jesus instituted that
night, reminds us that suffering and death are involved in our redemption
and in the redemption of the world. This remembrance meal focuses our
attention on the amazing love of God to pay such a price for our lives.

Next, he spoke about kingdom service. He illustrated through his
actions that those who are the greatest are the ones who are the servants. He
illustrated self-giving love not only in the Cross, but also in the daily acts of
sacrifice that kingdom greatness demands.

Finally, Jesus spoke about the Person whose presence would empower
and enable the disciples' work. He was concerned that his disciples would
feel forsaken and deserted after his ascension, so he assured them that
another was coming to take his place. The Holy Spirit was to be their teacher
(John 14:26); he was to convince the world of sin, righteousness, and judgment (John 16:8). The Holy Spirit was to empower the disciples' witness
for Christ. He was Jesus' guarantee that the disciples would never be alone.

The fact that Jesus discussed the Cross, kingdom greatness, and the
Holy Spirit on his last night before Calvary indicates that these were the
things that were closest to his heart in the last moments of his earthly life.
Certainly these emphases should be valued by us if we profess to love him.

- We must bow in adoration and praise at the love that purchased salvation for us at such a frightful cost.
- We must be willing to humble ourselves in service for others as he
  thus served.
- We must open ourselves to the One who takes Jesus' place in the
  world: the Holy Spirit.

march 31

making a leader

exodus 2

*By faith Moses, when he had grown up, refused to be known as
the son of Pharaoh's daughter. He chose to be mistreated along with
the people of God rather than to enjoy the pleasures of sin for a short time.*
Hebrews 11:24–25

The birth and development of Moses is an amazing story. He was a child of
the hated Hebrews, who were in Egyptian bondage. The daughter of
Pharaoh, who had commanded the death of every Hebrew son, found him.
Pharaoh's daughter adopted him, and he was made an heir to Pharaoh. His
own Hebrew mother was paid by his adopted Egyptian mother to nurse him.
Moses' mother's name, Jochebed, means "Yahweh is glorious" or "Yahweh is
the great one." She believed that God could save her child, and he rewarded
her for her faith. God delivered Moses from death, and then he used Moses
to deliver his own people from slavery. God delivered the deliverer.

Moses was aware of his origin, and he desired to help his own people.
It speaks well for him that he was willing to identify himself with them, a
slave people. Unfortunately, he took matters into his own hands when he
killed an Egyptian who had struck a Hebrew. As Abraham and Sarah had
tried to help God's plan along by giving Hagar to Abraham, now Moses tried
in his own strength to help his people. But he was not ready for his life's
work; nor was Israel ready for their deliverance. Moses needed to be seasoned and instructed, so God sent him to Midian to tend sheep. God
removed him from Egypt so he could receive the training he required to be
the deliverer of the Israelites.

We often regret the time God uses in training us. We become impatient
under it, but God took forty years to get Moses ready. We dare not despise
the time he takes to prepare us or the place he puts us to accomplish our
training. For Moses, it was quite a jump from prince to shepherd, but in the
solitude of the wilderness God trained his man. We must know something
of solitude if we are going to know God's ways, which cannot be learned in
the rush and hurry of life. We must know a quiet time. During his time of
training, Moses learned the way of the land through which he would lead
God's people. His days as a simple shepherd were not wasted. No days are
wasted when we are in God's will. All things serve his purpose.

fearing only myself

numbers 13

*Joshua son of Nun and Caleb son of Jephunneh, who were among those
who had explored the land, tore their clothes and said to the entire
Israelite assembly, "The land we passed through and explored is
exceedingly good. If the LORD is pleased with us, he will lead us
into that land, a land flowing with milk and honey, and will give it to us.
Only do not rebel against the LORD. And do not be afraid of the people
of the land, because we will swallow them up. Their protection is gone,
but the LORD is with us. Do not be afraid of them."*
Numbers 14:6–9

The only thing we have to fear is ourselves! Only we can preclude the future
God has for each of us. Therefore, we must fear intruding our self-centered
way into our own futures. It will only complicate things. A prophet once
heard God speak a word that is ours for the taking: "'For I know the plans
I have for you,' declares the LORD, 'plans to prosper you and not to harm
you, plans to give you hope and a future'" (Jer. 29:11).

Twelve young men stood and faced God's future at a place called Kadesh
Barnea. Ten chose their future on the basis of their anxiety and unbelief.
Their names were Shammua, Shaphat, Igal, Palti, Gaddiel, Gaddi, Ammiel,
Sethur, Nahbi, Geuel. No one ever names children after any of these men.
Only a rare historian even recognizes the names.

Two men chose their future on the basis of a personal knowledge of,
and full commitment to, Yahweh and his plans for them. They wholly fol-
lowed the Lord, and their names are still spoken thousands of years later.
We still name children after them. The world needs more Calebs and
Joshuas. Only such persons can lead us into the future, into the Promised
Land that we need and for which we long.

Look up! Draw near to God and claim the future he has made for you!

the path of life

psalm 16

You have made known to me the path of life;
you will fill me with joy in your presence,
with eternal pleasures at your right hand.
Psalm 16:11

The psalmist writes not of the path *to* life but of the path *of* life. The one who finds it lives. Psalm 16:11 is the Old Testament version of Jesus' "I am the way and the truth and the life" (John 14:6). Our life is in him. The psalmist believed that humans could dwell in the presence of God right now and know real life.

Could it be that our highest duty is to come to know God and his ways so the petition in the prayer Jesus gave us could in some measure be fulfilled? "Thy will be done in earth, as it is in heaven" (Matt. 6:10 KJV). There is no higher calling available, no higher privilege than dwelling in his presence and feeding on the pleasures there. The key to living here is the wisdom found in God and in his Word.

We live in a very unheavenly world. The nonreligious and the unbeliever will be the first to tell you how unheavenly it really is. Could it be that the drab disaster we call contemporary life is simply a witness to the fact that humans have lost the true God and have therefore lost themselves? Our path of life is found in Jesus Christ and in his Word to us.

april 3

hell's reality

luke 16:19–31

*If they do not listen to Moses and the Prophets, they will not
be convinced even if someone rises from the dead.*
Luke 16:31

In Luke 16 Jesus tells the parable about the rich man and Lazarus, in which
he speaks about eternal destinies. This parable indicates that one's eternal
future is the result of one's choices in this world. It is not due to chance or
even the goodness of God. By deciding to accept or reject God's salvation,
we determine our own destiny. A second lesson to be drawn is the corollary
of this: sin has eternal consequences. Most people feel that their sins are of
only the most temporal consequence and that if they wait long enough, the
guilt will simply disappear. The story of the rich man and Lazarus shows us
that our transgressions on this earth, if not forgiven through the grace of
God, reap for us an eternal weight of condemnation. The end of this life is
not the end of our sin unless we have been forgiven.

A third point of the story, which may seem obvious, is that the consequences of sin are not pleasant. Jesus pictures them as "torments." It is a serious thing to leave this life if one is not rightly related to God. That
seriousness is seen in the fourth point of this story. Jesus pictures no second
chances after this life. A great gulf is fixed between the redeemed and the
lost. As far as Jesus revealed our condition after this life, the day of grace and
mercy is past and the opportunity for redemption is over. To hope for more
is a gamble based only on desire. Eternal torment is pictured as a conscious
existence in which one is filled with remorse and regret. This story is
intended to caution readers so they will miss such a destiny. It is out of love
for the Pharisees and the wealthy that Jesus gives this parable as a warning.

We do not like to talk about hell, but Jesus did. Are you living in such
a way that you will have no regrets on that final day? Are you living in such
a way that your neighbor will have no regrets on that day because he has
seen Jesus in you?

the sacrifice of a son

matthew 27:32 – 56

Now my heart is troubled, and what shall I say?
"Father, save me from this hour"? No, it was for this very reason
I came to this hour. Father, glorify your name!
John 12:27–28

God is sovereign. But that does not mean he will protect his own from the difficulties of life. The people of Judah had many problems, but as long as they walked with God, their problems were God's opportunities. In the life of Jesus, a man's leprosy became Jesus' opportunity to show that he was master over that illness. A man's blindness was his opportunity to show that he could give sight. A man's lameness became his opportunity to show that he could make a person's body whole. God let troubles come to Israel so the entire world around them could see the redemptive power of Christ. If you let him have your whole heart, it does not mean you will not have troubles. His sovereignty means that those troubles can be a means for his glory. If your greatest joy is the glory of God, then you can even glory in your problems.

A man who had grown up in North Carolina was called by God into Christian service, so he decided to become a missionary doctor. He studied theology as well as medicine so he would be prepared to be a missionary. He ended up with three doctoral degrees, one in medicine and two in theology. Then he and his pregnant wife headed into the remotest part of Africa. They worked with one tribe for four years without any response. Every week they would meet for worship, but no African ever joined them. Then one day their son became very ill and died. That missionary made a coffin for his boy and carried him out to bury him. He was all alone except for the presence of one African man. When he shoveled the soil onto the rude casket, he was overcome with grief and buried his face in the fresh dirt and sobbed. The African man picked up the missionary's head by the hair and looked into his face. Then he lowered the man's head carefully back into the dirt and ran into the village, crying, "The white one cries like we do." The next time the husband and his wife met for worship, the place was packed. Now a church exists because of that family's suffering.

There is only one way the world can be saved. God showed it at Calvary. He sacrificed his Son. And that tribe was won through the sacrifice of a son.

The greatest sacrifice is not that of physical death; the greatest offering is when we take our hands off our lives so Christ can live in us victoriously and joyously. If our hearts are not clean, we will fight him or resent him. When we let him have our whole heart, then we delight to do his will, and there is a sweetness in it. That sweetness comes from precious fellowship with the One with scarred hands. There is no earthly joy like this. Don't miss it.

april 5

god cares

isaiah 63:7 – 9

For God so loved the world that he gave his one and only Son,
that whoever believes in him shall not perish but have eternal life.
John 3:16

The ancient Greek understanding of God and the biblical view of God are radically different. The difference stems from two contrasting understandings of perfection. For the Greeks perfection meant changelessness. For them perfection had to be static. If an object were perfect, it could not change without denying its own perfection. This meant that the divine had no feelings because one who has feelings can change. Therefore, God could not love or suffer. Greek philosophy had a term for this: *apatheia,* the origin of our word *apathy.* It was used of the divine and means "without feelings; without suffering."

What a different picture of God we see in the Scriptures. God loves Israel. He gets angry at injustice. He can be grieved. Jesus weeps at the death of Lazarus and dreads the thought of the Cross.

What makes the difference? The gods of the Greeks were impersonal forces. The God of Scripture is very personal. He is a Father, and as a Father he has a Son. Their relationship with the Spirit is one of love, and it is out of that fellowship of love that God created his world. When we sinned, God cared. That was what led to the Cross. The God of Scripture is not without feeling. He is passionate love. We are the objects of that love. We should worship him.

immanuel

exodus 40:34 – 38

*"The virgin will be with child and will give birth to a son,
and they will call him Immanuel"—which means, "God with us."*
Matthew 1:23

The God we worship is a God who has emotions. He is love, and he has chosen to pour out his love on us. When Adam and Eve turned from him, he looked for a people to love him and among whom he could dwell. He desires to be near the ones he loves just as human beings enjoy proximity to their beloved ones. God found a man named Abraham who was willing to love him and walk with him. Out of Abraham's descendants God established a nation of chosen people. That nation built a house for God in their midst, and God himself came and dwelt with them in all of his glory. He became the center of their existence.

God wants to be in the middle of our lives too, the point of reference for everything in our existence. This is the reason he names himself Immanuel, which means "God with us." Can there be a more amazing reality than Immanuel? God wants to be a part of our daily lives, closer to us than anyone else in the world. If we ever truly understood his desire for us in the light of his greatness and our insignificance, we would be on our knees in awe and thanksgiving. Don't let anyone ever tell you that God is not love.

a broken vessel

acts 9:1 – 19

*He touched the socket of Jacob's hip so that his hip was
wrenched as he wrestled with the man.*
Genesis 32:25

I once thought that during a time of consecration one should stand up. This is the way it traditionally happened in my church youth circles. We would have candles and everyone would say, "Yes, I want to give my life to Christ." It was such a noble and beautiful thing, and we courageously and proudly offered ourselves to Christ. However, that is not the way it was in the story of Jacob, which gives us a clue as to a more promising way.

It is God who wrestled with Jacob. God is always the initiator in our liberation. And before he blessed Jacob, he touched Jacob's thigh. God has to break a person before that person will surrender. The Christian community really ought to talk more about surrender than about consecration, because human beings resist God until the end and then must ask him to break the resistance and take control of their lives and hearts. God broke Jacob so he had a crippled leg, and then God came and began to bless him.

I never knew a person who was filled with the Holy Ghost who did not have some brokenness in him. We want to stand straight and be self-contained and poised, but God cannot use us or bless us when we are in that position. He wants to break us so that instead of our own power, we have the Holy Spirit's power. Are you willing to be broken for him? This is the toughest of all battles, but it determines whether we will be free or in bondage.

We need to have our own Peniel where we meet Jesus face-to-face. We must see ourselves for what we truly are. We must cry out to God for heart cleansing, and we must let him come and fill us with His Spirit. We must allow him to break us so he can make us into prevailers, conquerors, and overcomers.

fighting the blessing

genesis 32:1 – 32

I will not let you go unless you bless me.
Genesis 32:26

As the battle of Jacob's life approached, Jacob found himself alone with God. Esau and his four hundred men were advancing on Jacob's family, and after Jacob had done everything possible for protection, God found him alone and began to work on him. Jacob had been scheming to save his own soul, and God knew that all the scheming in the world would not get Jacob to be the man God wanted him to be. God wanted to change Jacob's heart, so he began to wrestle with Jacob.

Most of us believe that Jacob was trying to force a blessing from God, and most of us believe we also have to convince God to bless us. The reality for Jacob and for us is that we fight him to keep him from blessing us. God wants to cleanse our hearts completely, possess us totally, and set us free. But all the time he is trying to set us free, we fight him. We fight for our chains when he is doing his best to give us liberty. God fought with Jacob all night long, and when daylight came, Jacob looked up and God said, "All right. I have tried. I am leaving."

Jacob faced the most desperate moment that anyone faces when coming so close to God and yet continuing to fight him. God's answer was, "If you do not want my best, I will leave." Then Jacob panicked. "You are not going to leave me like this, are you? I have lost my cattle, my sheep, my goats, my wives, my children. I have lost everything, and now do I lose you too?" This was a blessed hour for Jacob because he saw the value of God alone.

Are you fighting God, even unwittingly, to keep him from giving you the best he has for you? If you continue to fight against him, he will eventually leave. Have you learned the value of God? Are you desperate to retain his presence?

what is your name?

genesis 32:22 – 32

The man asked him, "What is your name?"
"Jacob," he answered.
Genesis 32:27

At the climax of the long story of God's work in Jacob's life, God was no
only trying to bless Jacob, but he was also attempting to transform him
Jacob, whose name means "he grasps," is the classical example of th
schemer, the manipulator who is ever pulling strings to promote his own
self-interest. Now he faced a hostile brother, from whom he could no
escape. He had schemed to the end and was now completely alone and
afraid. There was nothing more he could do. He needed God's help if h
and his family were to survive. So he wrestled with the One who had been
wrestling with him all those years. Finally, Jacob surrendered and asked fo
God's blessing.

God responded to Jacob by asking him about his name. That was
moment of supreme self-discovery for Jacob. He could not escape this time
but had to face who he really was: a grasping, manipulative sneak and thie
who was also a cheat and a heel. The name *Jacob* expressed who he really was

It is significant that this event came twenty years after Jacob met Go
at Bethel. It takes a while for most of us to realize how deeply the self-interest
of sin permeates our beings. The Holy Spirit has to bring us to the end o
ourselves. Our deliverance can never come until we see who we are and
acknowledge it. So God asked: "What is your name?" The acknowledgmen
made possible the breaking that led to Jacob's deliverance. The scheming
manipulator became a prince with God. His new name, *Israel,* was given to
the people of God. Are you among those who have experienced such deliv
erance? Christ's Cross and the gift of the Holy Spirit make it possible for us

the grasping human heart

genesis 32

Your name will no longer be Jacob, but Israel.
Genesis 32:28

The story of Jacob is an amazing chronicle of the grace of God, reminding readers of the labyrinth of selfishness from which he has brought us. Jacob symbolizes all human persons living in sin. Jacob's name is illustrative. He was a twin, and when he was born he grasped the heel of his twin brother; therefore, the name *Jacob* means "the one who takes by the heel" or "the one who supplants." His character is one of "graspiness" and is the essential biblical picture of sin: pushing to achieve one's own way.

Incredibly enough, God loved Jacob, and it was through Jacob that God intended to raise up the nation out of which would come the Savior of the world. It seems unbelievable that God could use such a deceitful person to continue the process of redemption. However, God indicated the way his plans would be fulfilled in the new and transforming name he gave to Jacob, the supplanter. It was *Israel,* meaning "let God rule." The sovereign God who cares enough about a single, self-seeking person to turn him or her into a world changer is that person's only hope. Those who allow God to rule in their lives and to overrule their own self-interest will be blessed and will become a blessing to the entire world. In God alone there is hope for the transformation of the grasping human heart.

sweet surprises

hebrews 11:8 – 12

*Leave your country, your people and your father's household
and go to the land I will show you.*
Genesis 12:1

When God called Abraham, he asked him to leave his home, his family, and his land. God did not tell him what the journey would be like. He simply told Abraham that he would be with him and would give him a family, land, and a home. When God calls us to follow him, he does not tell us what our journey is going to be like. If he did, we might be too terrified to go. He wants our attention on him, not on the way we will travel. He wants us to entrust ourselves to him.

God's way for us is seldom what we would have chosen. This is one of the sweet surprises that God has for us. When we trust him and follow him along unexpected ways and to unexpected places, we find as we look back that the ways and places always fit. We recognize that they were just right for us.

When Bill Borden died, his friends found three things written in his Bible: "No reserve. No retreat. No regrets."

- "No reserve." That was how he began his walk with Jesus.
- "No retreat." That came from the middle of the battle.
- "No regrets." That was how he looked back on his walk with Jesus.

Abraham would say an amen to that approach to life. Can you? In Christ, our fears are never justified, but our faith always is!

a journey with the spirit

galatians 5:16 – 26

Live by the Spirit, and you will not gratify the desires of the sinful nature . . .
Since we live by the Spirit, let us keep in step with the Spirit.
Galatians 5:16, 25

There is a certain tension that comes when we have been in the manifest presence of the Spirit of Jesus and then we have to return to the normal routines of daily life. When God moves in a special way in our midst, we wish the exhilaration of that time could last forever, but it does not. In a sense, it is easier to be filled with the Holy Spirit than it is to walk in the Holy Spirit, but this is not a reason for discouragement. It is actually a reason to rejoice because God is forcing us to face the question of how we can live life in the spirit and live with his blessing. How can we live without losing his anointing and his joy?

Learning to walk in the Spirit is a deeper lesson in the life of faith. Christ wants you to know how to live a holy life with a clean heart, how to serve him hour by hour in the routines of life. He will lead you in the small things as he leads in the big things. In fact, the small things may be the keys to the big ones. If he directs you to study or clean or mow the lawn, then that studying, that cleaning, that mowing is as sacramental as a prayer meeting. However, if he is leading you to a prayer meeting and you are studying, cleaning, or mowing, then you have stepped out of his will, and the sense of his presence will grow dim.

Life must be lived with one hand lifted in praise to God and with the other hand immersed in the necessary activities of daily life. We must learn the delicate lesson of listening to his voice. Here is the place we learn how to live a Spirit-filled, Spirit-led, sanctified life.

life from barrenness

genesis 15; 21:1 – 7

"Sing, O barren woman,
you who never bore a child . . .
because more are the children of the desolate woman
than of her who has a husband,"
says the LORD.
Isaiah 54:1

Scripture insists that God is capable of bringing life out of barrenness. When God came to Abraham, he told him that all of human history would be different because of Abraham's life, that out of Abraham's descendants would come a lineage that would lead to the redemption of the world. I can imagine Abraham and God's conversation after God told him that. I can hear Abraham saying, "You obviously aren't from around here."

"Oh, really, what do you mean?" God asks.

"If you were from around here, then you would know that when a man is seventy-five and his wife is sixty-five, there is no chance for them to produce a child."

"That is right; I am not from around here. In the place from which I come, there is One who makes the impossible possible."

I am sure God has a sense of humor. He made Abraham wait twenty-four years before he started the fulfillment of that promise. How could one get a better illustration of the fact that God is the kind of God who can bring life out of barrenness? God is saying that he is the One who can bring water from a rock, fruit from sterility, life from death. Note the accounts in Judges 13, 1 Samuel 1, and Luke 1. Samson, Samuel, John the Baptist, and Jesus are all witnesses to what God can do.

God can bring something out of your barren and sterile heart too. If you open your life to him, you will find the unexpected. Out of you will flow living water that will reach a world for his glory. What could be a higher privilege?

april 14

touches of the spirit

john 20:19 – 23

*So I say, live by the Spirit, and you will not gratify the desires of the
sinful nature. For the sinful nature desires what is contrary to the Spirit,
and the Spirit what is contrary to the sinful nature. They are in
conflict with each other, so that you do not do what you want.
But if you are led by the Spirit, you are not under law.*
Galatians 5:16–18

God wants all of his children filled with his Spirit. That is why on the night
before the Cross, Jesus talked to his disciples so much about the Spirit. When
he commissioned his disciples, he asked them to receive the Holy Spirit
(John 20:19–23). He said that the Father was very eager to give the Spirit
to every believer (Luke 11:13). Paul had the same concern for all of his
friends (see Gal. 5:16–18). But why? What are the evidences of the Spirit
in the life of the believer?

One of these is simply an appetite for spiritual things. He is the quickening Spirit (Rom. 8:11), and he brings alive within us a hunger for God's
Word. The Scripture becomes a staple without which we cannot live. It
becomes the food of our soul.

A second characteristic is the desire to pray. We long for the Spirit's company. When we love people, we want to be with them. Fellowship with him
is not a burden but a delight.

A third characteristic is a love for the fellowship of his saints. We long
to be with those of like faith because in their presence we find the Spirit.

A fourth characteristic, and perhaps the one that speaks most loudly of
the Spirit's work within, is a hunger to share our knowledge of the Spirit
with others. The love of God is an other-oriented love. As God reaches out
to us, we will reach out to those who do not know him if that divine love
is in us.

How healthy are you today? Is the Spirit doing his quickening work
within you? If so, rejoice. If not, seek his face.

walking with god

genesis 5:21 – 24

He has showed you, O man, what is good.
And what does the LORD require of you?
To act justly and to love mercy
and to walk humbly with your God.
Micah 6:8

Enoch is one of the heroes of the Scripture even though the only characteristic we know about him is that he "walked with God" (Gen. 5:24). But that is enough. Walking with God is what the Christian life is all about.

We see it in the Creation story: In the cool of the day God came down to talk and walk with his creatures. We are told that Noah was a righteous and blameless man who walked with God (Gen. 6:9). The walk did not come out of the righteousness and blamelessness. No! Blamelessness and righteousness came out of Noah's walk with God. Note 1 John 1:7: "But if we walk in the light, as [God] is in the light, we have fellowship with one another, and the blood of Jesus, his Son, purifies us from all sin."

Abraham was the father of the faithful. We never read of him as a preacher, missionary, or social worker, but we do read that he walked with God. He is called "the friend of God" (James 2:23; see also 2 Chron. 20:7; Isa. 41:8). The preaching, the missionary witness, and the social service come, but they are authentic only when they come out of a walk with God.

Are you walking with him?

words of wisdom

acts 1 – 2

I know, O LORD, that a man's life is not his own;
it is not for man to direct his steps.
Jeremiah 10:23

Jeremiah recognized that the way of fulfillment for us is never in ourselves. It comes from beyond. I believe that if he were here today, he would say two things to us.

First, "Know under whose authority you live." The centurion whose servant was sick said to Jesus, "I myself am a man under authority" (Luke 7:8). We all are. We may be under the authority of self, but that is the way of death. This is why God gave us his Word: so we can know how to let God be saving within our lives. A daily perusal of its message will enable us to see and follow the path of light that means freedom and righteousness.

I think Jeremiah would also say, "Know where the power you need comes from. Recognize that it does not come from you. It comes from beyond." Zechariah recognized this when he said: "Not by might nor by power, but by my Spirit," says the LORD Almighty (Zech. 4:6).

The resources that we need to reach the goals God has for us are not in ourselves. They are in the One who was the key to the life of Jesus, the Holy Spirit. That is why we need to be sensitive to this heavenly Guest, who can lead, enlighten, cleanse, and fulfill our very being.

remember the future

1 chronicles 16:7 – 36

It is God who works in you to will and to act according to his good purpose.
Philippians 2:13

In Philippians 2:12–13 Paul tells the people in Philippi to work out their own salvation with fear and trembling, for "it is God who works in you." He never indicates that God will work redemptively in our lives in spite of us. God wants to work *with* us for our future, transforming us into the people he desires us to be.

Do you ever feel uneasy about the future? One of the best antidotes for that uneasiness is to look back upon the past and see the miracles of God's prevenient grace: how he worked in your life even before he brought you to himself. It helps to consider how many strings he pulled and what power he used to bring us to the place where we found Christ. Notice his providential, sovereign hand on you since that day, and remember that God's will toward you has not changed. His will toward you is just as good today as it was yesterday, as good as it was when you were a sinner who did not know him and he was lovingly working to bring you to himself. And he will continue to work and bring you to ultimate, final, and full salvation.

That is why Paul can joyously look at circumstances that seem negative. When he is in prison (Phil. 1:7) and when he is in need of financial support (Phil. 4:12), he can rejoice. He knows what the will of the One who is sovereign over all is toward him. It is good, and it will not change. How appropriate to work with that will.

worship and study

isaiah 40:28 – 31

His understanding no one can fathom.
Isaiah 40:28

Worship must be at the heart not only of our spiritual life, but also of our academic and intellectual pursuits. Life is supposed to be a seamless whole because it all has its source and its sustenance in the one God. It is he who gave us the challenge to study and know all that relates both to the creation and to himself.

This is our Father's world, and he has given it to us to master as his stewards. A spirit of worship toward the One who gave it all to us will make us more open, sensitive, and creative in our pursuit of knowledge and truth.

Faith and learning are not antinomies. Our faith is no enemy to knowledge. Anselm said, "I do not seek to understand in order to believe, but I believe in order to understand." Rejoice in the freedom God has given us to learn, and let the Spirit who first breathed upon the deep lead you. God is glorified when we learn.

The earth is the Lord's and everything in it,
the world, and all who live in it;
for he founded it upon the seas
and established it upon the waters (Ps. 24:1–2).

depending on him

joshua 1

*No one will be able to stand up against you all the days
of your life . . . I will be with you.*
Joshua 1:5

In Joshua we find that God is ready to do something new for his people.
The Israelites had been slaves in Egyptian bondage and in their agony had
cried out to Yahweh. He heard their cries, and he delivered them out of their
slavery to be his people. Now, however, because of their sin, they were wandering in the wilderness on the backside of the Jordan River, with no land
of their own. They began to long for something more stable, and God
wanted to give them that security. It is interesting to recognize how many
of the aspirations in the human heart have their origin in the heart of God.
He looks with pleasure on the basic human desires because he gave them to
us, and he wants to be given the opportunity to meet those needs.

We must realize our dependence upon God for the meeting of our
needs. We must choose not to force circumstances to fit our desires. We
must trust him. If we are receptive to him, there is no earthly power great
enough to keep us from enjoying the good that he wants to give us. God's
promise to Joshua emphasizes this truth: "There shall not any man be able
to stand before thee all the days of thy life: as I was with Moses, so I will be
with thee: I will not fail thee, nor forsake thee. Be strong and of good
courage" (Josh. 1:5–6 KJV). Oftentimes we look at our circumstances and
feel that there are too many obstacles and too many enemies for God's promises to actually reach fulfillment. It is only our shortsightedness that causes
us to doubt him. His promise is that there is nothing outside of us that can
keep us from enjoying what he wants to give. Nothing has the power to frus-
trate the purposes of God for me—except me.

a kingdom of priests

hebrews 7:26–8:6

You will be for me a kingdom of priests and a holy nation.
Exodus 19:6

What does it mean for Christians to be a kingdom of priests? Priests do not live for themselves; they live for the ones they serve. The nation of Israel was to be a whole nation that lived not for itself but for others. This self-giving existence is the plan God conceived for Israel and the plan he conceived for the church. This is the reason a church without a missionary passion and a missionary budget is not the church that Christ envisioned.

Priests are mediators. They stand between other people and God. Their significance comes from the ones between whom they stand. God has left Christians here so the world can know about our Father in heaven. Believers are to stand between the world and God, mediating between them. Followers of Christ must have God's signature on them so the world knows to whom they belong. When Christians have been washed by the blood of Jesus, they begin to look like Jesus. His character is to be the defining quality of their lives.

One important thing about the priests in the Old Testament is the garments they wore. A priest could not serve unless he wore the priestly garments. To serve as mediators between a world without God and God himself, we must be dressed in the righteousness of God so the world can see his presence in us. We cannot just have a cloak of righteousness that covers our sins; we must allow the Spirit to change us from the inside out so that we actually begin to be like Jesus.

Jesus is our High Priest. He placed himself between God and us and caused God's grace to meet our need, and therefore we were redeemed. As Christians we stand between Christ and his Cross on the one hand and the world in its lostness on the other. Our business is to cause that grace of Christ and the need of the world about us to meet. As the Father sent Jesus to us, Jesus sends us to his world and ours.

april 21

living like jesus

matthew 14:3 – 12

When Jesus came to the region of Caesarea Philippi, he asked his disciples,
"Who do people say the Son of Man is?"
They replied, "Some say John the Baptist; others say Elijah; and still others,
Jeremiah or one of the prophets."
"But what about you?" he asked. "Who do you say I am?"
Simon Peter answered, "You are the Christ, the Son of the living God."
Matthew 16:13–16

When Jesus asked his disciples, "Who do people say that I am?" their reply was very interesting. Jesus had been going through the countryside, preaching and healing. He had restored the sick, cleansed the lepers, given sight to the blind, made the lame to walk, and even raised the dead. His ministry had been marked by signs and wonders. So it is interesting that when the disciples cited who Jesus was like, two of the three men they mentioned never performed a miracle as far as we know. John the Baptist and Jeremiah were not miracle workers. They were men of a message, and they were men who suffered for that message.

There is something greater than power and much more desirable. That is personal holiness. John the Baptist and Jeremiah knew the way of the Cross, and they followed it. Signs and wonders speak only of deliverance from temporary problems. The Cross speaks of the nature of God and what he wants to make of each one of us. Signs and wonders speak of deliverance from suffering. The Cross speaks of embracing suffering so that those about us can see Christ himself. Paul understood this. Note Philippians 3:10, where Paul speaks of his supreme desire to "know Christ and the power of his resurrection and the fellowship of sharing in his sufferings, becoming like him in his death."

Is there any evidence of the message of the Cross in your life? Do people identify you with the Lord Jesus?

april 22

an offering to god

luke 18:18–25

Sell everything you have and give to the poor,
and you will have treasure in heaven. Then come, follow me.
Luke 18:22

One of my heroes is a man who never graduated from college. However, he may be as smart as anyone I have ever met. His Christian influence has reached around the world.

The key to his life was a conversation with Lettie Cowman, author of *Streams in the Desert,** who shared with my friend the determinative experience of her life.

When she and her husband were new Christians, they attended a missionary conference led by A. B. Simpson, founder of the Christian and Missionary Alliance Church. When Dr. Simpson finished his message, he said, "We must take an offering. This will be an unusual offering. You will notice that the offering plates are not empty. They are full of watches. These watches are not gold, but they are good watches. If you will put your gold watch in the plate, you may take one of these cheaper watches. We will sell your gold watch and send the message of Christ to those who do not know it."

When the plate came to Lettie, she handed it to her husband. To her shock, he took the plate, placed in it his gold watch that she had given him, and took out one of the cheaper watches. She reproachfully said, "I gave that to you." But the plate was gone.

Dr. Simpson then said, "We must take another offering. This time the plates will be empty. Many of us wear more jewelry than is necessary for good grooming. If you will put the jewelry which you really don't need in the plate, we will sell it and send the message of Christ to those that do not know it." When the plate came to Lettie, she handed it to her husband. He took the plate with his left hand, then reached over with his right hand and slipped her engagement ring off her finger. He placed it in the plate. Horrified, she said, "You gave that to me." But the plate was gone.

---

*Lettie (Mrs. Charles E.) Cowman, *Streams in the Desert* (Los Angeles: Oriental Missionary Society, 1925).

Then Dr. Simpson said, "Now we must take a money offering." When the plate came, she handed it to her husband and watched as her husband took from his pocket an envelope containing his paycheck for the previous two weeks. He put it in the plate. She said to him, "How are we going to buy groceries?" But the plate was gone.

Then Dr. Simpson said, "Now we must take the real offering, the offering of life. If you will give your life to carry the gospel to the world, stand up." Lettie Cowman's husband stood. Lettie said, "It was the determining moment of my life. I knew that if my husband said he was going, he would go whether I went with him or not. So I stood."

The impact of that story on my friend was such that he decided that he must give his life totally to Christ and live it totally for him. He did not become a preacher. He has spent his entire life as a businessman who lives to witness for Christ. The result is that his influence has been more extensive across the world and more fruitful in souls than that of anyone else I know. It is wonderful what God does when he gets all of one of us.

where did he go?

matthew 28:16–20

While he was blessing them, he left them and was taken up into heaven.
Then they worshiped him.
Luke 24:51–52

As a pastor I had never preached a sermon on the ascension. I had preached on Christ's birth, his baptism, the events in his life, his death, and his resurrection, but I had never preached on his ascension. Because I thought that there must be something significant in that story, I began to prepare a sermon on it, trying to understand what the significance is. As I worked, I thought of two questions: How far did Jesus go? And how long did it take him to get there? Then I laughed at my own stupidity. *How far* is a space question. He created space. He was there before there was space. He is not in space; he transcends space. Space is in him. *How long* is a time question. He created time because it is a reflection of space, a reflection of the creation. Days, hours, and minutes are part of created experience; they are not part of God's experience. He is not bound by time or space.

When I reached that point in my thinking, I had a moment of revelation. When Jesus returns, he will not have to travel through space; nor will it take him any time, for he is Lord of space and time. That means he is already here. He never really left. We just don't have the capacity to recognize his holy presence. We speak of having Christ in our hearts. The reality though is that we are in him because there is nowhere he is not. As Paul said to the Athenians, "He is not far from each one of us; for in him we live and move and have our being" (Acts 17:27–28). Suddenly I found that I had a sense of his nearness that I had never had before. When Jesus comes again and our eyes are opened to see him, I think we will realize that he has been here all along.

april 24

---

a thankful heart

daniel 6

He went home to his upstairs room where the windows opened toward
Jerusalem. Three times a day he got down on his knees and prayed,
giving thanks to his God, just as he had done before.
Daniel 6:10

The key to Daniel's life was that everywhere Daniel went, the Lord was with him. The men who hated Daniel had the king decree that no one could pray to any god for thirty days. After hearing the decree, Daniel went back to his room and opened his window toward Jerusalem. I love the fact that he faced Jerusalem. There was no magic in facing that direction, but Jerusalem was the place where Daniel knew God had dwelt. Daniel prayed in this way three times a day. I don't believe those prayers were merely routine. Daniel's heart was hungry enough that he wanted to keep checking in with his Source of guidance, security, and joy. As he prayed in this position, on his knees facing Jerusalem, he knew the potential consequence was death in the lions' den, and yet his prayer was one of thankfulness.

It is always easier to sense the presence of the Lord if you have a thankful heart. I once thought that it was the great preachers or those people who could give substantial sums of money who were the most effective Christians. I am convinced now that the most sacred and creative thing, the greatest work any person can ever do, is to thank God, to praise him, and to pray. The person sitting in a wheelchair in grateful praise and adoration may be of more value to God than anyone else in his kingdom. God does not play favorites; nor does he throw people away. No one need be useless. All of us can be thankful and pray. There is power in thankfulness and prayer.

april 25

false and fleeting fulfillment

psalm 46

God is our refuge and strength,
an ever-present help in trouble.
Psalm 46:1

One of the characteristics of human personhood is that we never find our fulfillment in ourselves. We must look beyond ourselves if we would ever really know fulfillment. As human beings we need purpose and meaning in our lives. We need something of which we can boast, something that gives us some self-confidence, self-esteem, and inner joy. But the effect of sin on us is such that we naturally look in the wrong places to find this fulfillment. We look for something when we should be looking for Someone. Our true fulfillment, the only ultimate fulfillment, is in God himself.

As we look for fulfillment, we also seek security. We seek it in creatures, institutions, possessions. Again, our sin blinds us and deceives us. All things other than Christ are only temporary refuges. David learned this and said, "God is our refuge" (Ps. 46:1). He is the haven to whom we should all flee. Peter was sensing this when he said to Jesus, "Lord, to whom shall we go? You have the words of eternal life" (John 6:68).

Are you looking for a refuge today? A place not only of security but also of fulfillment? Run to Jesus. He is the One you seek.

april 26

for better or for worse

deuteronomy 30:1–6

Place me like a seal over your heart,
like a seal on your arm;
for love is as strong as death.
Song of Songs 8:6

Jesus died to take away the distance between God and individual persons. He died to remove the reservations that alienate us from our relationship to him, to eradicate the hindrances that keep us apart. Circumcision was the mark of the people of God under the old covenant. It was a symbol of intimacy. At the most intimate place on a man's body, the place of love and of union, God put his own mark. But the mark on the body was only a symbol of what God wanted to do in every heart (see Deut. 30:6). Do you know that God can also circumcise our stubborn hearts at the point of deepest intimacy? He can do a divine surgery so that we can love him with all our hearts and all our souls. According to Moses, until we let him perform that surgery, we have never truly lived.

The culmination of the Christian faith comes when we let him transform our hearts so he is the delight of our lives. He wants to become the joy of our souls so we feel that the greatest privilege of life is to surrender to him. Our prayer can be, "Lord, I am yours for better or for worse, for richer or for poorer, in sickness and in health, to love and to cherish." And the beautiful thing is that even death cannot part us; it will only make us closer.

Have you come to the place where Jesus is your joy? Have you reached the point where you think it's safe to belong wholly to the Lord Jesus? The closest thing to this that we can know in experience is the joyous delight the groom finds in his bride; but not even a loving wife is as good as God. God wants to give himself to us the way a husband and a wife should give themselves to each other, and he desires us to give ourselves to him in the same manner: Completely! Unconditionally! Forever!

"be imitators of god"

ephesians 4:20 – 5:2

Be imitators of God, therefore, as dearly loved children and live a life of love.
Ephesians 5:1–2

One day as I was reading through the book of Ephesians, I found myself laughing aloud when I came across Ephesians 5:1, "Be imitators of God." How can someone like me imitate God? Many of his attributes immediately came into my mind. First of all, he is the omnipotent One. A few in history have tried to be all-powerful, but they have ended up as fools. Second, he is the omniscient One. He knows all things. But when I am in the process of finding an answer to a question, I discover that I have ten more questions, and so my experience is one of exploding ignorance, not knowledge. The more I know, the more I have to learn. Third, he is the omnipresent One. But I am confined to one moment in time and one point in space. How can I imitate him?

I looked again at the passage: "And live a life of love, just as Christ loved us and gave himself up for us as a fragrant offering and sacrifice to God" (Eph. 5:2). My laughter faded as I realized that God wants us to imitate his lifestyle, not his attributes. What Paul was telling the church to imitate was the life of love that issues in self-sacrifice modeled in the Lord Jesus.

Suddenly I found myself confronted not with divine attributes in abstraction, but with the very Cross of Christ. Then I realized that Paul was asking us to imitate the God we see on Calvary, the God who cares more for someone else than he does for himself. Paul says that self-sacrificing love pleases the very nostrils of God.

But how can I get out of my self-interest, which seems to contaminate every thing I do and touch? Paul gives us the key. It lies not in us but in the very love that sent Christ to Calvary. Paul believed that God can put his own love in us, if we want it and seek it.

If we let his Spirit fill us, we will find that his love comes with his presence. Then we can live as he lived because he will be living through us.

april 28

---

living water

john 4

Whoever drinks the water I give him will never thirst.
John 4:14

The story of Jesus and the Samaritan woman at the well provides a great example of the effectiveness of Jesus' witness. Jesus was tired and thirsty. The woman was deep in sin and conscious of the futility of her life. Jesus waited to help her. She was his inferior socially, morally, and spiritually, but there was no condescension in his manner toward her. In fact, he asked her to do something for him that put him in her debt, opening doors for dialogue that were not previously open. The important thing is not only that he asked her for something; what he asked for is also significant. When he asked for water and she questioned him in her surprise, he was able to offer her the gift of living water. Jesus had piqued the woman's interest and desire. She began to ask him about this living water, and Jesus revealed the key to it.

The thing that keeps persons from partaking of Jesus' life-giving water and enjoying his presence is sin. We must break with our sin if we want to know the refreshment, the healing, and the cleansing of his life-giving water. Jesus gently but firmly dealt with the Samaritan woman's sin problem. He exposed her sin, and she had nowhere to hide. This is a necessary aspect of our entering a relationship with Jesus. We must be willing to be clean and to be vulnerable to him. Amazingly, the Samaritan woman continued the conversation. She was so anxious for Jesus to give her living water that she was willing to open her heart to him. Are you willing to let him expose the secret places of your heart?

This needy and hungry woman, considered an outcast by the Jews in Jerusalem, is the first person to whom Jesus revealed his identity as the Messiah. What he could not safely say in the Holy City, "the City of the Messiah," he could tell to a poor, sinful woman who was hungry for salvation. His greatest secrets are kept not for the best but for those who feel the greatest need. Do you qualify?

calling the disciples

john 1:29–51

*Philip found Nathanael and told him,
"We have found the one . . . Jesus of Nazareth, the son of Joseph."
John 1:45*

The stories of the calling of the twelve disciples give us wonderful insights into the business of how men and women are reached for Christ. According to the gospel of John, only one of the first five disciples was reached directly by Christ. That was Philip. Jesus said to him, "Follow me" (John 1:43). The other four were reached by someone else's witness to Christ.

Andrew and an unnamed disciple, perhaps John, came as the result of John the Baptist's witness. Simon came because of his brother Andrew, and Nathanael came because of his friend Philip.

You and I have significant roles to play in the advancement of the kingdom of God. If people around us are going to find Christ, it will happen only as we bear a winsome witness to him. These first disciples were not ministers. They were laypersons who had been impressed by someone else's testimony about Christ. They had not known Christ long when they became soul-winners, and they turned first to their family and friends. We should begin our witness for Christ by reaching out to those to whom we are closest. They are our first responsibility.

What are you doing to bring others to Christ? Our lives and our lips must speak of him. And we should begin with those we love.

god, the source of life

1 john 5:1 – 13

With you is the fountain of life.
Psalm 36:9

The Christian story is this: When we chose to separate ourselves from God, we found that in ourselves there was no way back. We had no power to save ourselves. Only God could help. But he could not save us from his throne in heaven. That was not where the problem was; the problem was on earth, so he had to meet the need where it was—in us. Thus the Incarnation and the Cross became necessary. God had to become human and overcome the separation and death in us.

The central character in all this is not the Son but the Father, from whom the Son came. The Father sent the Son to become one of us, Immanuel. Our eternal death was overcome in that he took our sin with the consequent death on himself. The Father who is the source of all life gave back the Son's life in the Resurrection. We must never forget that the cost of sin is great. It brings about the sinner's death. But the cost of salvation is even greater. It means that One died not for his own sin, but for another's. In both cases separation from God makes death inevitable.

That is why we need to keep close to the Source of life, God himself. Our only security is an unbroken intimacy with the Fountain of life. Are you living there?

freedom from myself

philippians 2:5–8

Love . . . does not seek its own.
1 Corinthians 13:4–5 NKJV

Have you ever pondered the incredible delight of a negative freedom—not a license to do something, but a freedom from something? Do you know what a joy it is to realize there are some things you do not have to do? Perhaps the most thrilling of these neglected freedoms is that of not having to have one's own way. There is no greater slavery than that which insists you must have your own way—or try very hard to get your own way—in every situation. Nothing in the world destroys human relationships more quickly and more completely than this bondage to one's own wishes. This tyranny pollutes marriages, friendships, and parent-child relationships. The Word of God is very clear that we can be liberated from it.

When the apostle Paul states in 1 Corinthians 13 that love is not self-seeking, he is dealing with this insistence on fulfilling our own agendas. At the core of sin is my own self-will and demand that I get what I want. If I am to be a Christian, I must settle in my life once and for all that the law of my life is not my will, but Christ's will. His will has to be supreme, and that means that my will has to be crucified.

The Lord Jesus allows us to be wrong so many times in life in order to find out whether we can live without having to get our own way. We are wrong often enough that we ought to know we should never insist on our way unless it is divinely clear that it is his will we are seeking and not our own. It is surprising what healing and growth can occur in human relationships when we reach the place where we can bow to others and above all bow to him.

growing sweeter

philippians 4:4 – 8

I am not saying this because I am in need,
for I have learned to be content whatever the circumstances.
Philippians 4:11

We are not truly free until we are free from self-pity. Self-pity ensnares many people, but Jesus can establish us in a place where there is no room for feeling sorry for ourselves. Perhaps self-pity is more of a temptation for older people, although I have seen it in young and old.

My mother-in-law lived with us for the closing part of her life. It was one of the best educations of my life. She was in her seventies and eighties, and our family had a chance to watch her as she grew old. There were days when she could not do any kind of physical work, days when she felt useless. I can remember looking at her and, realizing that she felt useless, I would say, "Mother, you are the most important person in this house. All five of my kids behave better when you are here." And it was true. They had an opportunity to watch an aged woman getting sweeter and more contented every day. They would slip into her room, and there she would be sitting with a paper on her lap, and when they took a closer look, they would find their names written on it. She was praying through her prayer list. Instead of pitying herself, my mother-in-law used the last years of her life to give to other people through her prayers and through her presence.

I believe that if we will let God work in our lives, we can be an untold blessing simply because of the love of God shed abroad in our hearts through the Holy Spirit. Self-pity defies the nature, goodness, and wisdom of God, and I believe we can live without challenging him. Are you letting him make you a blessing to other people in whatever way he chooses?

freedom from appearance

2 corinthians 5:12 – 20

Love is patient, love is kind. It does not envy, it does not boast, it is not proud.
1 Corinthians 13:4

I am glad that Christ can get us to the place where we do not have to look good all the time in our own eyes. Have you ever lived around people who continually had to keep a mask on? No matter what event occurred, they had to come out of it looking better than everyone else involved. There is no way to come to humility if you are constantly concerned with yourself.

Many of us have a fetish about appearance. I am not talking about clothing and external appearance, although that can be part of it. I am talking about wanting to impress other people all the time, refusing to lose in front of other people, choosing not to accept even second best. Oftentimes we even become resentful toward relatives who make us look bad, and we shrink from being identified with them. What insufferable bondage it is for us and for those we love when we have to look good at every social engagement and in every situation.

This explains Paul's description of love as the person who does not have to boast and is not proud. How often we destroy priceless relationships by having to keep up our appearance when we ought to forget about ourselves.

freedom to not defend myself (part 1)

isaiah 53:7 – 12

He was oppressed and afflicted,
yet he did not open his mouth;
he was led like a lamb to the slaughter,
and as a sheep before her shearers is silent,
so he did not open his mouth.
Isaiah 53:7

There exists a glorious freedom for the few souls brave enough to entrust their reputations, futures, and lives to Christ. Have you ever been in a situation where someone attacked or criticized you? Perhaps you were misunderstood or perhaps you did something wrong, and someone pounced on your error. How quickly an alibi rises to our lips, or maybe even a good excuse. What a magnificent thing when we don't have to defend ourselves.

Let me ask you, who is freer? The person who has an uncontrollable impulse to speak to defend himself and does so, or the person who also has an impulse to defend himself but is free enough to stay quiet? Declining to speak on my own behalf requires much greater freedom and power than merely acting on the impulse to defend myself.

How much richer would some of our marriages be if we had that kind of freedom? How much richer our parent-child relationships? Our professional relationships? Are you as free as God wants you to be?

freedom to not defend myself (part 2)

isaiah 53:7 – 12

I had a philosophy professor at Princeton who had a profound influence on my life. Dr. Èmile Cailliet was a devout and godly man as well as an astute thinker. He had published a little book for laypeople called *The Life of the Mind*. One day in a course on Christian living he told us about an experience he had with a Princeton student who confronted him about this little book. "Dr. Cailliet, you're a professor at Princeton Theological Seminary, one of the most prestigious seminaries in the world. You have two Ph.D.'s, and you're an internationally known scholar. How is it that you could write something as simplistic as that book on the life of the mind and publish it under your name when you're as famous and as important as you are? It ought to be beneath your dignity."

The student continued, "Above all, it isn't psychologically sound. I really don't understand how you could put anything like that in print without dealing with the recent psychological work of one of your own countrymen, Foucault."

Dr. Cailliet said to us, "It's interesting to have one of your students deride you," then continued his story: "There was that first flush within me, that first impulse to defend myself. But the Spirit of God checked me and I said, simply, 'Thank you.' And I finished the class. After class I decided to walk down the street to cool off. As I walked, I remembered the three years I had spent working with Foucault and actually doing his research experiments. In fact, I knew as much about Foucault's work as Foucault did. But that student never knew that."

As Dr. Cailliet walked, a car pulled up by the curb and stopped, and a man jumped out and came running up and said, "Are you Dr. Cailliet?"

He said, "Yes, I am."

"Well," said the young man, "I just wanted to see you. I couldn't leave town without meeting you. I want to tell you about that little book you published called *The Life of the Mind*. It was like a light to me in a dark place. It gave me insights about myself and about life that I had never found anywhere else. And because of that little book, life's been richer and free ever since. Thank you, Dr. Cailliet."

Dr. Cailliet said, "I walked on down the street and lifted my heart i gratitude to God that I hadn't defended myself. That I had been free enoug that I didn't have to. God himself had become my defense."

freedom to be different

daniel 3

*If we are thrown into the blazing furnace, the God we serve is able
to save us from it, and he will rescue us from your hand, O king.
But even if he does not, we want you to know, O king,
that we will not serve your gods or worship the image of gold you have set up.*
Daniel 3:17–18

How many of us have known the enslavement and bondage of being in a
group and having to do something we did not want to do because we were
afraid of not pleasing the crowd? Then we are like Peter standing at the fire
when the girl looks at him and asks, "Aren't you one of his?" Peter did not
have the liberty to stand for Christ; he was bound and controlled by the
pressure of those about him, and so he betrayed the One he loved.

What a sad story. How much greater is the story of Daniel or of
Shadrach, Meshach, and Abednego, who looked the world in the face and
did what was right, regardless of the consequences. They were free to be different. We can never be free until we are free to be different from those
around us.

I was sitting in the home of a great Christian man, and he was telling
me about a sermon of his on "singing the Lord's song in a strange land." He
said, "You know, if you are ever going to sing the Lord's song, you will have
to sing it in a strange land. Only the people who have sung his song in a
strange land are going to sing it in his land." We will never be where God
wants us to be until we can stand for Jesus in a world that is indifferent or
even hostile to the message of Christ.

Let us today be willing to look the world in the eye and say, "I hope
you will be patient with me because, you see, I am a Christian."

love in spite of humiliation

matthew 27:35–44

My command is this: Love each other as I have loved you.
John 15:12

When Jesus sets us free from ourselves and all the entanglements of our desires, he can fill our hearts so full of love that we can love in the face of criticism, misunderstanding, and even rejection.

I was in the home of a very devout lady who told me her father's story. Walter had become a Christian, and after his conversion he had heard the message of perfect love and had sought it. God came and shed perfect love in his heart. A new preacher was sent to Walter's church, and before the first church service, Walter went to the barn and took out the very best ham so he could present it to the new preacher as a love gift. During the service, there was a testimony time, and Walter stood up and told how he was converted and then how the Spirit of God came and cleansed him from self-interest. In the middle of his testimony, the preacher stood up and said, "Sit down, Mr. Shehan. That is fanaticism, and as long as I am pastor, we will not have any talk of that kind."

After the service, Mr. Shehan surprised his family by going to the buggy to retrieve the ham. He took it to the pastor and said, "Pastor, we are so glad you are here. There are many churches without pastors, and our church needs a shepherd to lead and feed us. We love you, and if we can help you, let us know."

The next morning a strange buggy pulled into the lane. It was driven by the preacher. He said, "Mr. Shehan, I have come to apologize. If there is anything you want to witness to in one of my prayer meetings, go right ahead, because it is obvious that you have found something that I know nothing about. Blessings on you."

There is a power that comes when we are free from ourselves and free to love.

the black book

matthew 18:21–35

Love ... keeps no record of wrongs.
1 Corinthians 13:4–5

You will remember that one of the characteristics of love listed in 1 Corinthians 13 is that it keeps no record of wrongs. What a great way to live. Can you imagine how different our relationships would be if we would let God wipe them clean every day? Wouldn't it be liberating if we started every day with a clean slate, with nothing out of kilter from the day before? A great pastor told me about counseling a man and his wife who were in the process of getting a divorce. Finally he got the wife to consent to live with the husband, and then he turned to the husband and said, "All right, she is willing to make another try; are you?"

The husband looked at the pastor and said, "I will never sleep another night under the same roof with that little black book of hers."

After the pastor recovered from his surprise, he turned to the wife: "What is in your black book?"

She grudgingly replied that she kept a careful record of every mistake that her husband made.

There is enough love and enough power in the cross of Christ to enable us to forget past hurts and continue our relationships as if there had never been anything wrong. Even with the best intentions, this will never be done in human strength; only the Spirit of Jesus can enable us to forget our pains and hurts. If you choose to build up the memories of those hurts that other people have inflicted on you, you will pollute, corrupt, and destroy all of your relationships. Resentment has destructive power, but the grace of Christ has a deeper power to keep human relationships as clean and fresh as springtime.

It will take the love of God, and he can cause our love to forget.

poisonous wishes

philippians 4:10–13

*You shall not covet your neighbor's wife. You shall not set your desire
on your neighbor's house or land, his manservant or maidservant,
his ox or donkey, or anything that belongs to your neighbor.*
Deuteronomy 5:21

Discontentment is a poison that ruins friendships and destroys persons.
Only Jesus can enable us to live oblivious to the possessions of friend and
neighbor, content with what God has provided. Have you ever thought
about how much discontentment there is in the world just because each person notices that the person next door has it a little bit better? What avarice
and what greed there is in the human heart! I believe that the free person is
the one who can live on the least rather than the one who possesses the most.
Discontentment is the handcuff binding us to things that will not last or
ultimately even be meaningful. Could God place enough love in a heart like
mine so I could look at you when you have more than I have and rejoice for
you? That would be real love. That would be God's love.

Something inside me believes that this love is the kind that God planned
for me to have. Loving other people regardless of what they possess would
be freedom for me. John Wesley said that the tenth commandment, "You
shall not covet," is really a promise that God can deliver us from covetous-
ness; for we cannot obey God until we can live without wanting what someone else has.

free to let you win

1 samuel 24

*What you heard from me, keep as the pattern of sound teaching,
with faith and love in Christ Jesus. Guard the good deposit that was
entrusted to you—guard it with the help of the Holy Spirit who lives in us.*
2 Timothy 1:13–14

Jesus Christ can set you free from having to have the last word! We have all
experienced the incredible desire to walk out after lambasting another person with a brilliant and stinging finale to our argument. This is a classic pit-
fall for husbands and wives. Why must we have the last word? It is actually
not a sign of strength but of great and profound insecurity. We refuse to
look less than the best because if we do, our self-esteem plummets. It is a
marvelous thing when we become so free that we do not have to win in every
situation. We cannot be free, truly free, until we can lose without losing our
own self-respect.

All human relationships have a built-in rivalry. God lets it stay there so
we can learn how to lose—whether the victor wins justly or unjustly. He
wants us to reach the place where we do not have to come out on top every
time and we do not have to have the last word. We can face defeat without
being shattered by it.

free to fail

acts 17

*Peace I leave with you; my peace I give you. I do not give to you
as the world gives. Do not let your hearts be troubled and do not be afraid.*
John 14:27

I am convinced that there are some things we learn through failure that we could never learn through success. We can never be adequate witnesses until we have failed at some point, because the majority of people to whom we will minister will know what failure is. No person will ever be an adequate shepherd of souls (a Sunday school teacher, a mother, a neighbor, or a pastor) without having known the bitter spots in life. If we are not willing to face the Cross in our own lives, we limit our ability to glorify Jesus.

I am convinced that Abraham Lincoln was a great president because he failed so many times. He failed at almost everything he ever tried until he became president. He failed enough that he was no longer interested in winning but wanted to do what was right. There is a spiritual peer pressure among Christians. It is the pressure to do spiritual things for the wrong reasons, so we can look good. This has the same moral value as sin. We must come to the place where we do what is right whether the world views us as a success or a failure. We cannot do right actions to avoid failure or rejection. We must do right regardless of the consequences simply because it is right.

cracking fingers, setting free

john 21:15–23

So if the Son sets you free, you will be free indeed.
John 8:36

had been a Christian about six years when I realized that a substantial por-
on of my ambition was permeated by pride. I had my own ideas about
hat success in the ministry ought to be like, and the Lord confronted me
oout it. He asked, "Are you willing to let me take your life and spend it the
ay I please?"

"What are you going to do with it?" I asked him.

Quietly he responded, "You don't trust me, do you?"

"Well, it is not that I don't trust you, but it would help if you would tell
e what you plan to do with my life."

"No, I am not going to tell you my plans. You will never know full free-
om until you look me in the face and say, 'God, you can do what you please
ith me.'"

And so I tried to look him in the face and give him my full self. "What
that on the corner of your life?" he asked.

"That is my thumb. Can't I keep one finger on my life?"

"No, if are going to turn it loose, you have to take all fingers off."

I tried to remove the finger from my life, and I found that I could not.
ou see, it is only by his grace that we are ever set free. Finally, I looked up
nd said, "God, can you take that finger off?"

"If you will let me crack it hard enough and long enough, I can."

"Well, start cracking," I said, terrified. At that point, I quit kneeling and
ound myself flat on my face before God. Slowly, he began to set me free.

There is a power in the Cross that can set us free from the tyranny of
elf-interest that either controls or contaminates our lives. If we let him set
s free, we can relax and rest in him—no longer driven to strive for what we
esire for ourselves. We will find that his desires become ours. That oneness
the real freedom.

dangerous gifts

1 corinthians 12

Now to each one the manifestation of the Spirit is given for the common good.
1 Corinthians 12:7

One of the beauties of God's working with us is that he deals with us as a community. He gives you what I need, and miraculously he gives me something you are going to need. The Holy Spirit is the one who gives us gifts and he is the one who wants to control their use. Thus it is absolutely essential that a person who has a gift of the Spirit be filled with the Spirit. Because of the communal nature of spiritual gifts, our gifts are not only sterile, they are dangerous when used for ourselves or used apart from the Spirit of God. We easily damage ourselves and other persons when his gifts are not under his control. It is possible to have a gift and not have its Giver. Then we have an appearance of spiritual power, but it is tainted by self-interest, temper, a critical spirit, and a carnal attitude.

The spiritual gift I have must be under his control and not my own if it is to be truly fruitful. The Spirit must rule my life completely. When I come to the place where he controls me, then whatever he gives me belongs to him and can be used by him. When I have yielded myself to him, he is able to sanctify both me and the gift; then the gift becomes an instrument of his glory.

gifts for community

ephesians 4:1 – 16

It was he who gave . . . to prepare God's people for works of service,
so that the body of Christ may be built up.
Ephesians 4:11–12

he gifts of the Spirit are not related to our personal holiness. They are given
o us for the sake of others. God's gifts to us, except for the gift of himself,
re always other-oriented. They are intended to deal with the question of
ow Christians are to live together and how they are to function in a non-
hristian world. Ephesians 4 tells us that Christ gives gifts for the perfect-
ng of the saints, to equip them for service to others. Our gifts are intended
o help other people know the Lord Jesus more intimately.

We will never know our own faults and our own failings if we live alone.
. is in the friction that comes through our contacts with others that we find
ut who we really are. The Spirit's perfecting power is at work the most when
am in close association with other people. Because of God's gift of others
nd his gifts to others, I find perspective, balance, and grace. If I would be
hole, I must be a functioning part of the body of Christ.

So the gifts of the Spirit are given to others for our benefit and to us for
heirs. They are not given for personal privilege or pleasure but for the sake
f the others. Are you letting God use the gifts he has given you for your
rothers and sisters in Christ and for the world?

determining history

genesis 41:37 – 57; jeremiah 5:1

Terah took his son Abram, his grandson Lot son of Haran,
and his daughter-in-law Sarai, the wife of his son Abram,
and together they set out from Ur of the Chaldeans to go to Canaan.
But when they came to Haran, they settled there.
Genesis 11:31

As you read the book of Genesis you will find that it talks little about the international affairs of that period. Rather, Genesis records for us the history of a single family in a remote land. A patriarch had one son and then twelve grandsons, and those men influenced the course of human history more than anyone found in the headlines of the *Sumerian Times* or the *Babylonian Daily Chronicle*. The future was determined by these few men and not by the institutions or the international movements of that time. We live in a day when most people believe that institutions are the determining factors. They declare that if we could just change institutions, then we could change society. This is the appeal of the politician. Scripture tantalizes us with the amount of space it devotes to individual people rather than institutions. People seem to be the tools that God uses to bring change.

The implication is clear. Ultimately, persons determine institutions; institutions do not determine persons. The decisions that are made deep in the heart of an individual in the intimacy of aloneness with God are the decisions that will be historically significant for deciding the future. Those decisions may be made in such a way that even the people making them are not aware of the significance of their choices and the magnitude of the consequences. The most significant thing that ever occurs is when an individual person confronts his or her responsibilities before God and the opportunities and privileges of grace that are extended to each one in Christ. That is why intercession, evangelism, and discipleship are so important. And that is why you are so valuable—valuable enough that the life of God in Christ was sacrificed for you.

he makes no mistakes

mark 11:15 – 19

*If anyone would come after me, he must deny himself and take up his cross
and follow me. For whoever wants to save his life will lose it,
but whoever loses his life for me and for the gospel will save it.*
Mark 8:34–35

I remember one night during World War II when I spoke to a group of G.I.'s at an evangelistic service. One of the soldiers lingered afterward to talk. Once we were alone, he said, "I would like to become a Christian."

"Why?" I asked.

"Well, I don't want to go to hell," he replied.

"I suppose that is a good reason." I responded. "I don't know if it is the noblest reason, but it is a perfectly legitimate one. All right, then, will you give your life to Christ?"

The soldier stiffened, "Oh, I could never do that," he said. "Are you sure a man has to do that to be a Christian?"

I turned in my New Testament to read Jesus' words, "If anyone would come after me, he must deny himself and take up his cross and follow me. For whoever wants to save his life will lose it, but whoever loses his life for me and for the gospel will save it."

After a pause, he asked again, "Do I have to give my life to Christ to become a Christian?"

"Yes, you do. Why aren't you willing to do that?"

"Why, I have plans for my life!" he exclaimed. "How can I give my life to Christ if I already have my own plans for it?"

I wanted to shake that soldier's hand for his crystal-clear honesty. I had spent most of my life as a pastor dealing with people who felt that there was no contradiction between saying, "I will give my life to Christ," and saying, "I know what I am going to do with my life." That man sensed the contradiction.

The priests in Jerusalem felt that there was no contradiction between saying, "This is the Lord's house," and then running it in such a way that it was unfit for the Lord. Jesus had to walk in and declare, "You have made a terrible mistake. This is my Father's house. It must be managed his way." The priests reacted with panic.

Most of us panic when Christ comes into our lives like this. The foremost reason is our inordinate fear of what he will do with our lives when we allow him to take control. But is there any good reason to suppose that Jesus would make a mistake with our lives?

i can't live without you

ephesians 4:25 – 32

*Therefore each of you must put off falsehood and speak truthfully
to his neighbor . . . In your anger do not sin.*
Ephesians 4:25–26

What are the things that grieve the Holy Spirit? Ephesians 4 names two specific sins that grieve the Spirit. The first is lying. I believe Paul is talking not only of outright lies, but also of the small lies designed to protect the ego. When the truth is shaded just enough to keep ourselves from looking bad, and when we know that we ought to look bad, this is dishonesty. Embellishing the truth in order to appear circumspect is bearing false witness.

The second thing that grieves the Holy Spirit is losing our temper. One of the models for my Christian life has been a graduate of Asbury College who is from Greece. He spoke to us of an experience he had in which he grieved the Spirit. The man was a new immigrant and had just become a Christian. He was on a work team, shoveling coal. A coworker was quite profane, so he asked him to quit swearing. When the coworker continued the profanity, this Greek Christian punched him and knocked him out. His description of what followed was this: "All the rest of that day, I lived alone. The peace of God was gone. I went to my room that night and got down on my face and said, 'God, I can't live without you. What did I do wrong?'"

God responded, "You know what you did wrong." The next day he went back to that fellow who started it all with his profanity and asked for his forgiveness. He had lost his peace and did not regain it until he restored that relationship through confession.

Is there anything in your heart that you need to make right? As a great preacher once said, "When the Spirit grieves, the Spirit leaves."

blurred vision

mark 8:1 – 26

Jesus replied, "Go back and report to John what you hear and see:
The blind receive sight."
Matthew 11:4–5

The recognition of our sinful nature is the first step in becoming a Christian. Now, it is not hard for me to believe that *you* are fallen. My problem comes when I must believe that *I* am fallen. Even the best of men and women, no matter the nobleness of their hearts, find within themselves the impact of the fall. The fallenness of humanity fits the reality of the world in which we find ourselves. It particularly affects our ability to see clearly.

The mark of the new birth is opened eyes and clear vision. The question is how totally and how fully our eyes have been opened. Perhaps they were open at one time, but we have fallen asleep and our eyes have closed to the needs around us. Perhaps we have allowed distortions in our eternal perspective. There is nothing more dangerous than having blurred vision but thinking that it is clear.

If we measure our vision according to our own standards, how easy it is to draw an unrealistically positive conclusion about our eyesight. Instead we must test our vision according to the design of our Father for us and for the world, and the purpose of Christ for us and for the world's redemption. If we do, we will clearly recognize the blind spots with which we have been living. We will see the need of the world around us, and we will understand that it was our self-centered complacency that led us to believe our vision was sharp.

destined for a wedding

revelation 21

Come, I will show you the bride, the wife of the Lamb.
Revelation 21:9

In the early centuries of the Christian church, as theologians tried to understand the mystery of the Incarnation, an intriguing question arose. If human beings had never fallen, would God have sent Christ anyway? Some of them decided that, yes, if Adam and Eve had never sinned, the eternal Son would have still come and taken on human flesh. Their reasoning: God likes us, wants us to be near him, and wants us to be one with him.

A key factor in that thinking was the biblical claim that Christ came to the world to obtain a bride. John the Baptist saw Christ's role in that manner (John 3:22–30). Jesus saw his own mission in the same way (Mark 2:18–20). For both of them, the true philosophy of human history is nuptial. The final scenes in the book of Revelation (chapters 18–22) confirm this thesis. Those who believe in Christ are headed for a place on the very throne of God, where they are to sit with Christ as his bride. What a calling!

If we truly understood this truth, we would find flowing from that understanding a hallowing influence that would sanctify all of our lives. It would force us to see our sexuality as a parable of eternal things. Marriage would become a preparation ground for our ultimate destiny. And salvation would be seen in terms of self-giving rather than in terms of something we get. We would find ourselves seeking not a thing but a Person. I admit that I like the idea that Christ would have come even if we had never sinned, but the Scriptures do not address this question. They do make clear, however, that he seeks a relationship of intimacy with us in spite of our fall.

Are you enjoying the engagement period?

jesus, our model

mark 8:27 – 38

*For whoever wants to save his life will lose it, but whoever loses
his life for me and for the gospel will save it.*
Mark 8:35

Jesus Christ on the cross is the model for all Christians. The New Testament
explains this in two ways. The first deals with the scoffing and the sneering
of Jesus' enemies as they mocked him. They said, "He saved others; let him
save himself" (Luke 23:35). At this point, the model in Jesus is of a person
who chooses not to save himself or defend himself with words. This is the
example that Paul followed, and it is what he challenged the church to when
he said, "Follow my example, as I follow the example of Christ" (1 Cor
11:1). Paul describes Christ's example in Ephesians 5:1. "Be imitators of
God, therefore, as dearly loved children and live a life of love, just as Christ
loved us and gave himself up for us as a fragrant offering and sacrifice to
God." Christ did not save himself, but gave himself up for humankind, and
now Paul gives himself up for others. The word to us is clear: imitate this
example. Live in love and give yourself for someone else. This is the primary
business of all followers of Jesus: to choose not to save ourselves but to live
to save a world for Jesus.

The second way that Jesus is a model for us is his humanness. He is the
person that all human beings are intended to be like. He is our model. Since
Adam's sin, there has never been a person who was free from self-interest
and therefore every person has been less than a whole person. Now comes
Jesus, and he is free from self-interest, and because of that he is a whole person. It is only when we are in fellowship with this sin-free person of Jesus
Christ that we are saved. He comes into us and puts his life into us and turns
us inside out. He enables us to give ourselves away, to choose to lay down
our lives for other people.

sending timothy

1 corinthians 4:9 – 17

I have no one else like him, who takes a genuine interest in your welfare.
For everyone looks out for his own interests.
Philippians 2:20–21

elf-centeredness is one of the results of our fallen nature. Even after the
ew birth, we can still be filled with self-interest. There is no interruption
n the tyranny of self-centeredness apart from grace, yet even when grace is
resent, it is possible to care more about ourselves than about others.

I remember when I first found that plaintive little note in Philippians
:20–21. Paul writes, "I have no one else like him, who takes a genuine
nterest in your welfare. For everyone looks out for his own interests." Paul
ound himself in a pitiful situation when he looked around for an encour-
ger to send to strengthen the Philippian church and ascertain their state. As
e considered those about him, he decided that there was only one whom
e could trust to go. Timothy was the only member of his team who valued
he welfare of others more than his own.

Do you find yourself struggling with self-interest? It is possible for Jesus
o set you free so you will love others and care more about their welfare than
our own. When you let God bring you to that place, you find it is not
ondage but freedom.

If you had been a member of Paul's team, could he have sent you to the
hilippians?

may 22

---

is he calling you?

matthew 4:18 – 22

God called to him from within the bush, "Moses! Moses!"
Exodus 3:4

One day as Moses was tending sheep, he looked up and saw an inexplicable event occurring in front of his eyes. A bush in the desert was burning, but it was not consumed. As the flame leaped up, the leaves did not turn brown and become ashes. I suspect this is the way the majority of Christian lives begin: in some way God, at his own initiative, works his way into our conscious experience. Every Christian has an experience of the presence of Christ. We sense the reality of the Lord Jesus and know we are not alone, and we recognize that the One who accompanies us is not human. It is at this moment that we realize this other One is calling us to come.

I remember well when the call came to me in my early teens. I had been a church member all my life, going to church for four services on Sunday and occasionally my father would even drag me to Wednesday night prayer meeting. But I had no sense of the presence of God in my life. One day Jesus suddenly confronted me in such a way that there was no escape. I heard him say to me, "I want you. I want you to follow me." That call is an inescapable thing, and when it comes, you know that what is taking place is beyond the natural. You may not be able to take a photograph of Jesus, you may not be able to grasp him in your hand, but you know that you are in the presence of One who is greater than you, and that he has laid a claim on your life. What you do with that claim is what you do with your eternal destiny.

Is he calling you?

intimacy of trinity

john 14–17

And a voice from heaven said, "This is my Son, whom I love;
with him I am well pleased."
Matthew 3:17

Could it be that what the Father wants with me is the same thing he has known with his Son, Jesus? Basic to our belief in a religion of loving trust is the doctrine of the Trinity—three persons in one who love and give themselves to each other. At the absolute, ultimate beginning when there was nobody but God alone, there was not one alone. It was God in love—Father, Son, and Holy Spirit. Notice the intimacy of their relationship with each other.

Jesus spoke about his Father: "I tell you the truth, the Son can do nothing by himself; he can do only what he sees his Father doing, because whatever the Father does the Son also does" (John 5:19).

Or take the word of the Father about the Son: "This is my Son, whom I love; with him I am well pleased. Listen to him!" (Matt. 17:5).

Or listen to the words about the Spirit: "When he, the Spirit of truth comes . . . he will not speak on his own; he will speak only what he hears . . . The Spirit will take from what is mine and make it known to you" (John 16:13, 15).

There is an absolute intimacy and interdependence among the three persons of the Trinity; they live to give glory to the other members of that fellowship. That is what God wants from you and me; he wants our actions to be at his initiative so we glorify him. We are to be his beloved children, and we are to take what we hear from communion with him and share it with the world. Is it possible to be that close to him? The Scriptures make it clear that it is not only possible but the thing for which we are made.

out of devotion

john 15:9 – 17

He came to that which was his own, but his own did not receive him.
Yet to all who received him, to those who believed in his name,
he gave the right to become children of God.
John 1:11–12

If all God wanted was our obedience, it would be so easy to get it. He could get it in one of two ways. First of all, he could force obedience. I used to think obedience was all God wanted, and I thought if he could get me to obey, it would be miraculous. On one occasion Jesus said that he was able to ask the Father, and the Father would send a legion of angels to protect him (Matt. 26:53). He had power available to force obedience, but he deliberately chose not to use it. He did not want servile obedience. I think hell will be total obedience to the Lord Jesus without any love for him. Jesus is going to reign over heaven and over hell. He is the King of kings and the Lord of lords. Eventually, he will demand obedience from every person, but he desires something more than that. He desires that which he cannot coerce.

What God desires cannot be forced; nor can it be bought. If God wanted to, he could buy you and me. He has all the resources. Then he would have servants and slaves. He wants more. He wants sons and daughters for the Father and a spouse for the Son. A love relationship is more than a relationship of obedience.

How does God get this love relationship? Amazingly enough, the Creator stands before the creature, humbly and meekly. He wants us to choose him for himself, to join him in his work of saving the world, not because we are forced or bought, but out of devotion. God will never compel us to be part of his team, but he longs for us to be willingly obedient and invites us into a relationship of love.

"i like you"

exodus 25:1–9

*You are my friends if you do what I command. I no longer call you servants,
because a servant does not know his master's business. Instead, I have
called you friends, for everything that I learned from my Father I have
made known to you. You did not choose me, but I chose you and
appointed you to go and bear fruit—fruit that will last.
Then the Father will give you whatever you ask in my name.*
John 15:14–16

God loves his world and his people and wants to be in our midst. He wants
to be one among us. He likes us. It stirs my heart much more to think that
he likes me than to think that he loves me. We have used the term *love* in
such a way that we think that God is obligated; he is love, so he has to love
everyone. But do you know that he likes you? He may not like what you
do, but he is drawn to you. There is a vast difference between the relationships you have with people you love because you are supposed to love them,
and those you have with people you like. I notice that the people I like are
the ones to whom I want to get close, with whom I love to spend time. I
tend to migrate in their direction for fellowship and communion. I want to
get into my life some of the richness that is in theirs, so I seek them out to
enjoy the relationship.

That is the kind of God we read about in Scripture. He likes proximity
to us and wants to get close. That is why in the book of Joshua we find God
attempting to procure land for himself. He wants a little real estate that
belongs to him. He owns the whole world, but the world has repudiated
him. He longs for a bit of earth where the people look up and say, "We
belong to him. We like him. He made us. He sustains us. We are his, and
he is ours, and we like the relationship."

If you like a person, you will let that person invade your space. Do you
like God? Is your home or your office a place that belongs to him? Is he free
to rearrange your schedule and your plans? Is everything in your home acces-
sible to him? He is longing for us to look up at him and say, "We like you!
We belong to you. We like belonging to you, and this bit of the world in
which we live is yours, and we are glad."

tabernacle in your midst

psalm 24

Have them make a sanctuary for me, and I will dwell among them.
Exodus 25:8

The last sixteen chapters of the book of Exodus deal with the building of the tabernacle—a sanctuary in which God could dwell. If the Hebrews were going to be the people of God, God was anxious to come and dwell in their midst because he loved them. God's position is to be the center of our daily social life—indeed, of our total life. The key element in the true Christian life is a daily experience of worship and adoration of God as the center of our personal existence.

I have never known an effective Christian who did not have a regular, consistent devotional life. I have heard exciting testimonies, but they have not endured if the person did not establish daily time in the presence of God with his Word.

When I was a college student, God gave me a roommate who was an example to me. Every morning, I would wake up conscious of a light on in the room. I would look over and see my roommate kneeling by a chair, with his Bible open on the chair. I saw him there morning after morning, and something inside of me wanted to have what he had. I am the pious type and felt guilty about sleeping when he was on his knees. So very ignobly, I began to have my own quiet time with the same regularity that my roommate did. I will be eternally grateful to that roommate who shamed me into a pattern of consistent time with God. I do not care what it takes for you to start the pattern; once you begin to meet with God, he can take control and change your motivation so that what you want is him. Anything that forces you into the presence of Christ and into an openness to his Word will make a dramatic difference in your Christian life. He positions himself right in the middle of our lives so we can look at him and talk to him every day. He wants to tabernacle in us.

he is my delight

song of songs 2:3 – 4

Delight yourself in the LORD.
Psalm 37:4

When I was in my thirties, I had some difficulty physically, and at one point I thought I was going to lose my voice. I was filled with panic. I had never made any money except by preaching and teaching, and I had a family to support. Ever since I was sixteen years old, my life had been wrapped up in a ministry in which my voice was necessary. I began to say, "Lord, you cannot do this to me."

He said, "Oh? Which is it that you love: my work or me?"

To my delight, I found that I could say, "Lord, you are my love. Take my voice and anything else you want. You are the source of my joy." I enjoy the work of Christ, but he is so much richer than his work, and it is that personal relationship with him that is the most important relationship in life.

This is the reason the Holy Spirit is so important. It is he who bears witness to Christ; it is he who glorifies Christ. He makes us conscious of things within our lives that are displeasing to Jesus, and he brings our hearts into conformity with the pattern of Christ. We must be filled with the Holy Spirit in order that we may not grieve the Lord and so that Jesus Christ may find some delight in us as we find fullness of delight in him. It is a Christ-centered life to which God calls us, and it is the Spirit of Christ who makes it possible. Is he your delight?

making means the end

romans 1:18 – 32

*They exchanged the truth of God for a lie, and worshiped and served
created things rather than the Creator—who is forever praised.*
Romans 1:25

It is easy for us to take means and make them into ends, and that is the
essence of idolatry. The creation brings glory to God, but when we make
the creation or any part of it an end in itself, we are guilty of idolatry. Our
organizations, jobs, ministries, and our human relationships should be for
the glory of God. When our security and our fulfillment is in them, we give
them the place that God alone should have. It is easy for me, in my obscu-
rity, to criticize the fellow who publicly creates an empire for his own personal glory, but it is quite tempting for me to build a smaller kingdom
wherever I am. Are we taking God's creation and using it for our own glory?

This is exactly what happened to the Jews in Jesus' day. Remember when
Jesus said he would destroy the temple and raise it in three days? The Jews
were so horrified that they used this statement three years later to secure
Jesus' death sentence. Bystanders at the cross repeated his statement to taunt
him. We read in the book of Acts that Stephen's accusers remembered Jesus'
statement and used it against Stephen in order to kill him. The temple had
become sacrosanct for the Jews, and the thought of life without it was
incomprehensible. But this was idolatry. The building that symbolized God's
presence had taken God's place.

Six hundred years earlier, Ezekiel had recorded that the glory of God
departed from the temple and the priests of God never even knew when
God left. It is little wonder they missed him when he came in human form.
The Holy Place and its religious service were much more real to them than
the Holy One. God's Spirit is invisible. You can lose him and never admit
that he is gone. Remain sensitive to him.

losing his presence

Joshua 7

Stand up! What are you doing down on your face?
Israel has sinned; they have violated my covenant . . .
That is why the Israelites cannot stand against their enemies.
Joshua 7:10–12

The story of Achan makes many people shudder with fear. Achan was the man who, by sinning against the Lord, caused the Israelites to lose in battle. When Achan's sin was exposed, he and his entire family were killed. There is a concept in our day that if we accept Christ, then Christ is with us no matter what choices we make. This is not true. Christ is with us as long as we stay with him, but when we begin to go our own way in contrast to Christ's way, then the presence of Jesus will depart from our life. God cannot save us if we keep our back toward him.

This understanding is not simply an Old Testament principle, but an eternal truth. John the beloved said, "If we claim to have fellowship with him yet walk in the darkness, we lie and do not live by the truth" (1 John 1:6).

The Last Day will be a day of exclusion as much as one of inclusion. There will be a door, and all who do not pass through that door will be excluded eternally.

Perhaps some question then whether God is merciful. The last word in human experience is not going to be mercy, but righteousness and holiness. Mercy leads to righteousness. It is given in this life so we can come to know the holiness and the goodness of God. If we refuse his mercy, then we are left with only his holiness. Nothing will enter God's ultimate kingdom that is unclean or impure or deceitful. Note those tragic words that help close the Scriptures, "Outside are the dogs, those who practice magic arts, the sexually immoral, the murderers, the idolaters and everyone who loves and practices falsehood" (Rev. 22:15).

In truth, God never sends anyone to hell; we make the choice to turn toward him or away from him. Which way are you turned?

may 30

how close can you be?

luke 23:32 – 43

One of the criminals who hung there hurled insults at him:
"Aren't you the Christ? Save yourself and us!"
Luke 23:39

The Cross is the central fact of our faith. It is no accident that our thoughts continually bring us back to Golgotha. But the cross of Christ, though central, never stands alone. That day there were two other crosses on that hill. The God of providence, who ordered all time and history to point to this scene, would never have allowed an accident here. Those two thieves' crosses carry their messages for us too.

On one of these crosses was a poor soul who tried to find some relief by cursing Jesus. He added his voice to those of others as they taunted and mocked the Lord. This one whom Jesus was dying to save poured his bitter imprecations upon the One who was loving him until the death.

The striking lesson for us to learn here is how close a person can be to Jesus and still miss him. This thief could not have been more than a few feet away from him. He undoubtedly heard every whisper that came from the lips of Jesus. God had brought Jesus this close to the thief so the thief might make peace with him, yet the thief cursed.

It is possible to be this close to Christ and still miss him. One of his apostles did. One can be in the church and miss him. John Wesley did until he was thirty-five years of age. One can even be in the ministry and miss him. Remember that it was the chief priest who plotted his crucifixion. The supreme tragedy of human history is that many who are closest to Christ miss him and are lost.

He is closer to us than we think. We must not miss him!

how late can you wait?

luke 23:32 – 43

Today you will be with me in paradise.
Luke 23:43

On Golgotha that day were two crosses alongside Jesus' cross. Each has its own tale to tell. One is a story of salvation in the midst of judgment, love challenged by hatred, and life within the process of death itself. It is a story of hope that produces change.

The thief on that cross had begun the day like his criminal colleague on the other side of Jesus. He joined his voice to those of the crowd and his fellow thief as they cursed Jesus. His bitterness matched theirs. As the hours passed, though, he sensed the difference between Jesus and the others. He heard Jesus ask the Father to forgive those who were killing him. That produced thoughts that were unthinkable to him. Forgiveness? Could there be such for him? As he listened to Christ and sensed the Spirit that moved within him, he made a decision. He decided that if forgiveness was possible, he wanted it, and if anyone could give it, this strange One could. So he prayed, "Jesus, remember me when you come into your kingdom" (Luke 23:42).

The lessons here flood one on top of another. How far can one go in sin and still find forgiveness? How far from the church and its normal ministries can one be and still become a recipient of grace? How late can one wait before the hope of Christ's pardon is gone? This story makes it clear that no one, no matter how far from God, is beyond the reach of the love of Christ as long as breath remains. Thank God for that thief's cross as well as for Christ's.

june 1

work inside of me

john 3

No one can enter the kingdom of God
unless he is born of water and the Spirit.
John 3:5

Nicodemus was a natural leader. He was a man widely respected for his knowledge, position, integrity, and religion. He was a Pharisee and apparently one of the better ones. Nicodemus was a man of some honesty and had a sincere desire to do the will of God. He came to Jesus with his questioning mind and wondering heart and willingly acknowledged that Jesus came from God. His good works gave evidence of that. He wanted to know more of Jesus and his message.

Jesus dealt with Nicodemus decisively. He cut immediately to the heart of the matter and told Nicodemus that if he really wanted to see the kingdom of God, something must happen within him. Up to that point, Nicodemus's religion had been largely external. He had worked hard at keeping the Law and doing good, trying to please God through what he did. Jesus told Nicodemus that it was not a matter of his works, that instead it was a matter of the work of the Holy Spirit within him.

This is one of the greatest statements in Scripture on the doctrine of salvation by faith alone and not by works. Whether we are Christians is not a matter of what we do for God. It is a matter of letting God do something for us that we cannot do for ourselves. We are dead without him. He must give us life. Like Nicodemus, we are blind and cannot see. We must let him open our eyes. Every aspect of our relationship with God is a gift of his grace. If we are trying to please him with our own hard work and good intentions, we will fail. God is pleased and we are saved only when we let him do the work inside of us.

june 2

---

god wants to be close

revelation 3:14–22

*Here I am! I stand at the door and knock. If anyone hears my voice and
opens the door, I will come in and eat with him, and he with me.
To him who overcomes, I will give the right to sit with me on my throne,
just as I overcame and sat down with my Father on his throne.
Revelation 3:20–21*

God likes us and wants to be near to us, so he became one of us and lived
among us and eventually will return so we can all live together. The Revelation of John gives us an idea of the destiny for which we are all made. One
picture especially conveys the risen Lord's invitation: "Here I am! I stand at
the door and knock. If anyone hears my voice and opens the door, I will
come in and eat with him, and he with me. " (Rev. 3:20). It is possible for
the Lord to live inside of me and for me to live inside of him. The exalted
Christ also uses a second figure: "To him who overcomes, I will give the
right to sit with me on my throne" (Rev. 3:21). Every believer who walks
with Christ is headed for a position of remarkable intimacy in which we
share with Christ his life and his throne.

The value that God gives to human beings is inestimable. We are big
enough for him to come to us, eat with us, and live with us, and we are also
big enough to sit with him on his throne forever. Every person is a creature
of God with eternal potential and great value. God is preparing us for communion and fellowship with him. He wants to be close to us, but many
times we do not reciprocate that desire. We misunderstand his desire toward
us because we are afraid of him. We decide to protect ourselves from him.
So we build walls when we ought to be building a bridge in order to be as
close to him as we can be.

Are you living in fear of God? Have you built walls to protect yourself
from him? If you have, it is for one of two reasons. Either you do not understand the depth of his love and his desire to be with you, or you are living
with a sin that you do not want to surrender. If you are distant from him,
you are the one who is responsible. Why not close the gap?

marks of god's people

joshua 3 – 4

*The flow of the Jordan was cut off before the ark of the covenant of the LORD
... These stones are to be a memorial to the people of Israel forever.*
Joshua 4:7

In Old Testament times, God clearly disclosed the characteristics he wanted in his people. First of all, he wanted a people whose life centered around the ark of the covenant. That was to be the focal point for all the people of Israel. Two things made the ark important: the God who dwelt above the ark and the tablets of the Law, God's Word, within the ark. These two realities were to be the heart of Israel's life: God's presence and his Word. They were never to be separated, for the Word was the way into his presence. God himself could not be seen; to save his people from their own imaginations and delusions, he gave them the visible expression of the covenant. In order to be his community, we must be a community of the Word through which we come to him.

God also wanted another symbol in the lives of the Israelites. It was a pile of stones. When the Israelites came to the Jordan, God instructed them to pick twelve stones from the riverbed as they crossed, one for each of the twelve tribes. They were to place those stones in a pile as a reminder to themselves and to all future generations of the miraculous act of God that enabled them to claim the fulfillment of God's promises to them. They were to have a visible symbol of the redemptive act of God that would never let them forget.

Our lives should be similarly marked. The heart of it all should be his presence, which comes to us through his Word, and somewhere in our lives there should be the visible symbol that speaks of the miraculous act of redemption through which he saved us.

Is your life so marked?

june 4

---

living in the spirit

galatians 5:22 – 26

Live by the Spirit, and you will not gratify the desires of the sinful nature.
Galatians 5:16

As a seminary student, I found myself with the privilege of hosting one of the great Methodist preachers of the twentieth century, Dr. John Brasher. He was lecturing at Asbury Seminary, which was founded by Henry Clay Morrison, another Methodist giant. As we talked, Dr. Brasher said to me, "Son, Henry Clay Morrison was a great man." I nodded in agreement. Dr. Brasher responded, "No, son, you don't understand. Morrison was a *great* man." Then he told me a story.

Morrison and Brasher were preaching at a camp meeting. With an unusual anointing, Brasher preached to a large crowd on Sunday morning. He said that it was a glorious service with numerous people seeking God.

That evening Morrison preached. His text was on the giving of the Law at Mount Sinai. Morrison had a flair for the dramatic and, as Brasher recalled, "The lightning flashed, the thunder rolled, and the ground shook under our feet." As Morrison preached, Brasher became uneasy and began to suspect that Morrison was trying to outdo the morning service. He told himself, "Morrison knows that he is a greater preacher than I am. We had a great service this morning, and he thinks that we must have a greater one tonight."

After the service Brasher slipped into his tent and went to bed. Slowly the lights on the campground went out as people ended their Sabbath. In the darkness Brasher heard a noise outside his tent. It was someone fumbling for his tent flap. The person found the flap, entered the tent, and stumbled around until he found Brasher's cot. He knelt at the foot of the cot, buried his head in the covers over Brasher's feet, and wept as though his heart would break. It was Morrison.

Brasher did not say a word. Nor did Morrison. Spirit spoke to spirit. Brasher said to me, "Son, it is one thing to walk in the Spirit, but it is another thing to live continuously in the Spirit. The best thing to do when you have slipped into the flesh is to choose again to walk in the Spirit." Then he thoughtfully affirmed, "Son, Henry Clay Morrison was a great man."

What is the flesh? It is just putting my finger in things. Morrison knew that he had sinned and felt he had to make it right. That sensitivity was and is the key to greatness.

june 5

who is richer?

mark 10:17 – 23

For to me, to live is Christ and to die is gain.
Philippians 1:21

One verse of Charles Wesley's hymn "Jesus, Lover of My Soul" begins with a remarkable thought:

Thou, O Christ, art all I want;
More than all in Thee I find.*

Wesley continues by speaking of how Christ can raise the fallen, cheer the faint, heal the sick, and lead the blind. He seems to be saying that the answer to any human need is in Christ. Whatever I need to have done for me or to me, he can do.

The opening lines seem, though, to speak of something else. They speak of neither God's gifts nor his acts. They speak of Christ himself, that he is better than anything he can do for us or give to us. Wesley seems to be saying that Christ himself is enough. To have him is enough. We need no more.

It is fair to ask whether a person who has everything plus God is really any richer than a person who has only God. A person, if we could find one, who has only God is certainly not in poverty; he is as rich as the person who has everything plus God. God is enough.

Perhaps this is some of what Paul is saying when from prison he tells his Philippian friends that for him to live is Christ, and that therefore he has learned to be content in any state (Phil. 1:21; 4:11). It is certainly what Jesus is saying when he tells the rich ruler to sell all that he has and follow him. Jesus is not calling the young man to less. He is calling him to more, to himself, and he is enough. Have you found him so?

---

*Charles Wesley, "Jesus, Lover of My Soul," *The United Methodist Hymnal* (Nashville, Tenn.: United Methodist Publishing House, 1989), no. 479.

june 6

a new song

2 chronicles 29:20–28

Hezekiah gave the order to sacrifice the burnt offering on the altar.
As the offering began, singing to the LORD began also, accompanied
by trumpets and the instruments of David king of Israel.
2 Chronicles 29:27

Singing is a very important aspect of the Christian walk. The religion of historic Israel and that of the Christian church has been marked by music as no other religious heritage in human history.

Israel's birth as a nation was celebrated in song. Moses and Miriam sang as they looked back on their deliverance from devastation in Egypt (Exod. 15). Deborah and Barak joined their voices in song when God set the Hebrews free from Canaanite oppression (Judg. 5). Jerusalem rang with the song of instruments and choirs when the ark was brought to the temple (1 Chron. 15:16–28).

Song characterized the life of the people of God in Old Testament times when they walked faithfully before him. They sang when they worked, when they played, when they loved, and most of all when they worshiped. The adoration of God was difficult for them to conceive without a song. His presence quickened the joyous impulse to sing.

This continued in the early church. Paul and Silas sang after they were beaten, imprisoned, and put in stocks. A Christian without a song is an anomaly. No greater mark of the difference between Christianity and other religions of the world can be found than that of a Bach choral piece, Handel's *Messiah,* or an ordinary hymnbook in a Christian church.

When the believer maintains a relationship of intimacy with Christ, joy is an inevitable by-product, and its natural expression is song. David knew this, and so he sang: "I will sing to the Lord because he has dealt bountifully with me" (Ps. 13:6 NKJV). When we let our relationship with Christ languish, our song dies and we grow silent.

Is today a day of song for you?

june 7

sanctified by faith

psalm 24

Blessed are the pure in heart,
for they will see God.
Matthew 5:8

When we are born again, there comes a consciousness of the presence of Christ in our life. We then begin to walk with Christ. As that fellowship deepens, we begin to be conscious of how deeply our sinfulness has permeated our personal being. We realize that it is one thing to have our sins forgiven, and another matter to have our inner heart cleansed. The church has not always been clear about the power of Christ's blood through the work of the Spirit to purify and sanctify individuals deep within. But there have always been some who have probed the depths of grace and found that Christ's words "Blessed are the pure in heart, for they will see God" (Matt. 5:8) are a promise as well as an admonition.

But how is this possible? We certainly cannot cleanse our own hearts, for the very will that would choose to be clean is itself unclean. All salvation is a work of God, a work of grace that comes in response to faith. Sanctification is as much the result of faith as justification is, because it is something only God can do. This is what Paul was talking about when he told the Colossians, "Once you were alienated from God and were enemies in your minds because of your evil behavior. But now he has reconciled you by Christ's physical body through death to present you holy in his sight, without blemish and free from accusation" (Col. 1:21–22).

This is what Paul was telling the Thessalonians when he prayed for their sanctification. He knew they could never sanctify themselves. That is why he concludes, "The one who calls you [to holiness] is faithful, and he will do it" (1 Thess. 5:24). The call is a promise. Trust his blood that was shed for you.

salvation out of judgment

jeremiah 29

God did not send His Son into the world to condemn the world,
but that the world through Him might be saved. He who believes in Him
is not condemned; but he who does not believe is condemned already,
because he has not believed in the name of the only begotten Son of God.
John 3:17–18 NKJV

The God of Scripture is both just and merciful. Therefore, he both judg
and saves. Most of us believe that judgment and salvation are widely sep
rate experiences. The reality, though, is that they are two sides to one coi
and biblically they go together. The One who judges is the Savior, and t
Savior is the eternal Judge.

We see this in the lives of the people of Judah during Jeremiah's mi
istry. The people of Jerusalem were worshiping the queen of heaven insi
the temple. Their idolatrous worship was expressed in sexual orgies as th
sought the blessing of the fertility gods. They even sacrificed their childr
to the pagan gods to secure the favor of the deities. God's response was o
of horror, and he permitted the Babylonians to capture and destr
Jerusalem and the temple. Then God permitted his people to be carried in
exile in distant Babylon. For seventy years they lived amid an idolatrous cu
ture. The result of that exile experience was that the Jewish people were pe
manently cured of idolatry. The judgment of God had a saving face.

The same truth is seen in the Exodus story. The salvation of Israel fro
Egyptian bondage meant destruction for Pharaoh and Egypt. Paul w
thinking of this when he told the Corinthians:

But thanks be to God, who always leads us in triumphal procession in
Christ and through us spreads everywhere the fragrance of the knowledge of
him. For we are to God the aroma of Christ among those who are being
saved and those who are perishing. To the one we are the smell of death; to
the other, the fragrance of life. And who is equal to such a task? Unlike so
many, we do not peddle the word of God for profit. On the contrary, in
Christ we speak before God with sincerity, like men sent from God.
2 Corinthians 2:14–17

What was a fragrance of life to one, Paul said, would be the smell of death to another. God said it to Moses: "See, I set before you today life and prosperity, death and destruction . . . Now choose life, so that you and your children may live and that you may love the LORD your God, listen to his voice, and hold fast to him. For the LORD is your life" (Deut. 30:15, 19–20).

God is at work in every life. We determine whether it will be for salvation or for judgment. God's preference is that his acts in our lives should be saving. Even his judgment can be redemptive.

receiving and following

john 1:35–51

The next day Jesus decided to leave for Galilee.
Finding Philip, he said to him, "Follow me."
John 1:43

We often tell people that they should receive Christ. Yet we must remember the words of Jesus: "Follow me." The two appeals have very different connotations. The first appeal implies a certain need in us, an emptiness, guilt, a lostness. The center of concern is the human self and the fact that Christ can meet each person's need.

The connotation of "Follow me" is quite different. The central focus is on Christ, not on ourselves. It means refocusing our lives, not around ourselves and our lacks, but around him and his call. It speaks of our losing control and yielding to him. Suddenly our whole horizon changes, and it includes the Cross. That is where Jesus was going when he asked Philip to follow him.

It is not wrong for us to ask people to receive Christ, because without him we are empty when we should be full; we are loaded with burdens that we were not meant to carry. But we cannot leave people there. We must let them know that if they are to keep what they have found in Christ, they must hear that second word from him, "Follow me."

Beware of any presentation of the gospel that stops with receiving and does not talk about following. Salvation is not in an experience. It is in Christ, and we must walk with him if we would experience that saving power. Salvation comes through his presence.

John understood this when he said, "If we walk in the light, as he is in the light, we have fellowship with one another, and the blood of Jesus, his Son, purifies us from all sin" (1 John 1:7).

Are you following him?

never read a good book

2 timothy 3:14–17

*And he said to me, "Son of man, eat what is before you, eat this scroll;
then go and speak to the house of Israel."
So I opened my mouth, and he gave me the scroll to eat.
Then he said to me, "Son of man, eat this scroll I am giving you and fill your
stomach with it." So I ate it, and it tasted as sweet as honey in my mouth.
Ezekiel 3:1–3*

It is surprising how much a few hours spent with the right person can change one's thinking. One day it was my privilege to be the chauffeur for A. W. Tozer and to spend several hours with him. He had already influenced me deeply through his books and editorials. I had been impressed with his wide knowledge of the Christian classics, so when my opportunity came, I quizzed him about his reading habits and the books that had influenced him the most.

"Don't ever read a good book," he said, to my surprise. "You don't have time. You will never read all of the best books. For goodness' sake, don't waste your time on a good one!" He spoke with an explosive conviction. "There is a difference between having read widely and having read well. I would much rather be well-read than widely read. That is why I often reread an old work rather than search for a new one. If it is a great book, it deserves more than one reading."

Decades have passed since that conversation, yet the wisdom of that slight little man is still poignantly impressive to me. It is not possible to read even all the best books, and the number of books one can know with any thoroughness is hauntingly small. So each book that we choose is of great importance. The popular titles will come to have less of a hold on us, and some classics will beckon us to read them again and again. What matters is not the quantity of material that we read, but the truth we gain with understanding.

june 11

my ear, my thumb, my toe

leviticus 8

May God himself, the God of peace, sanctify you through and through. May your whole spirit, soul and body be kept blameless at the coming of our Lord Jesus Christ. The one who calls you is faithful and he will do it.
1 Thessalonians 5:23–24

The priest had a special place in the life of Israel. It was he who stood between Israel and God. To play that role, he had to be clean. Therefore, he was bathed and clothed with a tunic. A bull was sacrificed as a sin offering and a ram as a burnt offering. Then the blood of a ram was placed on the tip of the priest's right ear, the thumb of his right hand, and the big toe of his right foot. Isaiah later would say to the priests,

> *Depart! Depart! Go out from there,*
> *Touch no unclean thing;*
> *Go out from the midst of her,*
> *Be clean,*
> *You who bear the vessels of the LORD.*

> *Isaiah 52:11 NKJV*

Why the blood on the ear? God wanted the priest's ear to be separated to God. The Hebrew phrase for obedience is "to hearken to the voice of the Lord." If we are to be of service to God, we must be able to discern his voice amid the noises of life, and we must obey it.

Why the blood on the thumb? It is the thumb that enables us to hold things. The Lord wants to be Lord over our grasping and our holding. The priests of Israel had no portion when the land was divided. The Lord himself was to be their portion. Their hands were made to hold only that which was holy and clean.

The right big toe? The biblical term for the Christian life is *walk.* In the Old Testament, Enoch and Noah walked with God. God's special word to Abraham was, "Walk before me and be blameless" (Gen. 17:1). In the New Testament the word is, "If we walk in the light as He is in the light, we have fellowship with one another, and the blood of Jesus Christ His Son cleanses us from all sin" (1 John 1:7 NKJV).

Were the priests of Israel an elite spiritual corps with special demands on them? God told Moses that Israel itself was to be "a kingdom of priests and a holy nation" (Exod. 19:6). The truths symbolized in the life of the priests were to be realized in the life of every believing Hebrew. In 1 Peter 2:5, Peter tells his readers that they are "a holy priesthood" and are to offer "spiritual sacrifices acceptable to God." And what is an acceptable sacrifice before God? A life that listens to God's voice and obeys, that grasps after nothing but God and his will, that walks in all his ways. The wonderful thing is that God has made available the blood of Christ to cleanse us and the Holy Spirit to bring our ears, our hands, and our feet into consonance with his Holy Spirit.

plans for your life

jeremiah 17:5 – 8

*I know the thoughts that I think toward you, says the LORD,
thoughts of peace and not of evil, to give you a future and a hope.
Jeremiah 29:11 NKJV*

God's plan for all of us is infinitely bigger than we have ever dreamed. W
have limited vision, and we look at our own resources and plan according
We should lift our eyes to God and ask for his plan for our life. We w
always build smaller than God wants to build. God desires to take us, to
as far as he can possibly go with us, and to exhaust all the resources that a
in us in order to make us a blessing to the world. Many of us would ha
been more faithful to God and would have risked a little more if we h
dreamed how good God was going to be to us. Do not determine what Go
wants to do in your life by what you can see. Let him decide that.

F. B. Meyer has said that the biggest disappointments in heaven (if the
can be disappointments there) will come when God reveals what he wou
have done with our lives if we had let him. Unbelief is the fear that if I l
God have my life, he will hurt or deprive me. The fact of the matter is th
God never wills evil to any person. He wills only good. The reason he as
for absolute control of my life is that anything short of total surrender w
force the perversion and abortion of the good plans he has established f
me. God's plans for you are infinitely bigger than you thought; in fact, th
are bigger than you. Those plans can never be known or accomplished unl
you relinquish your future to him.

What are you planning for your walk with God or your outreach
others? Are you measuring it in terms of your own resources or in terms
your resources in God?

the priority of the personal

psalm 16

I have set the LORD always before me.
Because he is at my right hand,
I will not be shaken.
Therefore my heart is glad and my tongue rejoices;
my body also will rest secure.
Psalm 16:8–9

One assumption Christians make is that God guides those persons who belong to him. In fact, it is right for every child of God to expect this divine leadership. However, God does not provide direction for us by setting down his prearranged plan in all of its particular details. Although at times we long for more clarity, there is a reason for God's secretive approach. If he informed human beings of every detail of his plan, we in our ignorance would focus on the plan instead of on Jesus. We would begin to build our lives around God's purposes for us instead of around God himself. Christ did not come to call us to follow his ways; he has asked us to follow him. The difference between following Christ and following his way may seem subtle enough that many will not distinguish between the two. However, there is an incredible difference between following a path and following a person who leads us along that path.

The priority must be on the personal. Our prime business is to know Christ. The life that does not arise out of a personal, intimate knowledge of Jesus will ultimately, no matter how good, be frustrating, sterile, and unfulfilling. But the life that is lived in the immediacy of daily, hourly, continual contact with him will be fruitful and joyous.

pictures of god

psalm 119:9–16

No one has seen God at any time. The only begotten Son,
who is in the bosom of the Father, He has declared Him.
John 1:18 NKJV

Many people have a faulty conception of God. Perhaps it is inherited from parents or learned in church or school. Perhaps it is a reaction to one's own situation, or perhaps it stems from ignorance. Whatever the reason, most people tend to imagine God as they think he should be or accept the belief of the corporate group of which they are a part.

The only safe thing we can do to understand God is to make a lifelong study of Scripture. We must choose not to read our own presuppositions into Scripture, but to study Scripture to see what it actually says. Because Scripture is true, we will get a glimpse of what God is really like. Otherwise we would be left to our own projections. In the pictures that are given to us by the prophets and apostles and the Lord Jesus himself, we learn about the nature of God himself.

Scripture indicates that there is nothing in us that can bridge the chasm between the creature and the Creator. We have no ladder to climb to heaven. The citizens of Babel, who tried to build a tower to heaven, found they were unable to do it. God's face is hidden to us unless he chooses to disclose it to us, and he has revealed his face to us in the person of Jesus Christ, the Son of God and the Word of God.

Never settle for a secondhand picture of God. Search the Scriptures to find the true picture of God, and when you begin to glimpse his true nature you will find he is better than you could have ever dreamed.

nathanael and philip

john 1:43–51

"Nazareth! Can anything good come from there?" Nathanael asked.
"Come and see," said Philip.
John 1:46

Scripture is full of fascinating vignettes about the lives of people who had the privilege to encounter Jesus. One of these stories is told about two of Jesus' disciples, Philip and Nathanael. Nathanael, Philip's friend, was unimpressed when he learned that Jesus was from Nazareth. The Jews believed Galilee to be particularly contaminated because of the Gentiles there. Philip's excitement was contrasted by Nathanael's skepticism.

Nathanael wondered aloud if the Messiah could possibly come from such an insignificant and unclean place. Philip wisely chose to let Jesus speak for himself. "Come and see," he invited. Is there any better argument for the skeptic? Philip's response indicated that he had found in Jesus that for which he had been waiting, and he challenged Nathanael to decide for himself about Jesus' reliability and integrity. Philip's loving challenge to Nathanael indicated his trust in the faithfulness and trueness of the Lord Jesus.

Although Nathanael was surprised by Jesus, Jesus was expecting Nathanael. He had seen him sitting under the tree and said, "Truly, truly . . . you shall see the heavens opened, and the angels of God ascending and descending on the Son of Man" (John 1:51 NASB). Jesus immediately identified himself with the divine. Jesus showed Nathanael what he needed to see in order to believe. He does not insist that all people come to him like Philip, in childlike trust. He has grace for and wisdom enough to deal with skeptics like Nathanael. Jesus wanted both men on his team of disciples. When skeptics are confronted with Jesus himself and not just with words about him, they will find Jesus' goodness and truth.

Are you as confident in Jesus as Philip was? Is your witness as effective as his was? We must invite people to come and see what Jesus is really about. The people who see him find that he fulfills all the things for which the human heart longs.

june 16

encounters with god

acts 9:1 – 9

As he neared Damascus on his journey, suddenly a light from heaven flashed around him. He fell to the ground and heard a voice say to him, "Saul, Saul.
Acts 9:3–4

The history of the world could be written in terms of people who have had an encounter with the living God. Many of these people lived difficult and challenging lives; yet through difficulty, discouragement, and even despondency, they remained faithful to the One they had met. How was that possible? History tells the stories of these men and women who met God, knew he was real, and found in that knowledge an undeniable power. These faithful ones refused all alternatives to God himself, no matter how tempting they were, because they knew that only his way represents true life.

Abraham knew God well enough that God called him his friend. They walked and talked together. Moses met God in a burning bush and continued meeting him all his life. He stood face-to-face with God, and his life was arguably more determinative for human history than any other besides that of the Lord Jesus. King David met God and led the Israelites victoriously. Jeremiah met God and was faithful to the bitter end. The disciples met God. The apostle Paul met God. That is also what happened to Augustine in the fourth century, and his influence is still felt across human history. Martin Luther and John Calvin and John Wesley all met God, and the world has been different because of those divine encounters.

God is at work in human history, and he does his work through the lives of people who respond in faith and trust their personal encounters with him. Are you one of those people?

june 17

truth as a person

john 7:14 – 19

Jesus answered, "I am the way and the truth and the life.
No one comes to the Father except through me."
John 14:6

Jesus talked a lot about truth. Note how often the word occurs in the gospel of John. When he spoke about truth, Jesus spoke in personal terms. You will remember that he refused, much to the dismay of many people, particularly the philosophers, to speak of truth in abstraction, as though it existed in itself. He wanted to relate truth to himself and to his Father in an existential way. He even went beyond that; he ultimately identified truth completely with himself and his Father.

The temple authorities, troubled by Jesus and wanting to know the truthfulness of his message, challenged him. He responded, "If anyone chooses to do God's will, he will find out whether my teaching comes from God" (John 7:17).

Jesus thus affirmed the truthfulness of his own teaching in terms of a relationship to his Father. Sometimes we would like to translate that answer into "Anyone who does the truth will certainly know it." But that is not the way Jesus spoke or thought. We should never be fooled. There was no truth for Jesus apart from the Father. Truth was simply the Father's will. Thus personal categories are appropriate when we speak of truth because the ultimate categories are all personal. Ultimately, Jesus is the truth.

If we develop a love affair with the truth and pursue it far enough, we will find the truth. When we find it, we will have found Jesus and that he is the one we need. The shortcut to it all is found in his simple words, "Come unto me." Have you come?

june 18

pathos and hope

jeremiah 31

"This is the covenant I will make with the house of Israel after that time,"
declares the LORD. "I will put my law in their minds and write
it on their hearts. I will be their God, and they will be my people."
Jeremiah 31:33

The picture Jeremiah gives in his message to the people of Israel is remarkably realistic. He knew the human heart, and he told the people of God about the tragedy of trusting in the flesh. Jeremiah provided the groundwork for much of the New Testament teaching about grace. He also saw into the future. He was watching the old covenant of Moses come apart and the old legal relationship that bound the people of God together break into pieces, but Jeremiah realized that this was not the end. A new covenant would come, and it would be written not on tablets of stone but on the human heart. Then humanity would do the will of God, not because of an external force, but because they knew God and desired to do his will.

Jeremiah wrote a message of hope mixed with pathos—the hope of God's new covenant and the desperate reality of human sin. When we meet God and live with him, we discover who we are in the light of who God is. God is the one who gives a realistic picture of human life. When he presents that realistic picture to the human heart and we accept it, an unshakable realism comes into our life and witness.

With that realism comes the assurance that God can turn the "ought" of his Law into delight, as the psalmist declares (Ps. 1:2; 119:14–15, 47, 92). Jeremiah did not give up even when he wanted to because he knew that God would prevail and that he, through God's grace, could prevail. The message is applicable to us too. His way can be our delight as well.

out of control

daniel 1

But Daniel resolved not to defile himself with the royal food and wine, and he asked the chief official for permission not to defile himself this way.
Daniel 1:8

There is something remarkable about Joseph and Daniel. Both of them were able to live in a world that was alien to them. Joseph lived in Egypt and Daniel in Babylon, centers of worldly power. Separated from God's people, they were able to live victoriously in the midst of idolatry and paganism. One of the reasons for their triumph was that they came to grips with a truth that many people struggle to accept: life includes many factors outside of our immediate control. There is nothing harder to accept than things that happen to you that you cannot control or change. Sometimes we are responsible for the mess in which we find ourselves, but sometimes the world simply caves in on us regardless of our actions. Then we find ourselves in the test of a lifetime. This is where Joseph and Daniel excelled.

Joseph was sold by his own brothers, put in chains, taken to Egypt, and sold into slavery. Then because of his purity and integrity, he was unjustly thrown into prison and forgotten. A pretty good test of one's religion is what one does when one is rewarded with evil for good and then forgotten by the world.

Daniel was taken captive to a foreign land and put under the control of a king who did not believe in Daniel's God. The people around Daniel attempted to make him suffer for his faith in God and his success at court. Both Joseph and Daniel knew what it meant to live in circumstances they did not control. They were able to remain victorious when life was out of their control because they trusted that their God remained in control. Do you have the kind of serenity and trust that allows you to live in circumstances that are forced upon you? It is only possible if you really believe he is in control and will use it all for ultimate good. Joseph explained it to his brothers, "You intended to harm me, but God intended it for good to accomplish what is now being done, the saving of many lives. So then, don't be afraid" (Gen. 50:20–21).

my leader and provider

psalm 23

*Even though I walk
through the valley of the shadow of death,
I will fear no evil,
for you are with me;
your rod and your staff,
they comfort me.
Psalm 23:4*

One of the happiest things that occurs in salvation is that suddenly we find we are not alone. The Lord Jesus Christ comes into our life, and he is present there in the same way he was in the boat with the disciples when the storm came. He delivered the disciples from their fears and from the threat of the storm. After our conversion we find that he is not only present, but also at work in us and in our circumstances.

There ought to be evidences in a person's life when Christ is in residence. Other people ought to be able to sense the presence of the risen Christ. When Israel followed Yahweh, there were certain evidences of God's leadership. Likewise, when Jesus told his disciples to follow him, their lives became set apart from the rest of the world because of that primary relationship with him. This is the essence of the Christian life. When we turn our attention to Christ, we turn away from our own desires, plans, and purposes. We hear the call of Christ, and we follow. Christ's purposes then become our purposes.

When we allow Christ to separate us from all else in order to be in his presence, then God is able to provide for us in ways comparable to his provision for the people of Israel. When they were hungry, God provided food. When they were thirsty, God provided drink. When they needed protection, God provided deliverance. When they needed guidance, he provided a pillar of cloud by day and a pillar of fire by night to lead them. When we enter into a relationship with God, he becomes our Guide, our Leader, our Provider, and our Protector.

cutting the wick

1 corinthians 3

*No discipline seems pleasant at the time, but painful.
Later on, however, it produces a harvest of righteousness
and peace for those who have been trained by it.*
Hebrews 12:11

I remember that in my younger days on occasion I had to read by a kerosene lamp when I traveled for preaching engagements. I was used to electricity, and it was always hard to make the adjustment back to kerosene. I remember going over and turning the wick up so I could get more light to see. I also remember the soot dripping off the ceiling and the shade turning black when I turned the wick too high and left it up too long.

Too much wick meant soot. That is a parable for life. If someone pushes you too far, does the greasy, dirty soot of self begin to overshadow the light in your life? People will recognize that it is getting dark in your soul. I used to watch my grandmother take her scissors and cut that wick and clip off the extra that was creating the soot. Does God need to do some clipping on us?

There is a contamination that comes when we refuse to allow God to cut away the soot-producing, self-absorbing aspects of our lives. There is a defilement that comes when God's scissors have not been able to do their work. The Cross made it possible for him to transform us so we are free to be used in a way that glorifies Christ. He does not use a pair of scissors; he uses the nails of the Cross that pierce our ego until we are pure. When he cuts away the wick in us, we are clean, happy, and free.

need for each other

romans 15:1 – 7

*Why do you look at the speck of sawdust in your brother's eye
and pay no attention to the plank in your own eye? You hypocrite,
first take the plank out of your own eye, and then you will see clearly
to remove the speck from your brother's eye.*
Matthew 7:3, 5

It is not easy for humans to see clearly. All of us have trouble accepting the fact that we are fallen beings and are therefore capable of misreading things. Somehow because of the Fall, it is easier for me to see what's wrong with you than to see what's wrong with me. Did you ever notice how much easier it is to see another person's fault than your own? Perhaps we don't want to admit our fallenness because we don't know where to get help. However, we have been given substantial help, so if we continue in our blindness, it is our own fault.

First of all, we have been offered the Holy Spirit, who wants to live in us and transform us from the inside out. He wants to straighten out the crookedness, the twistedness inside you and me. We also have the Scriptures, which give us the picture of what a human person is supposed to be— the example of the Lord Jesus. We are to walk as he walked. A third help is one we so often miss: each other. Why can we not come to each other and say, "Help save me from myself"? We need to give thanks that God has given us each other. I need you, and I need you to help save me from me.

Wouldn't it be wonderful if we who call ourselves Christians wanted so desperately to please our Lord and were so interested in his cause that we would open our hearts to each other concerning family, finances, discipline, integrity, and a host of other things, asking, "How can I do it better?" If I would do that, I would find, perhaps to my surprise, that you are my friend and my help. That would help me to be a better Christian, and my relationship with you would be a more effective witness than any of us alone can ever give.

redemptive disaster

job 42

I know that You can do everything,
And that no purpose of Yours can be withheld from You.
Job 42:2 NKJV

It will make a world of difference in your life if you truly believe that God reigns. No man has influenced my life more profoundly than Samuel Logan Brengle, a commissioner for the Salvation Army. In my teen years I found some little books he wrote, and they influenced me profoundly: *Heart Talks on Holiness, The Way of Holiness,* and *When the Holy Ghost Is Come.*

These little books have a very interesting history that I only came to know years after I had first read them. Brengle was a brilliant young preacher whom God led into the Salvation Army. He became the Salvation Army's great spokesman for the message of personal holiness. One night a drunken man continually interrupted a service Brengle was leading. Finally, Brengle put the man outside the service. After the meeting was over, Brengle was the last one to leave, so he turned the lights off and stepped into the street. The drunken man was waiting for him. He struck one side of Brengle's head with a paving stone, and smashed the other side against the building. Samuel Brengle was in the hospital for an extended period, hovering between life and death. When he finally began to recover, it was a long time before he could resume his former activities, so the editor of the Salvation Army's magazine asked him to write some articles while he was recuperating in the hospital. Those little books, which have profoundly shaped many Christian leaders, were the fruit of that accident.

We must believe that God is running our lives. The devil can create minor complications, but God is in control whether you are in a hospital bed like Brengle, in a prison like Paul, or anywhere else. God can and will use your circumstances to accomplish his purposes. He is the only one who can produce fruit out of an apparent disaster.

june 24

false expectations

john 6

*When his family heard about this, they went to take charge of him,
for they said, "He is out of his mind."*
Mark 3:21

Jesus knew from the beginning that he would be rejected by those he came
to save. Yet he never swerved from the path his Father had set before him.
That did not mean it was easy for him. Because he was a normal human
being, rejection must have been as painful for him as it is for you and me.

His rejection by his own hometown and by his own family must have
been particularly painful. He had lived a model life of holiness and service
right in their midst, yet they would not believe. He did not fit their image
of what the Messiah was to be, so they spurned him.

Those who rejected Jesus hungered for more signs and wonders rather
than for a life of self-sacrificing love. They wanted a show, not humility; a
carnal display, not holiness. They wanted him to outdo the Romans at the
Roman game, but Jesus had come to play another game. They wanted him
to change their circumstances, not to change them. Jesus had come to
change them so he could change the circumstances of other people. They
had things backwards.

Does God perform acceptably for you? Does he act the way you think
he ought to act? If he doesn't, do you think it is because he is out of line, or
because your perspective is askew? Most of us want him to change our circumstances and other people's character, not our character and others' circumstances. But the only way he can change other people's circumstances
through us is to change us. And that is a different process. It meant a Cross
for Jesus, and if we want to follow him, it will mean one for us as well.

persevering faith

2 corinthians 12:7 – 10

*If I go and prepare a place for you, I will come back and take you
to be with me that you also may be where I am.*
John 14:3

I have at times been tempted to think that God made a mistake in the way
he ordered life because it did not work the way I thought it should work. My
idea was that if you lived the Christian life long enough, you would get to
the top of the hill and then coast into heaven. I was sure that the hardest
battles were in the early stages of the Christian life. Once you got through
them, you could enjoy Canaan Land, and there would be no enemies or trials. However, I find that the battles get more intense as we move along in
our walk with him. Not only do the battles become more intense, but our
physical resources become diminished.

This weakening that comes prompts us to tap nonhuman resources to
fight the battles that must be fought as we grow older. Now I find I am glad
that death is the ogre that it is, and that we go out of this world fighting. The
toughest choices of faith may be made in those final moments as we confront
the ultimate consequences of our faith in Jesus. Is Christ really supreme?
Will he take care of me and of mine? Our greatest adventure in faith comes
at the very end of life, when we have exhausted all human resources and are
thrown totally on the mercy and grace of Christ.

I had the privilege of knowing a lady who chose to believe in Jesus' provision until the end. When she was dying, she called her staff together. They
read Scripture, sang a hymn, and prayed once more, and she did not die.
"Well," she said, "we had better read again." So they read Scripture, sang
another hymn, and then she prayed, "Lord, this is foolish. These people have
work to do. Come and get me so they can get their work done." And Jesus
came. She trusted until the very end, and she went boldly into her new life
with Jesus.

he is committed to me

john 18:1–11

The Lord is not slow in keeping his promise, as some understand slowness.
He is patient with you, not wanting anyone to perish,
but everyone to come to repentance.
2 Peter 3:9

One of the most poignant moments in the life of Christ was in the Garden of Gethsemane when the soldiers and temple police came to arrest Jesus. He knew that this was the beginning of the end, that he would be humiliated, scourged, and crucified. We know this was not a pleasant fate for him because he had just finished asking his Father if this cup could be taken from him. Now the soldiers had come, and he accepted that there was no escape for his life. In this moment of no return, he was not thinking about himself. He was thinking about how he could protect his disciples.

He asked the soldiers, "For whom are you looking?" When they replied, "Jesus of Nazareth," He said, "I am he. Let these go."

It is a wonderful thing when we commit ourselves to Christ. The more amazing thing is the commitment that Jesus makes to us. It is difficult to drive him from our life. Remember his cry over Jerusalem: "O Jerusalem, Jerusalem, you who kill the prophets and stone those sent to you, how often I have longed to gather your children together, as a hen gathers her chicks under her wings, but you were not willing! Look, your house is left to you desolate" (Luke 13:34–35).

It is not Jesus who lets his people and his city go. It is they who shut him out. He is the gatherer, not the expeller. We, with our indifference or our rebellion, are the ones who break the relationship if it is ever broken.

Jesus knew that in a little while all of those men would run to protect themselves, and that Peter would deny that he knew Jesus. But Jesus moved to protect his wavering ones. Perhaps that was in Peter's mind when he later wrote that God is not willing that any should perish but that all should come to repentance (2 Peter 3:9).

In this scene in the garden we gain a glimpse into the very heart of God. What we see is a God who actually cares more for his creatures than he does for himself. They can reject him, but he cannot get them out of his heart. George Matheson understood this. That is why he wrote,

> O Love that wilt not let me go,
> I rest my weary soul in Thee;
> I give Thee back the life I owe
> That in Thine ocean depths its flow
> May richer, fuller be.*

God loves us. We should rejoice but not presume that this love will save us when we persist in our rebellion.

*George Matheson, "O Love That Wilt Not Let Me Go," *The United Methodist Hymnal*, no. 480.

"the lord remembered"

jeremiah 2

*The word of the LORD came to me saying, "Go and cry in the hearing of
Jerusalem, saying, 'Thus says the Lord:
"I remember you,
The kindness of your youth,
The love of your betrothal,
When you went after Me in the wilderness."'"*
Jeremiah 2:1–2 NKJV

At one time Israel knew God and walked with him, and then in the stubbornness of their hearts, they turned their backs on God and went their own way. They became lawless, choosing to follow their own desires in the easiest and most pleasant ways. Anyone who chooses the easier rather than the best, and self rather than God, inevitably loses. So the Israelites lost the presence of God and found themselves in Babylonian captivity.

In captivity they were away from the Holy Land and away from God. They had tried to be like other nations, so God designed their punishment to fit their crime. They were forced to live within the nation they had wanted to be like. Even in their backslidden state, the Israelites understood God enough to recognize that he was chastening his people. During the captivity they admitted their sinfulness and began to listen to the prophets of God. The result was panic and despair because they had forfeited their opportunity to obey.

The marvelous thing about God is that he is the God of second chances, and even third and fourth chances if a person will repent. God sent the Israelites a prophet to instruct them about what they needed to do. When God's people said, "There is no hope for us. God has forgotten us," God sent them Zechariah, whose name means, "The Lord remembered."

If you have turned away from God or if you find yourself in trouble, and if you assume that God has forgotten you, hear the word of Zechariah: "The Lord remembered." God has not forgotten you. He knows exactly who you are and exactly what your situation is, and he is sending you help.

the measure of your future

zechariah 4

"Not by might nor by power, but by my Spirit," says the LORD Almighty.
Zechariah 4:6

The Lord Jesus wants to expand every believer's influence. His plan for each of us is normally greater than we dream. We are to be his light in the world. If he really gets control of a life, it is amazing how far he can make the influence go.

In our self-consciousness, we tend oftentimes to wonder if God can really use someone like us. We think of our failures and our limitations. The measure of our potential future, though, is never found in these. He can forgive our failures, and he can give us the same Holy Spirit that was the key to the life of Christ. We do not need to live in defeat.

Nor do our limitations hinder our worth to God. Zechariah 4 explains that our effectiveness is not determined by our gifts and abilities. When the prophet says, "Not by might nor by power," he uses two Hebrew words that occur in the Old Testament to cover all human resources. One is used to speak of human strength, human ability, and personal power. The other is defined as strength, valor, efficiency, wealth, and military force. What God wants to achieve in our lives is determined not by our capabilities but by his. That is why the prophet speaks of the Spirit, for it is the Spirit who releases in our lives the very fullness of God himself.

The prophet Zechariah saw the way. The Holy Spirit is the one who can cause the light of the gospel to shine through us and penetrate the darkness of the world. Oh, may we be open to receive him and let him do his work through us!

the lord is with you

genesis 39–41

The LORD was with [Joseph]; he showed him kindness and granted
him favor in the eyes of the prison warden.
Genesis 39:21

We are told that Enoch, Noah, and Abraham walked with God (Gen. 5:21
24; 6:9; 17:1–2), and that as Isaac faced famine and as Jacob fled from hi
brother, Esau, and as Joshua began the conquest of Canaan, the Lord wa
with each one (see Gen. 22:3; 28:15–16; Josh. 1:5). God was with Mose
and they talked face-to-face (Exod. 33:12–14). The implication is clear. I
God is with you, that is enough to enable you to overcome, no matter wha
the circumstances.

The great tragedy occurs when we let sin or indifference slip into ou
lives and the presence of God is lost. Oftentimes, we lose him as Mary an
Joseph did (Luke 2:41–52) and never know it. Never take this relationshi
for granted. Keep the connections close. Let him know you can't live with
out him. And then rejoice in his nearness.

God made a difference in Joseph's life. In fact, it was so real that both
prison master and a pagan king recognized the presence of God in his lif
(Gen. 39:3–4; 41:38). Do those around you recognize God's presence i
your life?

When the Lord comes into a person's life, he brings many things wit
him. Things such as joy, confidence, faith, hope, and love! His presenc
breaks the hold of circumstance. It sets us free. Madame Guyon learned this
Note the joy and the freedom that were hers as she sat in her prison cell:

> *A little bird I am,*
> *Shut out from the fields of air*
> *And in my cage I sit and sing*
> *To Him who placed me there;*
> *Well pleased a prisoner to be,*
> *Because, my God, it pleases thee.*

Nought have I else to do;
I sing the whole day long;
And He whom most I love to please,
Doth listen to my song;
He caught and bound my wandering wing,
But still He bends to hear me sing.

My cage confines me round;
Abroad I cannot fly;
But though my wing is closely bound,
My heart's at liberty.
My prison walls cannot control
*The flight, the freedom of my soul.**

The presence of God hallows every place it touches.

---

*Jeanne Marie Guyon, "A Little Bird I Am," quoted by Lettie M. Cowman, *Streams in the Desert*, vol. 1 (Grand Rapids: Zondervan, 1925), 315.

the anointing

luke 11:9 – 13

But when he, the Spirit of truth, comes, he will guide you into all truth.
He will not speak on his own; he will speak only what he hears,
and he will tell you what is yet to come.
John 16:13

The great soul-winners of history have been those individuals with a personal identification, a total submission, and an inner sensitivity to the Holy Spirit. It is not as though the Spirit is a rival to Jesus in the believer's life. Rather, as Jesus said about the Spirit, he is the One who will guarantee that there is nothing in the life or in the spirit of the believer that is inconsistent with the glory of Christ. The Spirit does not speak of himself. He comes to us as Christ's gift to link us to Christ himself. He is the one who guides us into all truth, even into him who is truth. So John can say:

> *You have an anointing from the Holy One, and you know all things ... But the anointing which you have received from Him abides in you, and you do not need that anyone teach you; but as the same anointing teaches you concerning all things, and is true, and is not a lie, and just as it has taught you, you will abide in Him (1 John 2:20, 27 NKJV).*

That anointing is a person, the Holy Spirit. He is the Protector and Guardian of truth, not just of theological truth, but of the glory of him who is the Truth. When our spirit and purposes are one with those of the Spirit of Christ, then our full potential is realized. When we are fully controlled by God, then the very authority of Jesus, who declared that all authority had been given to him, is present and at work in us through the Holy Spirit.

the center of the story

colossians 1:15 – 20

Therefore let all Israel be assured of this: God has made this Jesus,
whom you crucified, both Lord and Christ.
Acts 2:36

Clearly the apostles' message described in the book of Acts is the one they had received. It was not of their own design or of other human origin. It was neither their own idea nor their own discovery. The message was sacred, given to them from the hand of God—given to reveal the very nature of God.

All of the witnesses in Acts spoke of Jesus' incarnation, his life, his death, his resurrection, and his ascension. Jesus is the heart of the church's story. In him and by him and through him salvation and hope have come to the world.

Jesus did not come on his own. The God who is God alone; the God from whom all things come, by whom all things are sustained, to whom all things must inescapably go; the God who revealed himself to Israel and whose word is found in the Old Testament—this God sent him. This God revealed himself in Jesus Christ.

Behind, beyond, above, and after all things stands no inevitable fate, no inexorable force, no impersonal law, no mechanistic first cause, but a Being who is personal. He has a personal name and has disclosed himself to us in Jesus. On the Day of Judgment we will confront not a force, but a person. The Judge will be the One who has shown his love in a life of mercy, strength, and goodness and in a death of personal sacrifice in order to let us know the depth of his commitment to us and our redemption.

Is the Lord Jesus the center of your witness? He ought to be.

the dungeon

Isaiah 26:1 – 4

For they drank from the spiritual rock that accompanied them,
and that rock was Christ.
1 Corinthians 10:4

On the coast of Scotland stands an old castle that contains a remarkabl
dungeon. It was cut down into solid rock and is called a bottle dungeon
The neck is a vertical shaft six feet deep and wide enough to drop a mar
through. Below the shaft is the dungeon, cut out in the shape of a triangle
It is perhaps ten feet across at the top, and the dungeon's circular wall i
slanted inward to a point at the bottom. The bottle part is too deep for a per
son ever to reach the neck. The result is that no one escaped after being
dropped into it.

The masters of the castle found that all prisoners placed in this dun
geon quickly went insane. Except one. That one prisoner was able to retair
his sanity even though he was incarcerated there for several weeks. His cap
tors drew him out and sought to discover his secret. To their surprise they
learned that it lay in six pebbles he had in one of his pockets.

The prisoner explained that the circular dungeon and the total dark
ness left him with no unchanging point of reference. When he felt his men
tal powers threatened, he would count his pebbles by moving them one at
a time from one pocket to the other. There were always six. With that
unchangeable point of reference outside himself, he was able to keep from
losing his mind. When his existence seemed an unending, unrelenting night
mare, there was one point of order external to himself, and his sanity rested
on that.

Contrary to much of modern thought, the key to the self is not *in* the
self. Without an external point of reference that will not move, we simply
wander and lose our touch with reality. This is yet another evidence that we
are made to relate to an Other. That Other is the God who made us. Perhaps
that is why Israel loved to call their God their Rock. Isaiah spoke of that Rock
and of the perfect peace of the one whose mind is stayed on him. We need
an unmoving center. We have one in Christ if we will accept him as such.

living water

ezekiel 47:1 – 12; revelation 22:1 – 5

The man brought me back to the entrance of the temple, and I saw water coming out from under the threshold of the temple toward the east.
Ezekiel 47:1

We should never despise small things if God is in them. Ezekiel 47 illustrates this for us. The prophet stood before the temple of the Lord in Jerusalem and saw a small trickle of water seeping out from under the threshold. The small stream flowed eastward.

The prophet was led out some 1,500 feet and found that the trickle had now become a stream that was ankle deep. He was led out another 1,500 feet, and the water was up to his knees. Another 1,500 feet and it reached to his waist. When he was led another 1,500 feet, he found that it was a river to swim in, a river no one could cross.

He noticed then that the stream was flowing down into the Dead Sea. To his delight he observed the waters of the Dead Sea being turned into waters moving with life. The salt water had become fresh. Animals came to drink. Fish leaped into the sea. Trees sprang up on the shore, bearing fruit of all kinds, and their leaves had power to heal. A scene of sterility, barrenness, and death was now a scene of healthy, productive life.

The final picture of the New Jerusalem in Revelation 22 picks up this scene. There the stream flows from the throne of God and the Lamb. The tree of life stands on each side, bearing a different fruit for each month. Its leaves are for the healing of the nations. The darkness is past. Mourning, pain, and death are no more. Everything is new. The thirsty are invited to come and drink of the water of life. The Lamb and his bride reign with the Father through the Spirit. And everything started with what appeared to be a trickle.

Someone has said, "Find where God is at work and join in." That work may be small, as the time-bound eyes of humans see it. But if God is in it, its future is as large as the promises of God.

july 4

the inner person

psalm 119:9 – 16

For as he thinks in his heart, so is he.
Proverbs 23:7 NKJV

The philosopher Blaise Pascal defined thinking as an inner dialogue. To think is to carry on an inner conversation with oneself. Human beings are unique in their capacity to stand outside of themselves and critique their own thoughts and behaviors. Our inner conversation comes when we analyze ourselves, others, and our context. A surprising thing is that the other person inside us, with whom we are in dialogue, is strangely unoriginal, little more than an echo who shouts back only that to which we have exposed him or her. Therefore, the care and feeding of the one within is of crucial importance.

That is one reason I would like as much education as I can get: I would like that person within me to be as intelligent as I can make him. If I am going to have to listen to him, I would like for him to have something worthwhile to say. That is also why I need as pure a heart as Christ's blood and the Holy Spirit can give me. There is enough in the world to defile and corrupt me without an impure stream flowing within.

This must have been what Paul was thinking about when he wrote to his friends in Philippi, "Finally, brothers, whatever is true, whatever is noble, whatever is right, whatever is pure, whatever is lovely, whatever is admirable—if anything is excellent or praiseworthy—think about such things" (Phil. 4:8).

If your inner dialogue is to be like that, you will have to expose the person within you to the cleansing power of the Spirit, and then you will have to feed him or her well. Psalm 119 is an excellent source of food.

july 5

crowded and pushed

john 2:1–11

On the third day a wedding took place at Cana in Galilee.
Jesus' mother was there . . . When the wine was gone,
Jesus' mother said to him, "They have no more wine."
John 2:1–3

The only people who ever call on God are people to whom God has already come and in whom he has already put a hunger for himself. A person becomes a Christian not because of anything noble in him but because he crowded and pushed into it by the Holy Spirit. When God comes and begins to move on a human spirit, he begins to put a hunger within—an aspiration. He creates a desire to be different, to be a better person. Our dreaming soul begins to long for holiness and righteousness; we begin to imagine what God wants us to be. In place of a life of inner apathy comes a spark of interest in ultimate reality and the dream of a new life.

God periodically sticks problems in your life and mine. Remember the wedding at Cana? Nobody noticed Jesus until they had a problem and the wine ran out. There were many weddings over the years in Cana that never had a miracle. The only wedding in which a miracle occurred was the one where Christ was present and the people recognized their need of him and allowed him to do what he could to do for them.

Do you feel crowded and pushed by life? If so, you are in an ideal spot for Jesus to come and do something for you. It is when our backs are against the wall that he loves to move in and meet us.

july 6

essential christianity

2 corinthians 5:14–21

And he died for all, that those who live should no longer live for themselve
but for him who died for them and was raised again.
2 Corinthians 5:15

God the Father, Son, and Holy Spirit, whose life is love, created us for
lowship with himself. We chose instead to center our existence in ourselv
and we stepped out of that divine love, all of us turning to our own w
This separated us from the One who is light, truth, holiness, love, and
itself. Disintegration, corruption, and death became our inevitable f.
because when we turned from God, we turned from the source of life a
from all that is good. We needed saving help, and we needed it where t
problem was—inside of us.

The Father, who is self-giving love, sent his Son to become one of
and reverse this process of destruction. Our relationship with our Sour
lost by our sin, had to be reestablished. God did this in the Incarnation
when the eternal Son of God was embodied in Jesus of Nazareth, the Jew
and in the Cross. Jesus took our sin and its consequences into himself. Wh
the Spirit raised him in triumph over death, a grace was released that ma
his life a source of life and holiness for us.

Thus Jesus took our judgment upon himself and provided a new
for us. Death was overcome by life, alienation by love, sin by righteousne
delusion by truth, and darkness by the light of his face. By this atoneme
our relationship to God through the Spirit became that of a child to t
Father and a bride to the Son. His life became ours so that we, God's peop
could fulfill his purposes for us: first, to be a kingdom of priests who li
not for ourselves but for others, especially for those who do not yet kn
Christ; and second, to be a holy people in whom God dwells and wi
whom the Holy One walks in eternal communion. Are you enjoying tod
the full riches of the life he offers us all?

july 7

---

out of the distance

exodus 3

Those who know your name will trust in you.
Psalm 9:10

What is the heart of worship? It is when God comes out of the abstract distance and into personal proximity, and we know that we are face-to-face with God himself. Worship occurs when we realize that he cares enough about us to tell us his personal name and to call us his children. This is enough to fill a person with praise, and if we are the people we are designed to be, our praise will never end.

When you tell another person your name, you allow that one to enter into a different relationship with you, a deeper relationship. The act of giving your name actually gives the other some control over you; it means that person now has the power to get your attention. You have invited that person into a closer relationship with you. This desire for closeness is a key reason the Old Testament emphasizes so strongly the name of Yahweh and the New Testament speaks so pointedly about the goodness of God in the name of Jesus.

This is the reason the psalms so often use the name of Yahweh (LORD in English translations). The psalmists are trying to say that God himself has become very personal to them. They are exulting in the fact that they know God by name, that they are God's friends. This is the heart of worship: that the God of all the world should want us to know his name, that he deigns to come so close to us, and that he longs for a deeper relationship with us. This is reason enough for continual worship.

our only hope

psalm 121

I lift up my eyes to the hills—
where does my help come from?
My help comes from the LORD.
Psalm 121:1–2

The greatest value of Psalm 121 lies not in a praise of nature but in its presentation of the contrast between nature and grace. The psalmist does not decry nature; he just knows its limitations and proclaims that there is no salvation in the natural world. Salvation comes only from above and beyond the creation. The hills represent nature at its best, but the best the earth has to offer is not big enough or good enough to rescue us from ourselves.

The answer to our need is neither within us nor within our world. It rests in the transcendent One from beyond the confines of the universe. When he comes, he brings supernatural resources to meet our natural needs. In this psalm the writer paints the background for the manger in Bethlehem where the eternal One broke into time and space, became a human person, and brought redemption to the world.

For those who can see, the need for this truth is apparent in every area of life. Modern people have tried every earthly source to solve their problems: government, education, economics, social sciences, psychology, and psychoanalysis. We have expected somewhere within us or within our world to find the key, the solution that we seek. Thousands of years ago there was a man, wiser than we, who saw the sterility of our vain efforts. He decided that help for humans comes only from Yahweh, who created and rules over all the factors and all the processes in which we place our hopes. Our only true hope and our only sure help is in the God who made heaven and earth.

my dread and my security

isaiah 44:6–8

He is my refuge and my fortress,
my God, in whom I trust.
Psalm 91:2

In Old Testament times, Yahweh alone was to be feared. He had neither rival nor competitor. He alone was humanity's ultimate concern, and he held humanity's ultimate destiny. In Old Testament times people did not make concessions to magic, idolatry, or the occult to deal with their daily fears and troubles. Whether they were anxious about the present or the future, there was no hope for help except in Yahweh. In the temple, in the home, or out in the field, Yahweh was the only answer to the problems the Israelites faced. He was to be their dread and their security. Fear of him was the beginning of wisdom.

Yahweh alone was God, and there was no savior beside him. Perfect peace was found by keeping one's mind stayed on him. This was not an easy religion, and it was dramatically different from the other ancient religions, in which people believed in magic, fate, and capricious gods. Old Testament faith pulled away all the normal crutches provided by society and insisted that a person must stand by faith in Yahweh alone, depending upon him in all circumstances.

In our day of swaying values and relative "truths," when the world pressures all Christians to accept some other help besides God, we need to remember that the God of the Old Testament is still our God. Jesus Christ reflects his Father's nature and puts the same demands on us that he placed on the Israelites; he insists that we be a striking contrast to the culture around us, which would have us be conformed to its own image. Society will offer a thousand crutches on which to lean, but each one will fail and will ultimately be destructive if we turn to it for security rather than to God himself.

july 10

---

a moment of divine touch

ephesians 2:8 – 10

How great is the love the Father has lavished on us, that we should
be called children of God! And that is what we are!
The reason the world does not know us is that it did not know him.
1 John 3:1

There is a great difference between what we can do and what God can do.
Our work has a finite character to it, but his is eternal. That is why one
moment of divine activity is worth more than a lifetime of human effort
and achievement. Between his work and ours lies the difference between
religion and grace, and religion without grace is sterile and ultimately
destructive.

Religion without grace inevitably leads to pride and arrogance. There is
an illusion within it all. Religion makes one feel superior to the irreligious.
Where God is at work, there is an inevitable humility because God is humble. Just look at Jesus. When God comes, our pride and our arrogance are
always broken. We do not feel superior. We know we are obligated. Meekness replaces self-sufficiency because our confidence, our trust, is no longer
in what we have done or are doing. When we live in grace, our confidence
is in what has been done and is being done for us. We know we are recipients more than we are givers.

The result of grace is a freedom that the merely religious never know.
Ours is the freedom of the child. Theirs is the bondage of the servant or
slave. Religious people, in spite of all they do, will never be spiritual children.
No human can ever achieve that by working. As recipients of grace we are,
not by our own working, children of the Father and enjoy the freedom that
comes with that relationship.

God wants us all to be his children, daughters and sons. We can't make
ourselves that. He can, and he can do it in one divine moment if we will
let him.

one holy passion

song of songs 3:1 – 4

My beloved is mine, and I am his.
He feeds his flock among the lilies.
Song of Solomon 2:16 NKJV

orge Croly was an Anglican clergyman. A man of remarkable gifts, he
s also a novelist, a historian, a theologian, a dramatist, a poet, and a
irist. When he turned away from all of his abilities and achievements to
e God, he hungered for a holy, consuming love for the Lord. Consider
efully his prayer.

Spirit of God, descend upon my heart;
    Wean it from earth, through all its pulses move;
Stoop to my weakness, mighty as thou art,
    And help me love thee as I ought to love.
Teach me to love thee as thine angels love,
    One holy passion filling all my frame;
The baptism of the heaven-descended dove,
    My heart an altar, and thy love the flame.*

Note the cry for totality: "through all its pulses move" and "filling all my
me." Croly knew that anything less than all was not a satisfactory offer-
 to present to God. He dared not be content with anything less. His offer-
 must, in accord with Old Testament thinking, be a whole burnt offering.

Too often the church has been willing to present a gospel that demands
s of its members than this. When it does, it is making no accommodation
 its adherents. It is actually cheating the needy. A partial surrender to
irist means a partial experiencing of his grace, and surely that is no gain.
 certainly as the Spirit is better than the flesh, a life in which the Spirit
 ves through every pulse and in which a burning, passionate love "fills all"
 "frame," is better than one with mixed loyalties. Surely the Christ of Cal-
 y concurs with Croly.

---

orge Croly, "Spirit of God, Descend," *Hymns for Praise and Worship*, no. 239.

true glory

ezekiel 10

THE LORD IS THERE.
Ezekiel 48:35

The temptation of the church is always to think according to the fashion the world. This is also the propensity of the human heart. After the temp was destroyed in Jerusalem, the Jews began to dream of another temp They remembered Solomon's temple with its gold and its architectural wo der, and they dreamed of the restoration of that glory. God, though, h something different in mind.

The true glory of the formal temple was not what Israel thought it w The true glory was something that could not be seen with the naked eye. was the real but invisible presence of the Lord himself, now departed fro Jerusalem. Israel had eyes only for the external and missed the real glory.

I once had a conversation with a young missionary who was living alo in the midst of primitive Indians in South America. He was the son of wealthy Midwestern banker. After his sophomore year, the young man h dropped out of the major university in his state to go alone and witho support to the mission field. I asked him why he could not wait until I had finished his training and matured a bit. His answer has haunted n across the years: "I was afraid I would lose the sense of intimacy I had foun with Jesus if I did not go."

More important than comfort or security—in fact, more importa than anything else to this young missionary—was a glory that his fami and friends could not see or sense. Was he right to go? His example may n be appropriate for anyone else. The rightness of his decision, though, h been confirmed by the creative results in one of the most fruitful lives liv for Christ in the twentieth century. Do you know where the real glory is? A you walking in it?

Ezekiel had eyes to see. He saw the glory leave the temple and the cit He dreamed of the day the glory would return. His book ends on a ve happy note. In the Hebrew the book closes with two simple words, the nam of the Lord and a word that is more commonly used as an adverb but is us here as a noun, *there*. We translate it "THE LORD IS THERE." Blessed is t one who has eyes to see the real glory—God himself.

the word of god

1 kings 22:1 – 38

As the LORD lives, whatever the LORD says to me, that will I speak.
1 Kings 22:14 NKJV

The world needs people who will stake their lives on the reality and truth of the Word of God. King Ahab of Samaria invited King Jehoshaphat of Judah to go into battle with him. Before they went, Jehoshaphat said, "Please inquire for the word of the LORD" (1 Kings 22:5 NKJV). Ahab called four hundred prophets to inquire of the Lord's will, and every prophet, down to the last one, decreed that God would bless Ahab's battle.

Yet Jehoshaphat found himself nervous. These prophets did not sound like the ones back home. In Judah the throne did not rule the prophets; God controlled them. The king depended on God's spokesmen to speak the truth. Jehoshaphat relied on a bony finger pointed in his direction and a man with enough courage to declare God's will and God's truth whether it was nice or not. Because of this dependence on another kind of prophet, Jehoshaphat requested that Ahab send for a prophet of Yahweh.

Reluctantly, Ahab sent for Micaiah, whom he hated. Micaiah had always spoken evil about Ahab because of Ahab's sin. As at other times, Micaiah now prophesied against Ahab, saying, "If you ever return in peace, the LORD has not spoken by me" (1 Kings 22:28 NKJV).

Four hundred voices had affirmed Ahab's plan, and there was only one dissenter, but the future of Ahab was not with the majority; it was not even in his own hands. The future was with the one faithful prophet controlled by God. Micaiah was put in prison until Ahab returned. Ahab did come back, but dead in his chariot!

These are the days when people must attune their ears to God's voice. What seems impressive may be the fad of today that has within it the seeds of tomorrow's funerals. The Word of God is what we need.

the truth of the message

john 4

Simon Peter answered him, "Lord, to whom shall we go?
You have the words of eternal life."
John 6:68

The early Christian church was a force of great power as it challenged the religious world of the Mediterranean. It overcame Roman political power and Greek culture. What was the key to its success? Part of it was the strength and the vitality that inhere in truth. Paul knew that the message he proclaimed was self-authenticating. He knew that what he was preaching was neither "cleverly invented stories" (2 Peter 1:16) nor even the best of human wisdom. Paul knew that it was the very wisdom of the God who had made humanity, and that it fit the human psyche. He knew that regardless of the outward response of the person to whom the gospel is presented, within every single hearer there is at least a minority report that says, "You were made for this!"

The Word of God is never a completely alien word when it comes to human beings! There is an inherent compatibility between the creature and the Word of the Creator. God made us for himself, and we are incomplete until we find him. That should give us courage and confidence when we witness. We are not seeking to sell something the other person does not need. Nor are we trying to impose something we have found onto another's life. We are simply indicating where that for which the other person waits can be found. Do you have any friends or loved ones who do not know Christ? Think twice before you fail to share. They are waiting, whether they know it or not.

jesus' temptations

luke 4:1 – 13

Then Jesus was led by the Spirit into the desert to be tempted by the devil.
Matthew 4:1

ote the legitimacy of the temptations that Satan used to appeal to Jesus.
ertainly there is nothing wrong with eating when one is hungry, but Satan
d not merely tempt Jesus to eat. He wanted Jesus to step out of God's will
r him, and so he invited Jesus to use divine power to meet his own needs.
any of our temptations are attempts to get us to use God's gifts, given for
rvice to others, for the satisfaction of our personal needs, perhaps even
o needs.

In the second temptation Jesus was encouraged to show God's power
at once, quickly and powerfully revealing who he was. This seemed to be
effective way of proving his divinity. Yet Jesus refused to accomplish God's
rposes without using God's intended means and timetable.

The offer of all the kingdoms of the world was alluring because it came
thout the price tag of the Cross. Jesus knew that the kingdoms of the
rld would ultimately be given to him. They were and are his, but he had
follow God's way, and God's way involved the sacrifice of his life. There
a Cross involved in our obedience to the will of God, just as there was for
sus. Any temptation to bypass the sacrifice and settle for ease and security
from the evil one. Even God had no ultimate victory apart from the Cross.

The temptation of Jesus occurred at the beginning of his ministry. This
something that we must watch. Before every step of obedience, we will
d resistance that must be overcome, temptation that must be fought. We
ust not use God for our own advantage. We must not accomplish his will
our way or time. And we must not bypass the Cross. It is in the losing of
r way that we find it.

a second witness

deuteronomy 17:6 – 7; john 5:31 – 38

*When he comes, he will convict the world of guilt
in regard to sin and righteousness and judgment.*
John 16:8

There is a power in the personal witness or in the preaching of a person who knows the anointing of the Spirit. Part of that may lie in the genuineness and the integrity of the one who shares. With preachers the impact comes in part from the preparation and from fidelity to the Word. But there is more and the more is the most significant part. It is what the Scripture speaks of as a second witness.

The Old Testament exhibits a deep concern for justice. It states that no person could be convicted of a crime on the basis of the testimony of a single witness. The danger of a false accusation was too great. So a second witness was required to convict someone of a crime.

The New Testament honors this Old Testament principle in the witness of the Holy Spirit. He never wants to send us out alone. Conviction comes when an inner voice, the witness of the Spirit, confirms the message of the outer voice that a person hears. It is the double witness that gives the power.

There is comfort in this, but there is also admonition. It should encourage us to know that we never have to witness or preach alone. There is One who wants to go with us and confirm our word. He may not be visibly present, but it is his voice that seals it all. That is why we should become very sensitive to his voice to us and his anointing.

Early in my ministry a wise woman spoke to me about another preacher. Her comment was, "His preaching is like the sound of dried peas poured on a tin roof." Empty noise! Those words have haunted me ever since. The joy, though, is that our witness does not have to be like the sound of "dried peas on a tin roof." They can be the very Word of God, and it is the second witness that makes them so.

carrying in your heart

deuteronomy 1:29 – 31

I thank my God every time I remember you.
In all my prayers for all of you, I always pray with joy.
Philippians 1:3–4

Paul's letter to the Philippians gives a great example of the attitude Christians ought to have toward those to whom they minister. Read the first chapter of Philippians and you will begin to sense Paul's passionate love for these people. There is a tenderness in his love for them. It is the love of a father, of a brother, of a friend. He says to the Colossians, "We always thank God, the Father of our Lord Jesus Christ, when we pray for you" (Col. 1:3).

Merely thinking of some people brings joy and a sense of gratitude. Paul's attitude toward his Christian friends overflows with love, as if to say: "I feel better when I think about you. In my prayers, every time I pray for you I do it with joy. There is always joy in praying for you because of your fellowship, your friendship, your companionship in the gospel. You have become a part of my life, and you bring me joy."

Paul also says, "It is right for me to feel this way about all of you, since I have you in my heart" (Phil. 1:7). In the same way an expectant mother carries her baby in her womb, Paul carried these people in his heart. Is this not a magnificent model for Christians and the ones about whom they are concerned? Are you loving like Paul did? Are you carrying the people God has given you in your heart?

freedom to go boldly

hebrews 10:19 – 25

At that moment the curtain of the temple was torn in two from top to bottom.
The earth shook and the rocks split.
Matthew 27:51

When the New Testament speaks of those who live in the flesh, it speaks of those whose lives are oriented around themselves and who know only their own resources. Such lives are characterized by alienation and distance from God. For them, speaking of intimacy with God is not only improperly familiar, but also offensive.

A woman in a Bible class once said to me, "When you speak of the love of Jesus, I find that it nauseates me." One Sunday during our noon meal the phone rang. It was this friend from our Bible class. With a tone of urgency she asked if I could immediately come to her home. When I walked into her lovely house, she was standing in the hallway weeping. When I asked what was wrong, she said, "Oh, Pastor, I see it. I see it. For the first time in my life, I see it."

When I inquired as to what she saw, she said, "I was sitting in the choir in my church this morning, and it was Communion Sunday. When the pastor took the bread and broke it and said those words, 'This is my body that is broken for you,' I saw it. He did it for me! He did it for me!" She never spoke to me again about being nauseated by the mention of familiarity with Jesus.

In Old Testament times a veil separated the Holy of Holies, where God dwelt, from the people of Israel. When Christ died on the cross, that veil was rent in two. The way was opened for access to God—immediate access. The writer of the book of Hebrews tells us that now, because of Christ, we should come boldly to the very throne of God (Heb. 4:16). The Cross of Christ means access to God, intimacy rather than distance, love rather than alienation. We must exercise our privilege of access to God.

the nature of god

exodus 20:1–21

Blessed are they who keep his statutes
and seek him with all their heart.
Psalm 119:2

The Ten Commandments are a window into the very nature of God. He revealed his character to us in his Law. He knows who he is and wants us to recognize him as he is. He is God alone and there is no other. He created all things but himself. The creation is good, but nothing in it is good enough to replace him. He has given us his name so we can address him. That name should not be used lightly or in vain. All time, every day, is a gift from him, and he wants our calendars to reflect our gratitude.

Everyone in God's world has a father, who should be an image of him. We should honor our parents not only because they gave us life, but also because during our infancy and childhood they stood in God's place in our lives. Human sexuality was given to us so we would have an example of the total, unconditional, faithful, and unbreakable love relationship God wants to have with us.

Property rights are sacred and should not be presumed upon or violated. Language is a divine gift that only humans in our world enjoy. Symbols should represent realities. Therefore, words should never be used falsely to gain personal advantage or to damage another. And last of all, God wants us to be content with his will for us and not to lust for others' position, place, or possessions.

In other words, God is holy and wants us and all of our relationships to be hallowed. He is good and should be worshiped. His ways are right and should be obeyed.

no salvation without relationship (part 1)

john 17

Now this is eternal life: that they may know you,
the only true God, and Jesus Christ, whom you have sent.
John 17:3

There are two common excuses we make to get around God's Law. We know we are saved by faith and not by works, and that keeping the Law of God i works—our works. Therefore, we assume that the Ten Commandment have nothing to do with salvation. They may be rules for maintaining fel lowship with Christ, but the keeping of them has nothing to do with ou redemption. Salvation is a thing that God can give us and that no one can take away from us.

What troubles me about this is that salvation is understood as having an existence in itself apart from the active presence of Christ. But the Scriptures if we look at them as a whole, know of no salvation apart from the Savior. To receive him is to be saved. To turn away from him is to turn away from salvation because there is no salvation apart from him. Salvation is the result of the active presence of God at work in one's life. Adam and Eve learned this when they broke their relationship with their Friend. At the Red Sea, salvation for Israel was the result of the presence of the Lord in their midst. The difference between the fate of Israel and that of Egypt was simply his presence.

Over the centuries Israel learned they could not presume upon God's presence. When they grieved him enough, his presence withdrew. That is why Moses pled with God after the golden calf experience. He told God he would not go forward if God's presence was not going with them. Jesus wanted his disciples to understand this. On the last night before the Cross, he told them, "Those who love me will keep my word, and my Father will love them, and we will come to them and make our home with them" (John 14:23 NRSV). His disciples' security and fulfillment were to be in the abiding presence of the Father, the Son, and the Spirit within them. The Law of God spells out the conditions for that abiding presence. Our security truly is in God.

no salvation without relationship (part 2)

romans 4:1–8

*If, in fact, Abraham was justified by works, he had something to
boast about—but not before God. What does the Scripture say?
"Abraham believed God, and it was credited to him as righteousness."*
Romans 4:3

If the Law of God spells out the conditions for fellowship with God, immediately someone suggests that we are saved by faith but that we are kept by works, by our obedience to the Law. But that again is wrong.

If there is anything we know, it is that there is nothing in us that can enable us to keep God's Law. That is true before we find Christ. That is why we need to seek him. And it is just as true after we become Christians as it was before. There is no capacity for holiness within us, before or after conversion. The difference between the after and the before is simply Christ's presence. The new life that comes in the new birth is not ours. It is his holy life now living within and making the difference. This is what Paul was speaking about when he wrote to the Colossians about Christ within us being "the hope of glory" (Col. 1:27). The hope is never in us.

This means that the question is never one of what we can do. The question is about what Christ can do. The wonderful thing is that when Christ comes into a life, he brings his Holy Spirit with him. That Holy Spirit is the Spirit of holiness, and he comes into us with his holy power to transform us and to enable us to walk in Christ's ways. Thus Paul can say, "So if anyone is in Christ, there is a new creation; everything old has passed away; see, everything has become new!" (2 Cor. 5:17 NRSV). The newness does not originate in us. It originates in the Holy One who dwells within.

Little wonder that Jesus spoke so much that last night about abiding in him. See John 14–17. In that abiding is our security. Some find this frightening and want a locked-in relationship with him. They look at themselves and know how untrustworthy they are, and they panic. We need to look at Jesus; faith is simply keeping our eyes on him. When we look at him, what do we see? We do not see one who is watching eagerly to find a reason to run away in offense and leave us. No, instead we find the One who has relentlessly pursued us until we turned to meet him. We see the One who died to save us and will never leave us or forsake us. We just must not forsake him. If we do, he does not stop his pursuit, but surprisingly our desertion of him makes it harder for us to trust again.

no salvation without relationship (part 3)

Mark 10:17–22

One thing you lack: Go your way, sell whatever you have and
give to the poor, and you will have treasure in heaven;
and come, take up the cross, and follow Me.
Mark 10:21 NKJV

There is a second excuse that many of us use to get around the Law of God as it is given in the Ten Commandments. We reason that the standard given in the commandments is an ideal one that is really unattainable. It is a target for which to aim, but a person should not really expect to hit it. Plus, it is part of the old covenant that is now past.

Jesus apparently did not feel that way. When the rich ruler wanted to know how to inherit eternal life, Jesus pointed him to the commandments. In the Sermon on the Mount, Jesus takes portions of the Decalogue and extends their claims on us. He does not relax them.

We often speak as if keeping the Law would be a heavy burden. But how would keeping the Law be a burden? Do we really believe that living with a divided heart is easier than living with a single heart? Is our life any richer if we look to the creation for what only the Creator can give us? Must we deal profanely with holy things like the name of the Lord and his Sabbath? Are we better off having no respect for those who gave us life? Do we have to live with deadly hate for any of our fellow persons? Is there no deliverance from the defilement and the destructiveness of lust? Can we come to the place where we can use language truthfully, even if it means our own hurt? Can't God make us content with what we have so we do not have to perpetually covet what is not our own?

Just to frame these questions ought to bring us to the conclusion that the Ten Commandments were not given to be an onerous burden and a structure to bind us. Rather, the Decalogue is our charter of freedom. The commandments are not a set of demands to bind us, but a tenfold promise of the freedom into which the Spirit of Christ wants to release us. If I will let him flood me with his Spirit and with his love, there is not one commandment that I have to break today. That is good news!

no salvation without relationship (part 4)

psalm 119

You are my portion, O LORD; ...
I have sought your face with all my heart.
Psalm 119:57–58

God has given to his people his Law. It sets before us his character and his ways. It speaks to us of him and the lifestyle that pleases him. For some, that Law seems to be a burden. But should it be? John obviously did not see it that way. In 1 John 5:3 he relates God's commandments and God's love, saying they go together and that the "commandments are not burdensome." Jesus says that his "yoke is easy" and his "burden is light," that he has come to relieve us, not to weary us (Matt. 11:28–30).

The psalmist seems to concur with Jesus and John. The longest of the Psalms, Psalm 119, is a paean of praise for the Law. For 22 stanzas and 175 verses the psalmist sings again and again of his delight in the Law. Two Hebrew roots are particularly used to express his feelings about it. Both are translated into English as "delight." The first and more common one is used in Jeremiah 31:20 to speak of the joy that a father finds in his child. It also is found on the lips of Wisdom as she recalls her part, as God's master worker, in the creation of the world (Prov. 8:30–31). Another usage occurs in Isaiah 5:7, where the prophet speaks of the pleasure God has in his people, whom he calls "the garden of his delight."

The other word carries with it the connotations of exultant elation, a very special joy. Isaiah uses it in 35:10. He is describing the return of the redeemed exiles to Zion. They come with singing and everlasting joy, "Gladness and joy will overtake them, and sorrow and sighing will flee away."

Though he came before Christ, the psalmist apparently had found the truth of Christ's words, "For my yoke is easy and my burden is light" (Matt. 11:30). The way to rest is not in rejecting or chafing under his yoke but in embracing it. The key to it all is found in two lines of Psalm 119, "You are my portion, O LORD ... I have sought your face with all my heart" (vv. 57–58). We find him and embrace his way by seeking him with all our heart. Then his presence hallows all.

the symphony of scripture

luke 24:13 – 35

And beginning with Moses and all the Prophets,
he explained to them what was said in all the Scriptures concerning himself.
Luke 24:27

One of my professors in graduate school shocked a number of us when he said, "I get a bit afraid for many of you who underline what you like in the Bible." Furtively, I closed my Bible. He continued, "I suspect that I can tell you which verses you have underlined." And then he gave a remarkably accurate depiction of the portions that I had marked.

He explained his point, informing us that what we did not underline was as much the Word of God as that which we did. He warned us that we should not study just the portions of the Scripture that we liked. The Scripture must be faced as a whole.

Then he said, "You read a verse and it has meaning for you, so you highlight it. But what you want to do is move from a verse to a paragraph so you see the larger unit of which your favorite verse is only a part. You need to begin putting these units together so you can see whole segments of biblical truth. From that you will start to see biblical themes and how they are developed through the various parts of Scripture." If we did that, he insisted, we could begin to see the unity and beauty of the Word of God.

It was then that I began to see that Scripture is a whole, though it is divided into sixty-six books written across many centuries. It is like a Beethoven symphony with its various themes, each of which is different, but each of which contributes to the beauty and power of the whole.

I did not stop underlining special sections because of what I heard that day. I did, however, begin to pay much more attention to the larger units within which my special passages came. The fun began when I found myself catching glimmers of biblical truth that bound it all together, from Genesis to Revelation. To further that process, I periodically bought a new study Bible so I could make a new set of markings.

The Scriptures are an incredible treasure of divine wisdom. No one will ever master them all in this life. The joy, though, is in the discovery of their truth, and that privilege of finding new truth is as available to the beginner as to the seasoned saint. I know no greater gift from God than that of a hunger for the Word that causes one to bask in its richness.

a heart like his

2 corinthians 5:12–21

We are therefore Christ's ambassadors, as though God were making
his appeal through us. We implore you on Christ's behalf:
Be reconciled to God. God made him who had no sin to be sin for us,
so that in him we might become the righteousness of God.
2 Corinthians 5:20–21

When we come into the presence of God, we instantly realize that we need a covering. We recognize that we are undone and unclean. How can we stand before God? We must have something that can shield us from the piercing light of his holiness. The righteousness of Christ is what covers us. But as soon as we are covered and can stand in his presence, we have a second realization. We find that we are not content to be covered. God is not an enemy; he is our friend. He is not One to flee from; he is the One we want to be like. At this point, we begin to long for him to change us from the inside out. Our prayer becomes, "God, can you not merely cover me but also change me? Can you transform my heart into something beautiful?"

Answering that prayer is just what he is waiting and wanting to do for us. When we are reconciled to him, he begins to put his likeness into our lives. He wants to get us to the place where we love what he loves. If we are full of unholiness and he is holiness itself, then he must give his nature to us so there can develop between us that deep and satisfying compatibility for which our hearts yearn.

> *O for a heart to praise my God,*
> *A heart from sin set free.*
> *A heart that always feels thy blood*
> *So freely shed for me.*
>
> *A humble, lowly contrite heart,*
> *Believing, true, and clean.*
> *That neither life nor death can part*
> *From Christ who dwells within.* *

---

*Charles Wesley, "O for a Heart to Praise My God," *The United Methodist Hymnal*, no. 417.

a hungry heart

luke 1:46–55

He has filled the hungry with good things.
Luke 1:53

Edwin Hatch was an ordained priest in the Church of England, and in his day he was one of the foremost church historians in the world. His lectures forever established his name among the scholars of the world. But when he left the lecture room and went into his prayer closet, his heart hungered for more than academic truth or international fame. He prayed:

Breathe on me, Breath of God,
Until my heart is pure,
Until with thee I will one will,
To do and to endure.

Breathe on me, Breath of God,
Til I am wholly thine,
Until this earthly part of me
Glows with thy fire divine. *

Many of us expect God to work in other people in ways that are identical with the way he works in us. The reality is that God is not confined to our religious tradition or our language categories. He can take any hungry heart and breathe his Spirit upon it until that heart glows with his fire divine. Edwin Hatch may never have heard the language about the baptism of the Holy Spirit, but his heart cried out for God to do something more for him.

Is your heart hungry for more? God does not have to work within the confines of our language or our categories.

---

*Edwin Hatch, "Breathe on Me, Breath of God," *Hymns for Praise and Worship*, no. 470.

as close as he wants to be

psalm 91

*O Jerusalem, Jerusalem . . . how often I have longed to gather
your children together, as a hen gathers her chicks under her wings,
but you were not willing.*
Matthew 23:37

One of the reasons the Jews rejected Jesus was that they could not believe
how close he desired to be to them. They were ill prepared to make the
changes that a relationship with him would require. When people are born
again and truly come to know Christ personally, their language begins to
change, their family relationships begin to change, and their deepest and
most personal dreams begin to change.

The world wants Jesus to keep a respectable distance from them so they
can control his influence over their lives. However, if Jesus gave his life for
humanity, then there is only one legitimate response to him—to give yourself to him like a bride to a bridegroom. Then the Lord Jesus becomes the
Source of your life and your most precious treasure, and the changes that
must come are not terrifying but satisfying. It is this level of intimacy with
him for which human persons were made.

Are you intimate with the Lord Jesus today, or are you aloof? Do you
keep him distant? He longs to be a part of every area in your life in the same
way a beloved spouse would affect your daily activities and choices. Amazingly, the sacrifices made for a love relationship with Jesus do not seem like
sacrifices. They become joys, and they bring a deeper freedom than you have
ever known. He is longing for your devotion and love. Are you as close to
the Lord Jesus as he wants to be to you?

is he the center?

isaiah 43

Before me no god was formed,
nor will there be one after me.
I, even I, am the LORD,
and apart from me there is no savior.
Isaiah 43:10–11

All human beings have a center of their existence, and the nature of that center will determine their personal identity. There is a center that every human soul is supposed to seek and to know—the true Center, which is the Lord Jesus. If we do not know him as the hub around which our life turns, we will have no understanding of who we are, how the world works, or the way things relate to each other. That Center determines all other aspects and relationships of our lives. Knowing Jesus as the core of our existence allows us to see the purpose and meaning in the various elements that compose our lives.

The person who does not have this center will have no key to explain adequately the mysteries and the heartaches that force themselves upon each human soul. The door to finding fulfillment and understanding ultimate meaning will never open for the individual who does not have the key— the Lord Jesus.

It is absolutely imperative for those of us who claim that Jesus Christ is the center of our existence to live a life that truly reflects the reality of Christ. Without our having to speak a word, it ought to be obvious to other people that Jesus is the key that opens doors for us and the center around which our entire existence revolves. Don't claim that Jesus is the center of your existence if your life does not provide the proof of your claim.

forgiveness of sins

mark 2:1 – 12

*"But that you may know that the Son of Man has authority
on earth to forgive sins . . ." He said to the paralytic,
"I tell you, get up, take your mat and go home."*
Mark 2:10–11

The first thing God wants to do for us is to give us his gift of grace and for-giveness. Even among the people of God, I find a lot of people who live with great guilt. We will never develop into what God wants us to be until we find out what it means to have God's forgiveness. That forgiveness is a gra-cious gift that we can never earn. In fact, there is nothing we can do to receive it except to take it from his hand in repentant faith. When we have accepted his gift, we are on our way to grace and growth.

The story of the paralytic who was lowered through the roof illustrates this beautifully. This man's friends brought him to Jesus for physical heal-ing, but Jesus knew what the man's real need was, so he said to the paralytic, "Your sins are forgiven." Everyone thought Jesus was sidetracked from the real issue of physical healing, but Jesus was the only one who saw the prob-lem clearly.

The forgiveness of our sins is the doorway into a relationship with the Lord Jesus. Tragically, I have seen some people who cannot accept this gift. But we will never know any further growth or grace until we can say that our sins are nailed to his cross and that we are forgiven and free.

bearing the burden

numbers 11

*Bring me seventy of Israel's elders ... I will take of the Spirit that is on
you and put the Spirit on them. They will help you carry the burden
of the people so that you will not have to carry it alone.*
Numbers 11:16–17

In Numbers 11, we see a picture of a great leader overburdened by the load
God had given him to bear. Moses complained to God because of the enor-
mous responsibility of carrying the people of God in his "bosom" (v. 12
NKJV).

Can you imagine Moses' position? He had a multitude of people looking to him for spiritual guidance as well as physical provision and security.
He served as their leader, their priest, their judge, and their intercessor. The
burden of a people who were called to be God's but refused to trust him
became a load too heavy to bear alone, so Moses cried out to Yahweh.

Perhaps you are carrying a work of God in your heart. It may be a small
work or it may be an enormous burden that God has given you to carry. In
such cases, it is easy to forget that God is the One who is the burden-bearer.
We are merely his tools. When Moses complained to God, God's reply was
simple. "Bring me seventy of Israel's elders ... I will take of the Spirit that
is on you and put the Spirit on them." We are not indispensable to God.
His Spirit carries the work he puts on our hearts.

intimate association with guilt

psalm 86

For you, Lord, are good, and ready to forgive.
Psalm 86:5 NKJV

Psalm 86 was written by a person in great danger, presumably King David. He was begging God to save him from a band of ruffians. His life was in peril, and yet in the middle of the psalm he said to Yahweh, "For you, Lord, are good, and ready to forgive."

To be human is to have an intimate association with guilt. When you and I are in deep need and we come to pray, there lurks in our mind a fearful realization that we are totally unworthy. Why should he listen to me? In essence, David says that he needs physical protection and political deliverance, but I am so glad that Yahweh is forgiving. Where David has failed, God can cover and forgive because Yahweh God abounds in steadfast love."

God loves us so much that he listens to us, even though we do not deserve his attention. He is good, and he is ready to forgive. And many times, he wants us to acknowledge his goodness and our sin before he acts on our behalf. If you sense that he is not listening, look into your own heart. Is there sin in it? If there is, you need to confess your sin to him and ask his forgiveness so you once again enter into a right relationship with him. He wants us to come to him for protection, but first he wants us to let him clean our hearts.

a true perspective

psalm 86

Among the gods there is none like you, O Lord.
Psalm 86:8

Most of us turn to prayer in order to solve a problem. Our troubles become the motivating force behind our prayers. If we were the people we ought to be, we would pray whether we had problems or not. One of the beautiful things about God and about human life is that he does not leave us long without problems. He sees to it that we have difficulties, and he works at ordering our situations so we are not trouble free. This helps us to stay in relation to him.

In Psalm 86 David prays to God in great distress because his very life is in danger. The reader senses David's panic and desperation in verses 1–7 and then there is a psychological shift in verse 8. All of a sudden David's eyes turn away from his problem and become fixed on God himself. When David enters into the presence of God, he forgets the men who are hunting for him.

When a person spends enough time in the presence of God, problems begin to fade into the background and God's greatness begins to loom large. This psalm is a classic picture of the way the most serious and intense problems melt away in the presence of Almighty God, before whom they seem insignificant. As David faces God, he gets the true perspective on reality. His problems diminish and God's glory increases.

get the rebel out of my heart

psalm 86

Unite my heart to fear Your name.
I will praise You, O Lord my God, with all my heart.
Psalm 86:11–12 NKJV

Psalm 86 is written as David's plea for God to remove the rebels who are harassing him. The psalm begins to change its focus, however, as the psalmist comes into the presence of God. He admits that his heart is divided, that he has a division in his being. He prays to God, "Unite my heart," so he can give thanks to him with a whole heart and not with a divided heart.

I suspect that this is one of the most significant prayers to be found anywhere in the Word of God. Anyone who comes to know God will begin to hunger for this reality. In verses 1–7, the psalmist beseeches God to embarrass the rebels of his court. But when he enters the presence of God, he asks him to remove the rebel from within his own heart. His own rebelliousness becomes the pressing concern of this psalm. The treachery in his own heart poses more of a threat than the rebel in his court.

God desires that each follower of Christ make this pilgrimage: to move from praying for changed circumstances to praying for a united heart. Of all the human aspirations and dreams, I suspect that longing for inner unity is the deepest hunger of the human soul—to have a heart completely united in commitment to God. We want to be as committed to him as he is to us. He wants us to praise him with our whole hearts, without any "minority report" within us to hinder that praise.

blameless, harmless, and without fault

psalm 86

*Do everything without complaining or arguing,
so that you may become blameless and pure, children of God without fault.*
Philippians 2:14–15

Is it necessary for Christians to sin every day in thought, word, and deed, or is it possible for the blood of Christ to set us free from the necessity of sin? The psalmist seems to have a vision of a united and perfect heart when he cries:

Teach me your way, O LORD;
I will walk in Your truth;
Unite my heart to fear Your name.
I will praise You, O Lord, my God, with all my heart,
And I will glorify Your name forevermore.

Psalm 86:11–12 NKJV

The psalmist wants to walk in the way of the Lord, yet he knows that a divided heart will make it impossible. He cries out for God to unite his heart, so that it is not a combination of two wills. When his heart is whole, he can praise God with all his heart, as he knows he ought to do. This is what God means when he says: "Love the Lord your God with all your heart and with all your soul and with all your mind and with all your strength" (Mark 12:30).

Christians know that God wants and deserves a heart united in praise to him. We differ, though, on whether this is possible for us on this side of heaven. Our world is so fallen, our sinfulness so deep, that sometimes it seems impossible to be inwardly whole before the Resurrection. Some admit that this is the cry of the devout heart, but that we cannot expect fulfillment until we enter the other world, where we can love him as we ought, with no temptations. But Paul had a different opinion:

Work out your salvation with fear and trembling, for it is God who works in you to will and to act according to his good purpose. Do everything without complaining or arguing, so that you may become blameless and pure, children of God without fault in a crooked and depraved generation, in which you shine like stars in the universe.

Philippians 2:12–15

changing times

mark 13

*Only hold on to what you have until I come. To him who overcomes
and does my will to the end, I will give authority over the nations.*
Revelation 2:25–26

It may not be obvious to all that times change, but for twenty-first-centu
Christians there should be no doubt. The collapse of mighty empires in th
last century should establish that fact. Sometimes revolution comes wi
volcanic suddenness; at other times, change occurs so slowly that it almo
goes unobserved.

Currently there is a changing of the guard in theological circles. Now
the time for those who believe in orthodox Christianity to stake our clai
and stand our ground. When I was young, I was applying to the universi
of my denomination in my home conference. My desire was to take o
graduate course on Plato. The graduate dean was uneasy. He feared that
might complete the course successfully and then want to pursue a gradua
degree there, and he assured me openly that they did not want to give the
degrees to evangelical Christians.

However, times have changed, and although those who fight again
orthodoxy may sound as shrill as ever, there is an echo-like character to the
protest that belies their arrogance. Their dominance of the center has end
as all other options besides Jesus begin to show their emptiness. It is time f
us to explore the mysteries of the biblical faith, to find its message for o
moment in time, and to proclaim it with all of the clarity and power G
can give us.

One thing should encourage us. The graveyard of human history h
many stones to mark the passing of various ideologies that have for a tim
enamored the human spirit. One marker is not there. It is the marker for hi
toric biblical faith, which lives and will continue to do so, for God's Wo
is eternal.

august 5

christian missions

matthew 28:19–20

"My name will be great among the nations . . ." says the LORD Almighty.
Malachi 1:11

The church has reversed the order of its priorities. Jesus said, "Go ye into all the world, and preach the gospel" (Mark 16:15 KJV). In Christian missions, we go out and minister primarily to the physical needs of people, and then if we get to put in a word about Christ, so much the better. Christ intended us to go because of a burning passion to tell the world about his goodness, his glory, and his love. Evangelism is to be the number-one motive for all Christian service. If the order is reversed and we minister to spiritual needs only after we have met the physical, the spiritual part is lost. The physical needs can never all be met. It is the love of Christ that must concern us primarily.

If you do not care about a man's soul, do not talk with moral superiority about the concerns of his body. You can only demonstrate that you care for the whole person by caring first for his soul. The perpetual temptation is to take care of other problems so we do not have to make ourselves vulnerable by asking, "Are you a Christian? Have you been reconciled to God? Do you know Jesus Christ?" It is only when Christ becomes supreme that we can minister to a person at every level of need.

if i had ten lives to live

isaiah 42:6–9

Therefore go and make disciples of all nations.
Matthew 28:19

A pure heart is an essential ingredient for accomplishing the mission that Jesus has given Christians, which is the redemption of the world. We are to surrender totally and completely to the One who gave himself for all people, and when we do, he uses us to accomplish his purpose: that all persons might know him.

I have found that most people are saved because of selfishness. We do not want to go to hell, and so we willingly accept the new birth as a protection against an eternity of judgment. However, the new birth does not accomplish in us all that needs to be done if we are going to be used by the Lord Jesus to save a world for him. After my conversion, I did not have any question about the fact that God had saved me, but I had many questions about whether I understood his call on my life in terms of the Cross. One indication that American Christians need a deeper work of grace is evident in the number of them who live lukewarm lives, without any passion for the lost, without any burning desire to spend and be spent for the salvation of the world.

Once I heard a missionary speaker say, "If I had ten lives to live, I would give them all to Jesus in missionary service." What an astounding comment! He had no interest in the world's values. No desire for wealth, power, prestige, or success. All that this man had and all that he was he desired to use to tell the world the wonderful news of Jesus Christ. That depth of passion and commitment to others only comes when our hearts and lives are totally surrendered. This is the only way the world will ever know Christ.

friendship: a gift from god

1 samuel 20

May the LORD be between you and me,
and between your descendants and my descendants, forever.
1 Samuel 20:42 NKJV

God bestows on his creatures the gift of friendship as an expression of his love. The relationships we possess are not something we create. They are gifts God gives as a symbol of his own nature, which is the communion love of three Persons. All the love that exists has its origin in God. If you lose God, your friendships will sooner or later disappear because the good will run out, and there will be nothing new to replenish the supply.

A tragedy occurs when we choose the old sinful ways because of the friendships we don't want to lose. Sooner or later those tainted friendships will be gone because sinners are separated from God. Scripture speaks of this great horror as the lostness of a soul. The lost soul is alone, separated from all, without the comforts that come from friendship, love, and companionship. God is the source of friendship, and in order for relationships to be pure, healthy, and continuous, he must be recognized as such.

Who would want to live in a world without the gifts of God? Those precious gifts will atrophy and disappear if we try to hold them separately from him.

i will bless the lord

psalm 34

I will extol the LORD at all times; his praise will always be on my lips.
Psalm 34:1

It is an exciting venture to take a particular psalm and guess what in the life of the author provoked him to write it. First, read the psalm carefully to see what it says, and then try to read between the lines, relating different aspects of that psalm to life. The question becomes, "What kind of human condition would cause a person to write a psalm such as this?"

One of things I have noticed is that if we study the book of Psalms long enough, we will find a psalm for every human situation. For moments of difficulty, moments of exultation, moments of tragedy, and moments of praise; there is a psalm that corresponds to each personal story.

Another thing I have learned about the Psalms is that many times the psalmists give their conclusion at the beginning, in contrast to the more familiar style in which a writer builds to a climax and then presents the conclusion. The psalmist will give the solution, and then the reader must work through the psalm to see what the situation was that brought the psalmist to that answer. Psalm 34 is one of the psalms whose conclusion is at the beginning, and what a conclusion it is! "I will extol the LORD at all times; his praise will always be on my lips." Wouldn't it be great if at the end of today that was the song on our lips? Let us make that conclusion the answer to our problem of today.

continual praise

psalm 34

I will extol the LORD at all times;
his praise will always be on my lips.
My soul will boast in the LORD.
Psalm 34:1–2

he writer of Psalm 34 possesses the attitude that a person should contin-
ally have toward God. The psalmist adores him, praising and blessing him
l the time. At some points he gets carried away with his praise of Yahweh.
it possible that we could come to the place where we bless the Lord at all
mes? Perhaps you immediately think of the circumstances surrounding
ur life and say to yourself, "If he only knew my situation, he would never
k such a thing from me. Life is too hard to be always praising God."

The psalmist apparently thought that blessing the Lord was not only a
ssibility but also a joy. "At all times" leaves nothing out. It means that
ere is not a moment when we think about ourselves. "Always" means that
ur adoration has no interruption; God's praise is always on our lips. Boast-
g in the Lord indicates that I find my delight in talking about him.

Abandon all the stereotypical images in the mind about praising God.
raise brings happiness because I focus on the perfection of God instead of
y own weaknesses. Continual praise means that whenever there is a lull in
y days or my activity, my thoughts immediately turn to God and are full
 praise of him. He becomes the beautiful thought that exists always at the
ack of my mind as the presence of a beloved is carried in the mind of a
ver. Christ is always present to me in the midst of all that I do; if I have a
oment, I think on him, and if other people are with me, I speak of my
eloved to them.

august 10

---

he is the key

psalm 34

I sought the LORD, and he answered me;
he delivered me from all my fears.
This poor man called, and the LORD heard him;
he saved him out of all his troubles.
Psalm 34:4, 6

Have you ever wished you could get rid of all your fears? I once thoug
that if I were a real Christian, I would have no fears. I also once thoug
that as I grew older, I would have fewer and fewer fears. I have found th
this is not true. What then should I do with my fears?

The psalmist sought the Lord, and the Lord delivered him out of all h
troubles. The Hebrew word for trouble, *megurah*, has in it the idea of drea
and terror. It is the kind of pressure that takes one's breath away. That
what fear does to us.

The psalmist found help. It is significant that he did not seek to get r
of his fears. Rather, he sought the Lord. When he found the Lord, he als
found that the Lord could break the smothering hold that fear could hav
on him. I love the realism of the Scripture. It never says that believers, youn
or old, will get to the place where they have no fears. It tells us, thoug
where to get relief. If we turn to the Lord, we will find that he can break th
constricting hold of our dreads and set us free to actually embrace them. H
does not want to save us *from* all of the storms of life. He wants to save u
in those storms, for it is there that we find we cannot afford to live withou
him. The storms can drive us to his breast. Then we can give thanks for th
storm because in it we found him.

available resources

2 kings 6:8 – 23

The angel of the LORD encamps around those who fear him,
and he delivers them . . .
The eyes of the LORD are on the righteous
and his ears are attentive to their cry.
Psalm 34:7, 15

One of the key differences between non-Christians and Christians is that in Christ many resources are available to the believer. Psalm 34 speaks of the angel who surrounds and delivers those who fear God. Remember the stories of Daniel and Elisha? When Daniel was in the lions' den and when the Syrian army surrounded Elisha's town, the angel of the Lord was with them, and he delivered both Daniel and Elisha without any harm. We need the eyes of faith to see that those who are on our side are greater than any enemy.

Another resource Christians have is the favor toward them that is found in the face of God. Do you know that God looks with favor on the ones who belong to him? He is waiting for his children to cry out to him so he can help them by delivering them and providing for them.

"The eyes of the LORD are on the righteous and his ears are attentive to their cry" (Ps. 34:15). Finally, when our heart is righteous before the Lord, we have a direct connection to the heart of God. It is this relationship that places us in a position in which God can deliver us. The angel of God, the favor of God, and the ears of God represent the advantages that are available to the Christian. Are we availing ourselves of these resources?

fear is never the last word

psalm 34

A righteous man may have many troubles,
but the LORD delivers him from them all.
Psalm 34:19

The words of Psalm 34 do not mean that whoever comes to Christ and lives for him will have no fear, no trouble, and no need. Instead, the psalmist says that the person who trusts in God will find that fear is never the last word. Trouble is never the final answer. Need is never the ultimate reality. When the story is over, the fear will be conquered; God will have delivered. The troubles will be mastered, and God will have freed the believer. The needs in life will have been met, and God will have provided for every need.

There would have been no impetus to write this song if the psalmist had never had any fear, any trouble, or any need. It is when you have been scared to death and God has brought you out of the trouble, that you can sing God's praise. When you are in a tight place and cry out to Yahweh, who is your only hope, you are in a situation ripe for a miracle. When you have no way to pay your bills and God provides, then you walk away while singing his praises.

The trouble itself turns our minds to Christ and gives him the opportunity to show himself good and powerful in our lives.

taste and see

psalm 34

Glorify the LORD with me;
let us exalt his name together . . .
Taste and see that the LORD is good.
Psalm 34:3, 8

In Psalm 34, the psalmist not only praises Yahweh constantly, he wants the reader to praise him too. It is bad enough when other people always praise God, but when they look at me and expect me to join in, I become tense and uneasy. The psalmist says, "Glorify the LORD with me; let us exalt his name together." He wants to turn the song that he has been singing into a duet. His praise is so exuberant that in the eighth verse of Psalm 34, he begins to talk about tasting the goodness of God. He challenges readers to taste for themselves how good God is, or how "sweet," as the Hebrew word is sometimes translated: "Why don't you take a taste of his goodness?"

When you and I begin to grasp how sweet God is, we will never want to stop singing his praises. We will not want our thoughts to rest on anything but him, and our hearts will overflow to tell others of his goodness.

Have we really tasted how good God is? Do we tell him how sweet it is to know him? Can other people see his sweetness in our lives? There is an exuberant joy overflowing from the psalmist's heart. Is there anything overflowing out of your heart today?

august 14

"get behind me!"

mark 8:27 – 38

But when Jesus turned and looked at his disciples, he rebuked Peter.
"Get behind me, Satan!" he said.
"You do not have in mind the things of God, but the things of men."
Mark 8:33

The first time that Jesus informed his disciples about the necessity of the Cross occurred immediately after Peter declared that Jesus was the Christ. After Peter made his declaration, Jesus began to explain to them what it meant to be the Christ, but Peter would not listen. He had his own vision of the Messiah's role, and there were no crosses involved. It is interesting when a mortal man wants to lecture God on what God's right and proper role should be. Can you imagine how many times old Peter blushed about that incident in the days that followed?

Jesus responded to Peter's rebuke with the strongest language he had ever used: "Get behind me, Satan!" I believe that as soon as Peter began to say the Cross was unnecessary, Jesus was reminded of another who wanted him to bypass the Cross by bowing his knee. Satan had said that the Cross was unnecessary; if Jesus would simply bow down to him, he would give to Jesus all the kingdoms of the world. Jesus turned to his beloved disciple as if to say, "You are the devil for me this moment. Get behind me!"

Sometimes the ways of God seem contrary to everything we believe ought to take place. But if we attempt to manipulate God into doing our will, we are on the side of all the forces of evil. God's will must be done God's way, and God's way always involves a Cross.

blindness

mark 8:13 – 26; 10:46 – 52

Once more Jesus put his hands on the man's eyes. Then his eyes were opened,
his sight was restored, and he saw everything clearly.
Mark 8:25

In Mark 8, Peter announces that Jesus is the Christ, and then he whirls round and tells Jesus what it means to be the Messiah. Because of his arrogance, Peter receives the sternest rebuke in all of Scripture for responding as he did when Jesus began to speak of the Cross. After this story there are several others that deal with the disciples' inability to understand Jesus' message to them about the Cross. This section is bracketed by two stories about blind men. Before the account of Peter's confession at Caesarea Philippi is a story about a blind man at Bethsaida. He is brought to Christ, and Christ touches him. Later, in chapter 10, is the story of blind Bartimaeus.

I think Mark is trying to convey some theology through the way he has arranged these stories. Jesus did not have any trouble healing the man from Bethsaida of his blindness, and he did not have any trouble healing Bartimaeus. What he had trouble curing was the blindness of his own disciples.

Jesus can cure physical blindness with a demonstration of power. All he has to do is speak, and it is done. But do you know what it takes to cure your blindness and my blindness? It is not power. It is divine self-sacrifice. There was no way we could be delivered and redeemed without Christ's suffering. It did not hurt him to speak the creation into existence, but in order for a single sinner, like you or me, to be forgiven, it was necessary for him to come off of his throne, give up his attributes, and humble himself to become one of his own creatures. He had to suffer and die. Not even God can forgive sin without self-sacrifice.

the purpose of the law

psalm 19

The law of the LORD is perfect, reviving the soul.
Psalm 19:7

Psalm 19 speaks about the Law of Yahweh, the statutes of Yahweh, the precepts of Yahweh, the commands of Yahweh, and the ordinances of Yahweh. The psalmist emphasizes Yahweh's revealed pattern for life. Interestingly, he uses the personal name for God because the Law is never in abstraction; it is based in the personal presence of God himself. This Law is God's instruction on how human beings are supposed to live. It is given to us so our lives will be compatible with his desires for us. At Sinai God claimed the Israelites for his own and revealed to them the way they could live with a holy God. He disclosed the Law to them as a sort of uncovering of his face, a baring of his heart to his people, so they would know how their lives were intended to reflect his life.

In Psalm 19 the psalmist says that these instructions from Yahweh to his people are more precious than gold, even the finest gold. The Word of God and the way of God contain a sweetness known to the author of this psalm, so he compares God's Word to honey, the sweetest thing he would have encountered. God's way is more valuable than gold, and his Word is sweeter than honey because they enable people to know who God is; they symbolize the presence of God in our midst. The reward for keeping God's instructions is the opportunity to know Yahweh himself.

god's greatest gift

daniel 6:10

Blessed are those who hunger and thirst for righteousness,
for they shall be satisfied.
Matthew 5:6 NASB

The best gift God can give to any person is a hunger for himself. There is nothing we can do to make ourselves hungry for God. All salvation is from God, but if we will give him the chance, he will instill a hunger within. If that hunger is fed, he will intensify it until it is the burning passion of our life. I never would have found Christ if I had not had in my heart a hunger for him. Across the years of my life, the most stabilizing thing has been the hunger for God. He has never taken away my desire for him. The older I become, the more intense the hunger for him is, and I find myself thanking him for it and asking that he would intensify my appetite for him even more. If we are hungry, he will fill our need, and the greater our appetite for him is, the more of himself he will give to us. That hunger is a promise of his presence.

If he is near you, cry out to him. If you sense his presence, call out to him. If you feel him close, reach out, because in that moment he is findable, and you ought to lunge for him. He will not take all your troubles away, but he will protect you in the middle of trouble. When the storms come, he will be your hiding place, and he will endure them with you. The storm will rage around you, but you will be in the middle of him, and his presence is safety. He will even enable you to sing in the midst of the storm. That hunger for him becomes the greatest gift that anyone can be given.

Hallelujah, I have found Him—
Whom my soul so long has craved!
Jesus satisfies my longings;
*Thro' His blood I am now saved.**

Clara Teare [Williams], "Satisfied," *Glorious Gospel Hymns* (Kansas City, Mo.: Nazarene Publishing House, 1931), no. 61.

make me a captive, lord

romans 6:15 – 23

So now present your members as slaves of righteousness for holiness.
Romans 6:19 NKJV

The hunger of the human heart for God is one of the most awesome realities in human history. To be human is to pray. On occasion movements arise of people who want to deny the validity of this aspect of human life, but the eventual decline of those movements provides evidence that to be human is to be religious.

We are not ultimately content, though, just to seek God or to know about him. Our hearts in their better moments long to be possessed by him. In fact, they long to be possessed totally by him. That is why the biblical message about holiness can never quite die. Perhaps the greatest evidence of the authenticity of the holiness witness is the cry of the believer's heart to be just that, holy. The hunger will express itself in every body of believers no matter what denomination they are or what theology they claim.

George Matheson was a Scottish Presbyterian, a clergyman who had been well trained at Glasgow University. He was a brilliant scholar and gifted preacher, and his heart hungered to be wholly the Lord's. He wearied of the resistance he found in his own heart to the whole will of God, and so he wrote:

> *Make me a captive, Lord, and then I shall be free.*
> *Force me to render up my sword, and I shall conqueror be.*
> *I sink in life's alarms when by myself I stand;*
> *Imprison me within thine arms, and strong shall be my hand.* *

---

*George Matheson, "Make Me a Captive, Lord," *The United Methodist Hymnal*, no. 421.

got what they wanted, lost what they needed

genesis 3

*After he drove the man out, he placed on the east side of
the Garden of Eden cherubim and a flaming sword
flashing back and forth to guard the way to the tree of life.*
Genesis 3:24

The Hebrew culture seems to have had an obsession with the subject of sin.
They emphasized it not because they were a morbid people, but because
they saw much more clearly than we see. From their perspective sin separated
the sinner from God. The Pentateuch teaches that sin destroys one's relationship with God. It was just that simple and that radical.

The Old Testament is very clear that when people sin, it cuts them off
from God. Adam and Eve in the Garden of Eden were told by God to eat
anything they wanted. Eden was intended for their pleasure and enjoyment;
there was only one tree of which they were instructed not to eat. The forbidden tree, the Tree of Knowledge of Good and Evil, was the snare Satan
used to cause humanity to enter into a world of sin. The rest of the story is
history. God banished Adam and Eve from the garden and from his presence. They got what they wanted, and they lost what they needed. This is
the story of sin.

You and I desperately need God. From him flows all that is good, true,
and right. All good has its origin in God himself, and it must be maintained
in him or else it will become defiled and corrupt. We do not have the option
to take the goods and separate them from his presence. There is no good
away from him.

his holiness, our protection

hebrews 12:12 – 29

Our God is a consuming fire.
Hebrews 12:29

Sin has a transcendent character. It rises above natural law and personally affronts the Holy One. God is holy, he is the Almighty, and the difference between right and wrong begins and ends in him. If you do not have the triune God, it is impossible to distinguish truth from error, and everything blurs together in a great gray mass of confusion. We tend to be frightened of the holiness of the Father, Son, and Spirit, but in reality his holy nature provides the security in the world. We want God to be angry when a child is hurt or when a person is discriminated against because we do not want evil to win. We are glad that God gets upset when rich people take advantage of poor people. God finds sin offensive because he is holy and he does what is right—always.

When the Holy Three-in-One comes into our midst and begins to make us like himself, we should be filled with ecstasy because his holiness offers the only chance for our crooked world to ever be made right. God's holiness is the dream of all the utopian philosophers, whether they acknowledge it or not. He is the One in whom there is no falsehood, no wrong, no pollution. He is the Just One: absolutely true, completely good, and always right.

august 21

responsible for sin

james 1:12–15

She took of its fruit and ate.
Genesis 3:6 NKJV

One crucial difference between biblical religion and other religions of the world concerns the nature of evil. Evil in Scripture is not a co-eternal principle with good. Ultimately only God is good, and evil is simply the turning away from God. Evil, in Scripture, is not an eternal, metaphysical principle; it is a moral choice made by beings, human and angelic. The significance of this for individuals is that it forces us to be responsible for our own evil.

It is not necessary to have either Satan or the demonic to account for human evil. In fact, even the serpent was not necessary in the Garden of Eden for Eve to sin (Gen. 3). Eve and Adam sinned because of their own moral choices, and God refused to let Eve blame the serpent. The only power the serpent had was the power of allurement; it enticed her to misuse her freedom in the way the snake had misused its own freedom.

We have no excuse for the evil in us, no one on whom we can blame our sin. There is no evil principle that makes sin necessary; we simply are free to sin. Satan may entice us to sin, but he is a finite creature like we are. Ultimately, he will be subject to the same righteous judgment to which we will be subject. We are free to surrender to him, but he has no control over us that we do not give to him. We must take responsibility for our sin and never play the victim.

sin is not done with the doing

Revelation 20:11 – 15

But if you fail to do this, you will be sinning against the LORD;
and you may be sure that your sin will find you out.
Numbers 32:23

It is a common thought in the minds of most Christians that willful sin does not really matter because God forgives us after the deed is done, when we ask him for that forgiveness. What we tend to forget is the omniscience and the omnipresence of God. God knows every thought of our heart, every imagination allowed to flit through our mind, and every action completed in secrecy.

Even more alarming to consider is that God is omnipresent. He is actually present every time a sin is committed. He is between the two adulterers. He is present when a theft occurs, whether of goods, reputations, or relationships; whether by a common criminal, a preacher, or a politician. Nothing ever slips by without his knowledge and without his presence.

There is another, perhaps more serious aspect of the Holy One that we must consider. God is eternal. He is the beginning and the end of our lives. He is the one who gives each person a beginning, and he is going to be the end of every life. No one will finally escape a confrontation with him.

Human delusions about the insignificance of sin must be destroyed, for if sin is a problem to God and God is eternal, then that tiny sin committed in secret is not done with the doing. You can attempt to start a new day fresh, but yesterday's sin will be there just as much as if you were committing it that moment. Sin is only destroyed through self-giving love.

time does not remove sin

psalm 51

Wash away all my iniquity
and cleanse me from my sin.
For I know my transgressions,
and my sin is always before me.
Against you, you only, have I sinned.
Psalm 51:2–4

Time does not erase our moral transgressions. They are offensive to God, and time does not take them away. They transcend time because they are part of an eternal, infinite relationship. For a crime I commit against the state, I can pay my dues, and when I have paid for my crime, it dwells only in the past. I cannot be prosecuted for a crime for which I have already paid. This is not true with a sin in your relationship with God. Time does not remove it, hide it, or fade it.

A lady from my congregation called me one morning. Her tone was so flippant on the phone that I was insulted, and I started to hang up. Then I realized her flippancy was the result of an internal panic. In five minutes, I was at her house, asking her what was wrong. She sat in her living room and said, "It was eighteen years ago, and I thought it was all over and forgotten. No one was hurt, really; it was just something that I did wrong, and I have lived with it. I thought I could forget it, but since I have been attending your lousy Bible study, I cannot stop thinking about it. It is as real as if I had done it last night. Is there any hope for me? I feel that I am the most defiled person on the face of the earth."

The only place we can discover that we are sinners is in God's presence. We need to get into his presence so he can make us bring to our attention those defiling things that we have sought to forget.

triumphal procession

isaiah 50:4 – 9

*Thanks be to God, who always leads us in triumphal procession in Christ
and through us spreads everywhere the fragrance of the knowledge of him.*
2 Corinthians 2:14

The fragrance of the knowledge of Christ is spread in the earth through us.
To some it will be an aroma unto salvation; to others it will be an aroma that
leads to death because they will reject him. Who is equal to the task of spreading that knowledge? Paul tells us how to meet such a task: "But thanks be to
God, who always leads us in triumphal procession in Christ and through us
spreads everywhere the fragrance of the knowledge of him." Many scholars
agree that Paul mixed his metaphors: the first half of the verse seems to deal
with the Resurrection (the triumphal procession), and the second half seems
to deal with the Cross (fragrance comes only through crushing).

However, one day I found a paperback book on this passage of Scripture. It was a doctoral dissertation, and the scholar had researched this verse
and studied the Greek word *thriambeuo*, which is translated "to lead in triumphal procession." He found that it was an old Etruscan word, and the
Etruscans had a very different triumphal procession from the Roman one
that was led by the emperor. The king who led the Etruscan triumphal procession through the city was the captured, defeated king. He was spit upon
and beaten, and at the end he was sacrificed to the Etruscan gods who sup-
posedly had given the victory. The conquering king brought up the rear of
the procession. So Paul had not mixed his metaphors. He was picturing
Christ not as the conquering King, but as the conquered King, the One who
was to be the sacrifice.

If Christ leads the procession, then he leads us to an altar of self-sacrifice,
the Cross. It is a triumphal procession because out of the sacrifice of self the
fragrance of the gospel comes.

consequences of sin

matthew 18:6 – 14

If your hand or your foot causes you to sin, cut it off and throw it away.
It is better for you to enter life maimed or crippled than to have
two hands or two feet and be thrown into eternal fire.
Matthew 18:8

There are two serious results of sin. First, sin separates the child from the Father, and the Father is the Source of life. Sin infects a person remarkably like a virus. One day we can be clean and healthy, and the next day we can have death in our body and not even realize that it is there. Suddenly we begin to find that life is more trying and more taxing, and sometimes the virus leads to death. Sin does not just head us to the cemetery; it heads us for something infinitely worse, an eternity of separation from God, who is Life, Light, and Love. We must resist the temptation to minimize or rationalize the deadliness of sin.

Second, once we commit a sin, we have no capacity or ability to take that sin out of existence. It exists defiantly in the face of all our attempts to cover it or remove it. We cannot just turn over a new leaf and wipe the sin out of our life by willful choice. Sin is a treachery, and there is absolutely nothing we can do to repair the break we have made. The only hope for us is to allow God to do what only he can do. He alone cleanses a person's heart. He alone restores broken relationships. He alone is the answer to our sin.

If you are alienated from him, you are dying. If you are holding on to your sin, you are drowning in a sea of hopelessness. Turn to the One who is Light, who is Life, who is your Father.

language for sin

psalm 32

Blessed is he whose transgressions are forgiven,
whose sins are covered.
Blessed is the man whose sin the LORD does not count against him
and in whose spirit is no deceit.
Psalm 32:1–2

The Hebrew language is rich in vocabulary for moral realities, and particularly for describing sin. Interestingly, neither English nor Greek contains so many words to talk about the reality of sin. Hebrew has a word for willful transgression, when a person knows the Law and knows not to break it, yet breaks it anyway. It has another word for a sin when one sees what one is supposed to do and attempts to do it, but fails, or falls short. A third word describes the perverseness of the human heart. We know what is right, but there is something inside of us that wants to do the opposite. Finally, there is a word that is used for deceit, guile, or duplicity—when one wears a face that is not true to who one really is.

The psalmist says the person is blessed who is clean on all of these accounts. If a person reaches the place where trespasses are removed, shortcomings covered, perverseness and iniquity cleansed, and duplicity gone, that person is the model for other men and women. That person should be the standard—the one who on all accounts is clean of sin.

Does your understanding of sin include all that the Scripture includes? Is there any rebellion in your heart? Any shortcoming? Any perverseness? Any deceit? If there is, you need to let Christ cleanse your heart.

honest with god

psalm 32

*Then I acknowledged my sin to you
and did not cover up my iniquity.
I said, "I will confess my transgressions to the LORD"
and you forgave the guilt of my sin.*
Psalm 32:5

Only God can bring us to the place where we are free from sin. He is the only answer to the problem in every human heart. Since that is true, one would think that we would run to him. If he is the only one who can cure our problem, why do we hesitate to beat the walls down to get to him so he can cleanse, forgive, and save us?

The writer of Psalm 32 knew that he had sinned against God, and yet he decided to keep silent. As a consequence of that silence, his life deteriorated. His bones grew old and miserable, and there was a roaring noise inside his soul. That roaring tumult inside the human soul is the burden of guilt that saps our very life. Sin produces guilt, and guilt introduces static inside our heart and mind. It makes us so confused that we are distressed and disintegrating. Sin also blinds us to our true spiritual state by deceitfully whispering that we are not as bad as we, in our worst moments, imagine we might be. Sin dares us to try to take control of our own lives. In truth, we are a million times worse than we know, and our attempts to control our lives destroy us and the ones we love.

The psalmist says that eventually he confessed his sin to God. His confession is this: "You know my sins, my shortcomings, the perverseness of my heart, the games I have played with you. Now here I am." The astounding thing is that God forgave him when he was honest.

Is your soul so full of static produced by sin that you cannot even hear God calling or feel him nudging you to repentance? If so, confess your sin to him.

his witness to himself

john 18:1 – 14

And he touched the man's ear and healed him.
Luke 22:51

Malchus, the servant of the high priest Caiaphas, was the Father's last love note to Caiaphas. Malchus was the servant whose ear Peter sliced off during Jesus' arrest. In his gracious mercy Jesus restored Malchus's ear, and Malchus's witness to Caiaphas of that event was the high priest's last chance for repentance. It was God's final witness to him: he put someone right in Caiaphas's court who had been touched by the loving hand of Jesus. Oh, the unending mercy of God! If a person is lost, it will be in spite of himself and in spite of the evidence that God stacks up in his life. I am confident that Caiaphas did not employ Malchus for long after this incident of healing. I imagine that the sight of Malchus's ear made Caiaphas uneasy and nervous.

When we choose not to obey and do not act on the witness God gives to us, sooner or later we will banish that witness from our lives because we cannot tolerate its suggestive presence. The love of God continues to point to him in all areas of life, even in the lives of the most hardened unbelievers, but some of us refuse to see or hear it.

I remember being a student at a Jewish university. One day as I was sitting in the library, I heard some people singing. As my mind tried to absorb their music, I heard the line, "King of kings and Lord of lords, / And he shall reign forever and ever." Immediately, I thought, *It can't be true. I cannot be hearing Handel's* Messiah *in this Jewish university.* But I was. A group of absolutely enraptured students were listening to the "Hallelujah Chorus" from one of the greatest musical witnesses ever written to Christ.

Are you missing the witnesses to Christ that he has purposely placed all throughout your life? He witnesses not just to his own reality, but also to his love, his beauty, his truth, his goodness, his justice, and his magnificence. Are you listening and watching for the witness?

can man seize god?

john 18:1–14

*Then the detachment of soldiers with its commander and the Jewish
officials arrested Jesus. They bound him and brought him first to Annas.
John 18:12–13*

On the night of Jesus' arrest, what was it that bound the Lord to those
Roman soldiers? Surely the ropes and cords were not strong enough to hold
the Creator of the universe. If Sampson could break the ropes of the
Philistines, certainly the Son of God could do the same. No, Christ was not
bound by the soldiers; he was bound by his own compassionate, divine, loving heart that caused him to give himself to them. It was Christ's love for you
and me that caused him to go with those soldiers who eventually nailed his
body to the cross.

Can man seize God? Never! God gave himself away that night. Jesus
was in perfect control all throughout his arrest, trial, and crucifixion.

God will never let you get into a situation in which he is not in perfect
control. When you find yourself in circumstances that seem to be full of
chaos and confusion, look to Christ. If you belong to him, you will find
him there in perfect control of your situation.

It was Jesus, the One in whom all things exist, who sustained the Roman
soldier's life while he roughly placed the Son of God on the cross, and it was
Jesus who gave that soldier the physical strength to drive the spikes into his
hands.

august 30

ishmael and isaac

genesis 17:15–22

We are not children of the slave woman, but of the free woman.
Galatians 4:31

Have you ever stopped to notice that Abraham received the fulfillment of a God's promises through his son Ishmael? The promises of descendants, nations, and land all came through Ishmael's children. Ishmael had twelve sons, each son was a prince, and each son became a nation. There was only one thing Isaac gave to the world that Ishmael could not: the Christ. Jesus, the One who would bring redemption to the world, is the descendant of Isaac.

What made the difference between the two sons of Abraham? Ishmael represents humans working in their own strength. The results look productive, but there is no salvation in them, and ultimately they create violence and destruction. Isaac displays the action of God in human life, and the hope of the world is being fulfilled when we allow God to work through our lives. Ishmael is a result of an individual forming his own character, and Isaac is a result of a person allowing God to put his own character in the human heart. We are eternally barren if we attempt to work in our own way.

Have we slipped from the high ground where we let Christ form his character in us, down to the marshy lowlands where we attempt to define our own character? If Christ works in my life, then my focus will rest on him, and I will be open to him. If I am the only one at work in my life, my attention will be completely absorbed in myself, and that is always destructive.

Is your life an occasion for you or an occasion for him? In your answer to that question dwells the difference between light and darkness, between life and death, between God and you.

freedom to die

acts 6:8 – 7:60

While they were stoning him, Stephen prayed, "Lord Jesus,
receive my spirit." Then he fell on his knees and cried out,
"Lord, do not hold this sin against them."
When he had said this, he fell asleep.
Acts 7:59–60

Josepf Tson, one of the heroes of the faith during the Communist reign in Romania, told me a story about facing the secret police during an interrogation. They were trying to intimidate and destroy him. After a particularly grueling session, he fell on his face before God in desperation and said, "God, they are destroying me. I cannot take any more."

Josepf told me, "I think I heard the voice of God saying to me, 'Josepf, Get up! Who are the secret police compared to the One who sits on the throne of the universe?'"

Josepf got up and returned to the interrogation with a new sense of fear, but it was not fear of his persecutors. Rather, it was a reverence for and holy fear of God himself. One day the chief interrogator said to him, "Josepf, you are stupid, and you will never learn. I guess the only thing we can do is just kill you."

Josepf replied, "I understand, sir. That is your ultimate weapon, and when all else has failed, you can kill me. But sir, when you use your ultimate weapon, I will be able to use my ultimate weapon."

"What is your ultimate weapon?" demanded the chief mockingly.

"Well, you see, your ultimate weapon is to kill me, and my ultimate weapon is to die. When I die, I will be better off than I was before because every sermon I have preached will be sprinkled with my blood."

How do you get to the place of absolute freedom, where Jesus can do with you whatever he wills? Recognize that the One who holds you in the palm of his hand is greater than any force in the world. When he matters more to you than any other thing, even life itself, then you are free.

let not your heart be troubled

ezekiel 36:24–29

*Will you really lay down your life for me? I tell you the truth,
before the rooster crows, you will disown me three times!
Do not let your hearts be troubled. Trust in God; trust also in me.*
John 13:38–14:1

Perhaps two of the most amazing verses in all of Scripture are John 13:38 and 14:1. Have you ever put these verses together? The chapter division obscures a hidden gem of truth. I never even dreamed that the verse acknowledging Peter's failure and sin would be followed by one of deepest comfort. Jesus knew the desire of Peter's heart. He knew Peter did not want to deny him, that Peter dreamed of being a hero and dying for the Messiah. But Jesus also recognized that as much as Peter wanted to do what was right, he would not. His response to Peter's failure was comfort. He was going to send One to Peter who would enable him to do what he longed to do, to be faithful. The Holy Spirit would make Peter all he wanted to be.

All the valor and heroic spirit in the world will not equal the Spirit of God in a person's life. Jesus knows your heart and your willingness to accept the Spirit, and he also sees your failures. He knows whether you are hungry for him, and if you are, he says, "Let not your heart be troubled. Believe in me. I will set you free so you can follow me with all your heart, all your soul, all your mind, and all your strength. I will set you free to be faithful."

The promise in Ezekiel 36:27 holds true: "And I will put My Spirit within you and cause you to walk in My statutes, and you will be careful to observe My ordinances" (NASB). Those are not commands to obey; they are promises that we will obey when we are filled with the Holy Spirit.

mark of the sanctified heart

isaiah 53

Yet He Himself bore the sin of many,
And interceded for the transgressors.
Isaiah 53:12 NASB

I have come to believe that the mark of the truly sanctified heart is that it cares more about another's salvation than it does about its own well-being. It is not the words you say or the deeds you do that really matter. It is whether deep down in your spirit you have taken the way of the Cross and come to the place where you care about what Jesus cares about and are willing to give up everything so people will be redeemed.

What do you do for your entertainment? How do you spend your free time? Is your constant concern the welfare of the world? If you get caught up in success, or if you get bogged down in defeat and forget to care about others, you have become sterile. You have walked away from the Spirit of Christ.

The key to every person lies in someone else. You are spiritually responsible for some other person or persons, and your obedience to the Lord Jesus will enable those people to obey. If you want your neighbor to come to know Christ, you have to start allowing Christ to work in your own life so that out of your clean heart he can draw your neighbor to himself. I do not believe that anyone's salvation starts in himself or herself. It began in the heart of the Father, and it should be continued in the hearts of those who love the Lord Jesus. The Father cared more about us than he did about himself, and so he gave us the best thing he had. The Son cared about us more than he did about himself, and so he died for our redemption. When we care more about the people around us than we do about ourselves, the Holy Spirit will be free to win the world for Christ.

the lord is your keeper

psalm 121

My help comes from the LORD,
the Maker of heaven and earth . . .
The LORD watches over you.
Psalm 121:2, 5

There are three words of promise for the believer in Psalm 121. First, God transcends and reigns over our circumstances: "He will not let your foot slip" (Ps. 121:3). Circumstances and forces over which we have little control surround you and me, but God is caught in none of these and can protect us in the midst of them. The person who knows and trusts God does not have to fear the insecurities and uncertainties that dog the path of the unbeliever.

Second, God is not caught in the exigencies of time: "He who watches over you will not slumber" (Ps. 121:3). He is the eternal One, so nothing wearies him. He neither slumbers nor sleeps. He has no need for sleep. There is no deficiency in him.

Finally, Yahweh has his eye on his people: "The sun will not harm you by day, nor the moon by night" (Ps. 121:6). Yahweh watches over them to protect them from anything that would hurt, from any evil. He is committed to his people and to their welfare. The forces and factors that others fear need not bother those who trust in Yahweh. The gods whom others seek to appease hold no threat. God created and controls everything. He will be our shade of protection.

Are you in a situation where you need Yahweh to keep your foot from slipping? Do you need him to guard you while you sleep? Do you need him to keep you from all evil? He is the God who reigns over circumstances, over time, and even over evil forces. It is safe to rest in his presence.

one for three

john 16:7–15

He will bring glory to me by taking from what is mine and making
it known to you. All that belongs to the Father is mine. That is why
I said the Spirit will take from what is mine and make it known to you.
John 16:14–15

The Spirit is the gift of the Father to the world through his Son. The Father sent the Son as his gift to a lost world, and now the Father and Son send the Spirit to finish the work of redemption. The Spirit is the divine gift to us. As Christ came from the Father and is of the same nature as the Father, so now the Holy Spirit comes from the Father and Son and is of the same nature as they. Jesus has been Immanuel, "God with us"; now the Holy Spirit will be God in us.

Jesus said that to receive him was to receive the Father, and to reject him was to lose the Father. Now Jesus says that if the disciples receive the Spirit, they will have all three persons of the Trinity, the Father, the Son, and the Holy Spirit, because they are Three in One. The relationship between the Father, the Son, and the Spirit is a picture of loving communication and common purpose.

Those of us who live after Pentecost have an amazing privilege and opportunity. It is possible for us to be in more intimate fellowship with the triune God, through the indwelling of the Spirit, than were the twelve disciples when Jesus dwelt among them. As Christians, we need to be living up to our privilege, dwelling in the place of intimacy and tender fellowship with the Spirit of Jesus.

reality of communion

matthew 26:26 – 30

Take and eat; this is my body.
Matthew 26:26

It has always awed and distressed me how much more serious we are abou
the symbols of communion than we are about its reality. No one ever mind
going to receive the symbols, but when one is invited to partake of the rea
ity, hesitancy and panic enter the human heart. Some people come wit
delight to take a wafer and the cup, but hastily back away from acceptir
Christ's life, which is freely offered.

The church is the body of Christ, and if God's world is going to b
reached with the gospel, it will be through his body. Remember that Chris
body was broken so you and I could be saved, and we will have to be bro
ken if others are to be reached. We have the privilege of sharing in Chris
sufferings for the sake of other people. God could not exempt even himse
from suffering because the only saving force in all existence is a life sacr
ficed in love, surrendered to something outside of, and bigger than, itsel
Jesus surrendered himself to the Father in death. What Christ has to off
to me and to you today is his life. We can live a life like the Lord Jesus whe
we are willing to let down barriers that we use to shield and protect ou
selves from pain. We must let Christ's life possess us so that we can be th
temple of Christ and not the temple of self-interest.

When we partake of communion, we must recognize that by our actio
we accept Christ's sacrifice and say to the Father, "Break me as you wil
Spend me as you spent Jesus."

If we will let God break us and spend us and possess us, we will live i
fellowship with Christ, and our lives will be fruitful.

receive the holy spirit

joel 2:28 – 32

He breathed on them and said, "Receive the Holy Spirit."
John 20:22

On the evening of the day of Jesus' resurrection the disciples are together in the upper room when suddenly Jesus appears in their midst. The most important conversation of the risen Christ with his followers occurs during his first post-resurrection encounter.

Jesus greets his disciples and shows them his resurrection body, which bears the marks of his passion. Then he commissions his church by giving them the same charge that the Father has given to him. "As the Father has sent me, I am sending you" (John 20:21). This concept of sentness is one that Jesus has presented earlier, during his talks about his own mission. Now he will return to the Father, and the disciples must become the "sent ones." He is entrusting his work to them. Finally he simply says, "Receive the Holy Spirit" (John 20:22).

John the Apostle must be remembering the baptism of Jesus by John the Baptist. As Jesus came out of the water to begin his redemptive work, the Spirit descended upon him. That anointing identified him as the Messiah. For three years the Spirit has been the dynamic force in Christ's ministry, and now Jesus sends his friends to complete his mission. If they are to do his work, they need his Spirit. So Jesus says that they too must receive the Holy Spirit. The parallel for our lives and ministries is clear.

the witness of the spirit

john 16:7 – 11

The Holy Spirit also testifies to us.
Hebrews 10:15

I had an opportunity to witness to a guy sitting beside me on an airplane. At the end of our flight he looked over at me and said, "Do you believe this conversation is an accident?"

I laughed. "No, I don't think this is an accident because I'm not supposed to be on this plane."

He laughed too and said, "That's funny because neither am I. When I bought my ticket, they told me it was a nonstop flight to Mexico City, and when I got on I found out that it makes two stops, one in Houston and one in San Antonio. At first I was as mad as I could be, but I don't believe this conversation is an accident either."

Right at that point the wheels of our plane hit the landing strip, and I had an overwhelming feeling of remorse. I didn't want to let him go; I was just getting to the place where I could really tell him about the Lord Jesus. Then something or someone said to me, "I am doing very well with him on my own."

I looked up in gratitude and said, "Yes, you are." I went on my way praying for the man and extremely thankful that he was in the hands of the One whom we cannot see.

The Holy Spirit has already prepared all the people to whom we witness, and he will use our witness long after the conversation is over. Christ witnesses about himself in every human heart. It is never because of you and me that people find Christ; it is only because of the Spirit of Jesus.

resurrection visits

john 20–21

So the last will be first, and the first will be last.
For many are invited, but few are chosen.
Matthew 20:16; 22:14

Sometimes I wish I could have been in charge of planning Jesus' post-resurrection visits, although I fear that I would have gone about it differently from the way the Father planned it. I would have taken Jesus to see Pontius Pilate. (Can't you see Pilate's mouth falling open in horror?) It would have been even more fun to visit Caiaphas and Herod and watch their faces turn red with anger and shock. For some reason, Jesus never paid any attention to those guys after his resurrection; it was as if they were inconsequential. The future is never in the world's systems of power.

Instead, Jesus went to find Mary Magdalene and then his disciples. He went to see the people who loved him. Jesus never concerned himself with impressing the leaders of society. He knew who the people were who would impact the world in the next two thousand years. It was Mary Magdalene, Peter, John, and the other disciples—those who had been with him.

It was not their devotion to Jesus that made them influential people; it was his presence in their lives. The future is never where the world thinks it is. The only thing that will make your life count for anything lasting and significant is inviting Christ's presence into your life. When he enters, he will bring with him salvation from sin; deliverance from the tyranny of selfishness; and freedom from defilement, sterility, and pride. He can bring us to the place where Mary Magdalene was, where Jesus is our only treasure.

september 9

ridiculous instruments

acts 2 – 3

Then Peter said, "Silver or gold I do not have, but what I have I give you.
In the name of Jesus Christ of Nazareth, walk."
Acts 3:6

Have you ever attempted to do something heroic for Christ in your own strength? Have you ever been like Peter on the night of Jesus' arrest, when he clipped off the servant's ear in an attempt to save Jesus? Can you imagine how stupid Peter felt about that night? Have you felt humiliated over your own attempt to help God?

Remember that it was this man, Peter, who acted in his own strength, making a fool of himself, who became the hero of the book of Acts. Isn't that a beautiful thought? When we act in our flesh, we are as ridiculous as Peter was that night, but if we continue to follow Christ, he will bring us to our own Pentecost, where the Spirit of Jesus comes and cleanses us and fills us with his character and power. Then the Father can take ridiculous instruments like you and me and make us instruments for his glory and for the furtherance of the gospel. What if Peter had given up in humiliation? History would have been much poorer, and Jesus' patient work with Peter would have been lost.

Are you living in a place where you know that you are working for God in the flesh? If you are, ask Jesus for his Pentecost. Ask him for his Spirit. Do not give up or let up until the Spirit fills you completely. He always comes to those who ask.

september 10

sacred by association

psalm 84

*My soul yearns, even faints,
for the courts of the LORD;
my heart and my flesh cry out
for the living God.
Psalm 84:2*

At certain moments in history the curtain between this world and the next one parts. A person is confronted with God. If God comes in grace, the glory is so great that the person's life is changed forever. Life is transformed, and all is different. One has only to think of Abraham, Moses, Peter, John, or Paul of Tarsus. What we know as holy history has resulted from such moments. All significant redemptive movements begin when God breaks through and speaks, and God desires to break through to every person. He wants to reveal himself to us.

It is quite obvious that this is what happened to the psalmist who gave us Psalm 84. God had come to him, and he could neither forget the experience nor get away from the impact it had on all areas of his life. It transformed all his relationships, and it left a hallowing touch on his view of places, people, and times. He met the Holy One, and as a consequence a whole succession of things in his life became sacred by association.

Have you had an encounter with the living God such that your life is transformed in every area? If you have not, he is waiting to meet you. Will you ask him to come and sanctify a moment of time by a personal encounter with his presence?

secrets in the dark

psalm 139

*If I say, "Surely the darkness will hide me
and the light become night around me,"
even the darkness will not be dark to you;
the night will shine like the day,
for darkness is as light to you.*
Psalm 139:11–12

I had a dear friend who had been a Methodist minister's wife. Her husband had died early, and she had become a Christian after he died. She was a soul winner and a passionate lover of Jesus. One day I heard that she was losing her eyesight, so I made a trip to see her. I had been in her apartment for about seven minutes before she shocked me with a question. "Dennis, you came to comfort me, didn't you?"

She asked the question like it was an accusation, and I knew I was guilty, so I said, "Yes, I did."

She looked at me and said, "Dennis, would you deprive me of the privilege of walking with Christ in the dark? There are secrets I can learn in the dark that I could never learn in the light."

Not too long after our conversation, she regained her sight, and then she lost it totally. But when she walked into total darkness, she walked into darkness while embracing it because she did not walk alone.

God gives us songs in the midst of our trials and teaches us lessons in the storm that we could never learn in the sunshine. If you have the eternal God with you, you have the source of all goodness, and if you have the fountainhead of all goodness with you, what else do you need?

seek first the kingdom

james 2:14 – 16

But seek first his kingdom and his righteousness,
and all these things will be given to you as well.
Matthew 6:33

If you do not believe that God is the Creator, Sustainer, and Lord, you will have trouble trusting him enough to obey him when it comes to taking risks that jeopardize your comfort, your family, or your life. I don't think we truly believe until we have risked greatly and God has worked for us. Faith that we maintain while sitting in a chair without any danger or vulnerability is not biblical faith at all. Biblical faith emerges when we take a risk and realize that if we do not receive divine help, we will be embarrassed.

Dr. E. A. Seamands was a missionary in India. One day a Hindu merchant who had decided to become a Christian came to him and told him that he wanted to be baptized. "Good," said Dr. Seamands. "We will baptize you in the pool in front of your business on market day."

The Hindu said, "If you do that, everybody in the countryside will know that I have become a Christian. What will that do to my business?"

"You don't want to hide the fact that you have become a Christian, do you? The best thing in the world is to let everybody know it all at once. It is much less painful that way." So the Hindu merchant, with fear and trembling, was baptized that day in front of his business establishment.

The only way you are going to take a risk is if you believe that God is the Creator, Sustainer, and Lord. Can you truly say, "Whether you take care of me or not, I am going to do what you ask"?

september 13

sent to the cross

john 19:17–30

Jesus came and stood among them and said, "Peace be with you!"
After he said this, he showed them his hands and side.
John 20:19–20

Have you ever connected Jesus' phrase "As the Father has sent me, I am sending you" (John 20:21) with the Cross? Peter and the disciples did not want to hear about the Cross and neither does the church in our day, particularly about the Cross for us. Christ came in the Resurrection to show his wounds and his scars, and I wonder if on Judgment Day we will be required to show him *our* scars. He will not care about our trophies and victories; he will care about the wounds and scars we have received because of him. Those are the cords that will bind us to him.

We naturally tend to follow the disciples' lead, refusing to talk about or attempt to understand the Cross, wanting instead to talk about position and power. Perhaps we will blush at our own titles on that Last Day when he asks to see our battle wounds. Jesus says to us, "As the Father sent Me, I also send you." Where is he sending us? To the Cross.

What the disciples did not understand, and what we do not understand, is that the only way a world can be redeemed is through self-sacrifice. Hear Amy Carmichael's poem:

> *Hast thou no scar? No hidden scar in foot or side or hand?*
> *I hear thee sung as mighty in the land.*
> *I hear them hail thy bright, ascendant star*
> *Hast thou no scar?*
> *Can he have traveled far who has no wound or scar?**

---

*Amy W. Carmichael, "No Scar?" *Mountain Breezes: The Collected Poems of Amy Carmichael* (Fort Washington, Pa.: Christian Literature Crusade, 1999), 173.

i am sending you

philippians 2:12 – 18

Again Jesus said, "Peace be with you!
As the Father has sent me, I am sending you."
John 20:21

The Good Shepherd commands his sheep to follow him! Following Christ is an all-engaging commitment of one's life and heart. Jesus says that this is how it must be; he must be the leader and controller of one's life. Therefore, we must have holy hearts. The human desire is to manage our own lives; we are hesitant to release control because we might face unexpected demands or unpleasantness. But we are never safe until we have taken our hands off the control knob and have forfeited our right to ourselves, so that Jesus is in full control.

If Jesus gains the right to spend us the way he pleases, there will be miracles in our lives. Just as he broke the five loaves and two fish, providing food to the multitude, so there will be fruit in our own lives. We will live as Jesus, who gave up his life for his sheep.

For every person there comes a day when Jesus says, "Follow me." Have you come to the place where you are ready to be a living sacrifice? Let Christ fill you, use you, and pour you out in the way he pleases. Let Jesus give you to whom he will. Take your hands off your life, and let him put his hands on your life.

There is a world out there. Jesus has shown us the way to win it: his Father sent him to lay down his life. Now he is sending you.

the sent ones

hebrews 11:13 – 16

As you sent me into the world, I have sent them into the world.
John 17:18

Much of the church has lost its evangelistic thrust and a substantial chunk of its missionary passion, yet there remain billions of people across the world and millions in our own land who do not know Christ. It must be astounding to God that we carry on the ordinary business of life as if we were not sent ones. But the One whom we claim to follow is the One who carries in his body the marks of his total surrender—his willingness to give all that he is and all that he has for one purpose: the redemption of his Father's world.

Jesus Christ is the one who has said to us, "As the Father has sent me, I am sending you" (John 20:21). So we are the sent ones, but we have either not heard or chosen not to understand. If we had understood our mission, the world would be a different place.

Can you draw a line between your position as a Christian and your passion for what Christ sent Christians to do? Our position and our witness will ultimately be measured against the task that he has sent us to accomplish. The task before us is impossible, and therefore daunting, unless our lives are given in total surrender and filled with the Spirit of the One who has called us. We can have a nice position and a respectable reputation as a Christian and yet never be available to the Christ whose name we bear. We will be judged accordingly.

purity and revival

matthew 5:27–32

*Speak to the Israelites and say to them: "I am the LORD your God.
You must not do as they do in Egypt, where you used to live,
and you must not do as they do in the land of Canaan,
where I am bringing you. Do not follow their practices."*
Leviticus 18:2–3

There is an important link between our purity in physical relationships and our vitality in spiritual relationships. It is quite clear biblically that God's purposes for us are tied up with our sexuality. He can only accomplish his purposes in human history, in human society, and in human lives if his followers use their sexuality according to his design and plan. I have noticed a startling truth in the history of the church: the Holy Spirit has a particular affinity for people who are very careful in the sexual aspect of their lives. You will have a difficult time finding an outpouring of the Holy Spirit among people where there is substantial sexual laxity.

For some reason, purity and revival are linked inseparably together; God seems to have a particular sensitivity for protecting his creation in this way. Perhaps human sexuality is especially important to God because it is a prime symbol of the depth of intimacy that God desires with each human person. God uses most effectively those individuals who are committed to personal holiness and purity, and he seems to have a special blessing for groups who are committed to corporate holiness and purity. In our day, when such holy behavior is an anomaly, we need to set our course by his standards and not by the standards of the world.

Whether you are married or single, young or old, are the thoughts, imaginations, and actions of your heart as pure as Jesus would have them be? If there is any impurity in you, you can expect spiritual impotence.

shackled in rome

acts 28:11 – 31

When we got to Rome, Paul was allowed to live by himself,
with a soldier to guard him.
Acts 28:16

I love the ending to the book of Acts, which is the final story of the apostle Paul in the early church. Paul was a courageous spokesman for the gospel of Christ. He had given his life for the message, and at the end of his life he found himself under house arrest in Rome. In spite of the fact that he had to live shackled to a Roman soldier, he spent his time teaching people about Jesus Christ and the kingdom of God.

If you had lived in Rome in those days, where would you have thought the future was? The typical person would have looked to Nero's palace for the power and the future, believing that the significant figure was the emperor ruling from his throne. The reality is that today, two thousand years later, we name our dogs Nero and our sons Paul. The world's ways are never the ways of God, and the world's people are never the people of God. The one who cast a long shadow over the next two thousand years was one who was tucked away in a simple house and shackled to a Roman soldier, not the one who sat on the throne, dictating to people how they should please him.

Do you feel that your life is being wasted? Are you in some sort of captivity? If so, take heart. I am sure that Paul felt exactly the same way. Instead of taking the gospel to Spain, he was chained to a guard in Rome, influencing only those who came to visit him. But God's ways are not our ways, and God used Paul in the place of his captivity, with all its limitations, to change all of human history.

sloshing sins

matthew 15:10 – 20

But the things that come out of the mouth come from the heart,
and these make a man "unclean."
Matthew 15:18

One of the most effective illustrations I have ever heard was told at a retreat by the Baptist preacher Peter Lord. He asked a young lady to come up to the platform, and he had in his hand a cup of water. He instructed the girl to grab the arm that held the cup of water and shake it very hard. After a moment of hesitation, the girl shook his arm, and water went flying everywhere. He looked at her and pointedly asked, "What made the glass spill water?"

Immediately she replied, "It spilled water because I shook your arm."

"Oh no," he said, "It spilled water because there was water in the cup."

He turned to the rest of us and explained. "A fellow at work irritates you, but it is really not he who irritates you; he just sloshes out the irritation that is already present in your own heart. Sin originates in you. A person receives a promotion a little faster than you, and you find that you are fighting jealousy. That jealousy is inside of you, and all that other person did was bring to the surface what already dwelt in your heart. No one can provoke inside of you what does not originate there."

Every human heart needs a deeper cleansing by the Holy Spirit. We ought to thank God for the person who irritates us or makes us angry or jealous. That person provides the means for God to teach us something about ourselves. That irritating person shows the true colors of my heart, and only once my heart is displayed in all of its corruption can it be washed white and clean.

finding myself in him

acts 9:1 – 30

*Brother Saul, the Lord—Jesus, who appeared to you on
the road as you were coming here—has sent me so that you
may see again and be filled with the Holy Spirit.*
Acts 9:17

The only time we can begin to see ourselves clearly is when we begin to see Christ for who he really is. As soon as we see his greatness, we begin to see our own inadequacy with new clarity. I never truly see myself until I face God. I can deceive myself as long as I look at other people. I can always find someone in the crowd who looks worse than me, and when I compare myself to that person, I look halfway decent. On the other hand, I can always find a person who looks better than I do, and that throws me into a fit of insecurity. So I find myself on a seesaw between the kind of self-confidence that comes from belittling other people and the kind of insecurity that comes from a covetous heart. Other people are not a reliable standard by which to measure myself, and I am not realistic when I allow them to control my picture of myself.

When I enter the presence of God and allow him to correct my sight by clearing away all that is in my line of vision except himself, then I see his beauty and my corruption, his purity and my dirtiness, his greatness and my insignificance, his goodness and my selfishness. That is why it can be uncomfortable for me to enter into God's presence, for I begin to see who I really am; for all of us, that is unpleasant. But I also begin to see what he can do with a life surrendered to him. It is possible for some of his beauty to rub off on me, for his purity to become my purity. He is even able to take away my selfishness and move me out of the insignificance that comes from a self-centered heart and into the center of all that is really important.

Are you in God's presence? Do you have his vision of who you are and who you can become? If you do not, you will spend your life being tossed between false confidence and ruthless insecurity, like a leaf in the wind.

the enemy of fruitfulness is myself

romans 8:1 – 17

*Because through Christ Jesus the law of the Spirit of life
set me free from the law of sin and death.*
Romans 8:2

believe that God wants to give each individual a clean heart, a heart cleansed from the self-will and self-interest that always traps us in futile and sterile paths. Scripture explicitly says that the Spirit gives life, but the flesh profits nothing. What is the flesh? It is simply my way in contrast to God's way. The self insists on keeping itself the center of my existence, yet the fruit of living with myself at the center is vanity, emptiness, and loss.

When a person has only one will and that is to do the will of God, the Holy Spirit can begin to build into that life the marks of his presence. He can transform that person's life into a temple of God's holy presence and make it a fruitful and faithful life. He can order it so that it shines with his glory, and he can place inside that person the witness of himself that he wants the world to see.

The greatest enemy to fruitfulness in my life is my own way. If I let Christ purge me and cleanse me so that I am wholly his, then the Spirit can begin to shape my life so it conforms to his master design. Do you know what it means to belong to God completely? If you hold on to even a small corner of your right to yourself, you will destroy all that he wants to do in and with you. Once Christ has given us a clean heart, he can give us the faithfulness and fruitfulness for which we long.

the gifts or the gift?

ephesians 1:3 – 12

My people come to you, as they usually do, and sit before you to listen to your words, but they do not put them into practice. With their mouths they express devotion, but their hearts are greedy for unjust gain.
Ezekiel 33:31

Sometimes I believe that Christians are not really interested in the gifts that Jesus desires to give. Each of us has some idea of what we would like for God to give to us: physical healing, a prosperous business, a happy family. The Jews had an identical problem; they wanted God to give them political freedom from Rome. This freedom became the goal toward which all things moved, and their expectations for the Messiah were in terms of liberation. This freedom would bring religious liberty, economic security, and mental equality. The Jews fell prey to the age-old temptation: they wanted God's gifts more than his presence.

We would rather have God's gifts than God himself, and if God removes his gifts, we abandon the Giver. This certainly characterizes the world of the twenty-first century, particularly in North America.

Is there a place in your heart where you are more interested in the things he gives than in him? Do you know what it means to have the life of God living in you, where you realize that he himself is the gift and better than any of his gifts? If you have all of Christ's gifts and miss him, you have missed life.

the god of life

2 corinthians 4:7 – 18

Even though I walk
through the valley of the shadow of death,
I will fear no evil,
for you are with me.
Psalm 23:4

Our God, the living God, the very source of life itself, invites us into his presence. It is a presence in which nothing evil, not even death itself, can stand. Little wonder then that the psalmist affirms his trust in God so that even as he walks through the valley of the shadow of death, he will not be afraid; the God of life is with him. Where God is, there is nothing to fear. This is the reason that people are to trust in him implicitly and completely.

Sometimes we who have the riches of the New Testament forget that the writers of the Old Testament did not enjoy our privilege. The author of Psalm 23 had never heard about the Lord Jesus. He had never read about the resurrection of Jesus from the dead; and yet, latent in his psalm lies a faith that challenges death itself. And that challenge is founded simply on the fellowship between God and the psalmist. The psalmist knew God, and he recognized that this God was Lord of life and that therefore there must be an unending potential in communion with him. "I will dwell in the house of the LORD forever" (Ps. 23:6).

Is your faith strong enough to face death itself and still believe? We who have the rest of the revelation have no excuse for a weak and paltry faith.

the great elementary teacher

psalm 24:1 – 2

For with you is the fountain of life;
in your light we see light.
Psalm 36:9

God is the best third-grade schoolteacher in the world. He has the ability to take anything in creation and use it as an object lesson to teach human beings about himself. The compatibility of this world to his purposes is such that it appears as if all things were made just for him and his teaching purposes. But we must remember who he is. Why should it surprise us that the world that he made should fit his character so perfectly that he can use all aspects of it to point to himself?

This whole world was designed so we could see God's reality. Why do so many of us miss it or see so dimly when we are surrounded by symbols of his presence? Charles Wesley confesses in a well-known hymn:

Long my imprisoned spirit lay
Fast bound in sin and nature's night;
Thine eye diffused a quickening ray,
I woke, a dungeon flamed with light.
My chains fell off, my heart was free;
I rose, went forth, and followed Thee. *

"Nature's night." How descriptive of our situation! We are so blind to the lessons all around us that God is waiting for us to see. His answer to our problem is a quickening ray of flaming light. I find myself praying, *Thank you, Lord, for what I do see. Give me more of your quickening rays and expose me to more of your lessons, so that I may see you.*

---

*Charles Wesley, "And Can It Be That I Should Gain?" *Hymns for Praise and Worship*, no. 115.

the hope of the world

matthew 23:27 – 28

Depart, depart . . . Touch no unclean thing!
Isaiah 52:11

The hope of the world is not in power, position, or wisdom, and it is especially not in money. The hope of the world is in those people who are clean. Isaiah 52:11 says,

> *Depart, depart, go out from there!*
> *Touch no unclean thing!*
> *Come out from it and be pure,*
> *you who carry the vessels of the LORD.*

If you are to be the witness for Christ that he asks you to be, if you are to have a future with him, you must be clean. The future and the hope of the world is wherever God is, and God dwells with and in his people when they are clean. He can get rid of our sins and take care of our failures and create in us a place in which he would feel comfortable living. Once we allow him to do that, there is no end to what the Spirit can do with our lives.

You may be trying to possess him. You may be trying to have Christ and keep some pollution in your heart. It will not work. If the future is to be realized, you must let him cleanse you so you are clean, pure, and holy. He wants possession of every area of our lives, and if you surrender your life to him, you will find yourself with a future. What Christ receives he cleanses, and what he cleanses he fills, and what he fills he uses. The hope of the world lies in the people who give themselves to him for cleansing and filling.

the ten commandments

deuteronomy 5:1 – 22

The LORD spoke to you face to face out of the fire on the mountain. "I am th
LORD your God, who brought you out of Egypt, out of the land of slavery."
Deuteronomy 5:4, 6

Have you ever thought about how all-encompassing the Ten Command
ments are? The first one, "Thou shalt have none other gods before M
(Deut. 5:7 KJV), means to let God be God. Get rid of all the rest, and l
him be God. There is a sense in which the other nine commandments a
commentaries on, or consequences of, that first commandment. When t
second commandment says, "Thou shalt not make thee any graven image
it is talking about our relationship to everything that is not God. We are n
to put anything in the place of God. So the first covers our relationship
God, and the second our relationship to everything else.

The third commandment has to do with the sanctity of language. Yo
cannot get any closer to a human being than dealing with that person
means of expression. The fourth one has to do with the sanctity of tim
Time is the boundary of the human experience. Therefore, the thing clo
est to us (language) and the thing farthest from us (time) come under God
Law. The fifth has to do with the sanctity of the home, the sixth with th
sanctity of life, and the seventh with the sanctity of sex. Every human beir
comes from a home, has life, and has a gender, and God wants to ensu
that we order our lives correctly so that all these areas will be areas of bles
ing and not curse.

The eighth commandment has to do with our relationship to posse
sions, and the ninth deals with our relationship to truth. Possessions are ou
most earthly reality, and truth is our most transcendent reality. Finally, th
tenth commandment deals with our desires. All aspects of our life are
come under his control, not because he likes to control but because he knov
what is best for the children he has made.

the law written on our hearts

matthew 5:17 – 7:29

*I will put my law in their minds
and write it on their hearts.
I will be their God,
and they will be my people.*
Jeremiah 31:33

Inside the temple of God, the Holy of Holies contained the ark of the covenant, and inside that ark were the tablets of the Law. I am enamored by the fact that the Law of God is in the most sacred place of his presence. When God spoke from Mt. Sinai and gave the Israelites the Law, he was not presenting them with rules to be followed. He was revealing his character, his nature, and his will for them. This God whom Israel was supposed to follow, and whom we are supposed to follow today, is the Holy One. The Law of God reflects his holy nature, and there is no way to bypass his holiness if we are going to come into his presence.

I used to think that the Law was an Old Testament phenomenon, but I found that when Jesus interacted with anyone, before the conversation was finished, he had introduced the Law into the dialogue. Jesus asked the woman at the well about her husband, he told the woman caught in adultery to go and sin no more, and Zacchaeus returned all that he had stolen. The key difference in the New Testament is that the Spirit of Jesus is given to enable humans to keep God's law. Now the Spirit of God writes the law on human hearts. Have you allowed the Spirit to write his law on your heart, and are you living by that law?

source of peace

exodus 33:12 – 17

But while Joseph was there in the prison, the LORD was with him; he showed
him kindness and granted him favor in the eyes of the prison warden.
Genesis 39:20–21

One of the most remarkable stories in the literature of the world is the story
of Joseph. Sold into slavery by his brothers, he found himself alone far from
home and all that was familiar. When tempted by his master's wife, he was
rewarded for his chastity by imprisonment. He is the classical example of
the person for whom everything goes wrong. Yet he refused to let despair,
bitterness, or unforgiveness control him. The result was that he rose to the
second highest position in the Egyptian government, and he became the salvation of the brothers who had sold him into slavery.

How does one explain such a life? Scripture gives a simple explanation.
It says the Lord was with him (Gen. 39:2, 3, 21, 23). From a biblical perspective this seems to be enough to explain such a remarkable life. The presence of God makes every misfortune and every injustice bearable. In fact,
this is the explanation given explicitly or implicitly for the lives of all the
heroes of the faith in the Bible.

What misfortunes or trials are you facing today? The presence of Jesus
can bring freedom in the midst of bondage, joy in the midst of sorrow, and
peace in the midst of the storm.

my festival

haggai 1 – 2

"All you people of the land take courage," declares the LORD,
"and work; for I am with you," declares the LORD of hosts. . . .
"From this day on I will bless you."
Haggai 2:4, 19 NASB

Haggai was a prophet whom God sent to the people of Israel soon after their return from Babylonian captivity. His name symbolized hope for Israel because it spoke of the festivals (*hag* in Hebrew means "festival") that were at the center of Old Testament worship. Three times a year Israel was to come to Jerusalem to the temple to worship Yahweh there. During their years in captivity after the temple was destroyed, that, of course, was not possible. So Israel mourned and dreamed of a day when they could return to Jerusalem and worship as they had in days of old. Now they are back in Jerusalem, but the temple has not been rebuilt. They have been more concerned about their houses than his.

In Haggai, the man's name and his message were the same. They were one of hope. To help us understand how it felt to Israel, picture this: it would be like the church of Christ being deprived for two full generations of the privilege of observing Christmas, Easter, Pentecost, or Thanksgiving, and then God, to encourage them, raising up a preacher named Mr. Christmas Easter Pentecost. God was telling Israel that if they would turn to him and put him ahead of their own desires that he would restore to them the temple and the festivals, and he would even send to them "the Desire of Nations," the One who would be God himself in blessing in their midst. Is it not wonderful the way God does not give up on us?

You may be in a place where you need a word of hope and encouragement. Let this strange name of Haggai be a word of hope for you today. God can restore to us all that we may have lost through our self-will and foolishness. He has no desire to abandon us. He wants all that has been good in our relationship with him in the past to be a promise of better things ahead. We must trust and obey. His will toward us is good!

god is mindful of me

psalm 8

What is man that you are mindful of him?
Psalm 8:4

The phrase "mindful of" is full of meaning in Scripture. It first occurs in Genesis 8 when we are told that God remembers Noah and his family and sends a wind to dry the earth for their comfort and safety. The second and third occurrences are in Genesis 9:15–16. Here God sets the rainbow in the clouds and promises that he will be mindful of humanity and all his creatures and will never let water destroy all life again. The phrase next appears in Genesis 19:29. As God prepares for the destruction of Sodom and Gomorrah, he remembers Abraham and saves Abraham's nephew Lot and his family. God is also mindful of Rachel (Gen. 30:22) and Hannah (1 Sam. 1:19) in their barrenness and gives them children. The context of this term in the Old Testament is one of grace and hope.

God's mind and heart are full of thoughts about individual persons. Even in our unworthiness he waits to reach out to us in loving-kindness and redemptive grace. He was mindful of Noah's safety, of the world's living things, of the family of Abraham, and of the longing hearts of Rachel and Hannah. The record shows that he will be mindful of each of us in any situation in which we find ourselves. God never judges human beings until he has shown his care and love by offering a way of reconciliation and deliverance. Let this be a word of comfort and joy to your heart today: God is mindful of you.

the power of god

psalm 8

Out of the mouths of babies and nursing infants
You have ordained strength.
Psalm 8:2 NKJV

The second verse of Psalm 8 is one of the most revolutionary in all of Scripture. It speaks of babies who are both helpless and dependent and says that from their mouths come strength. One could not draw a greater contrast to the idea of power and self-sufficiency than a nursing infant. Yet the psalmist says that it is from the lips of babes and sucklings, who cannot even explain their own needs, that God established the power to overcome his enemies and silence his adversaries.

What a dramatic way to express the fact that God's ways are not our ways, that his kingdom is not of this world and does not function the way that we think it ought to function! Implicit within this text is the whole argument of Scripture that the flesh profits nothing. It is not by might and power, as the world understands such things, that the ultimate victory will be won. A helpless baby began the undoing of the kingdom of evil, and it was in that very helplessness that the majesty of God was revealed.

What the world considers majesty and power, the true believer finds to be ephemeral show. The only biblical figure that portrays weakness more aptly and dramatically than that of a baby is the broken body of the Son of Man as he dies upon the cross. Paul understood this when he wrote, "The foolishness of God is wiser than man's wisdom, and the weakness of God is stronger than man's strength" (1 Cor. 1:25).

We need to allow God to reshape our thinking so that we see strength in the places where he sees it and not where the world sees it.

eternity in our hearts

2 corinthians 4:16 – 5:9

He has made everything beautiful in its time.
He has also set eternity in the hearts of men.
Ecclesiastes 3:11

Christians are to be people who love that which endures. The author of Ecclesiastes writes that God has put eternity within the human heart. This gift makes us yearn for life to be meaningful, so we are never content to give ourselves to that which will fade away. The eternal One has made us for the things that endure. Therefore, Christians will always be different. We can never simply run with the pack, giving ourselves to the things that pass away.

This longing for what is timeless and valuable causes people to reach for God because God is the eternal One. The Holy Spirit's work is to produce eternal fruit in the character and lives of his people.

It is from the anointing of the Spirit that we find the power to live for the things that endure. "The one who sows to please his sinful nature, from that nature will reap destruction; the one who sows to please the Spirit, from the Spirit will reap eternal life" (Gal. 6:8). This statement by Paul is the law of life.

Can you detect the difference between time and eternity? Have you found the power to give yourself to that which will endure? Even the most barren person who does so will be fruitful, and the most desolate person will know eternal joy.

the way of the cross

John 12:20 – 26

"For my thoughts are not your thoughts,
neither are your ways my ways,"
declares the LORD.
"As the heavens are higher than the earth,
so are my ways higher than your ways
and my thoughts than your thoughts."
Isaiah 55:8–9

A remarkable transformation occurs in the disciples between the events in Mark 8–10 and those in Acts 2. What made the difference in their lives before and after Pentecost? The key change is in the way they thought and understood. Before Pentecost they had a notion that power, position, and possessions could solve all human problems. They believed that if Jesus were on the throne in Jerusalem, he would clean up the world, and they were ready to be his prime ministers to help him accomplish the world-changing task. These earnest yet ignorant men did not have the foggiest idea of the price that had to be paid to bring redemption from one life to another. In their natural minds they assumed that redemption, like obedience, could be imposed and coerced. They desired to be part of a kingdom of power. Little did they realize the vastness of the gulf between their way and the way of Jesus.

Into the fabric of ultimate reality is written this law: if one person is ever to influence another, he has to forget about himself and lay down his life for another. The only hope of being a part of another's transformation is for that other person's welfare to become more important than one's own. Jesus' life demonstrated that our welfare was more significant to him than his own, and his death was the price he was willing to pay for us. Out of Christ's sacrifice for us comes the possibility of our redemption. If we follow Jesus, we must be willing to deny ourselves and take up his Cross. It will entail dying to self-interest and allowing someone else's interests and well-being to become more important than our own.

god's secret agents

Matthew 6:5 – 13

When you pray, go into your inner room, close your door and pray
to your Father who is in secret, and your Father who sees
what is done in secret will reward you.
Matthew 6:6 NASB

How is your prayer life? It is much easier to talk about one's prayer life than to actually pray. The older I become, the more convinced I am that the most important thing Christians ever do is pray. I once read a line by Francis Asbury that troubled me for a long time. He said that a person who reads the Scripture and yet does not pray has missed the most important part. Now my tendency is to awaken for my quiet time and turn to the Word and find my soul fed. Scripture is a joy to me, but Asbury said that prayers must accompany our reading of Scripture. Someone who reads without prayer is comparable to the insurance salesperson who makes a pitch about the policy but never requests a signature on the paperwork. Do you pray? Do you know anything about intercession?

God constantly looks for people who will intercede. To the knowledge of church historians, there has never been an outpouring of the Holy Spirit that did not begin in a secret, hidden place in some simple heart with a burden for God's work in the church. Heaven will show us God's secret agents, those people who have prepared the way for the Spirit to act through their prayers. Perhaps God has you tucked away somewhere in a place that seems to prohibit effective ministry. God may have simply set you in the place where you can do the most important task: pray for the world!

let the meditation of my heart be acceptable

psalm 19

Keep your servant also from willful sins;
may they not rule over me.
Psalm 19:13

Some of us need to realize that we possess hurtful patterns of behavior that are deeply seared upon our souls and our psyches. Have you ever been guilty of using a person for your own ends without even knowing it? Have you ever taken advantage of people without realizing you were hurting them? Have you watched while people in powerful positions crushed those underneath them? Have you seen parents manipulate children and vice versa? Many times we act in our own self-interest without being aware that we are doing so.

The psalmist wrote about this long before any psychology class was taught or any theory of counseling was developed. If you begin to let God's Spirit have his way in your life, you will find that he reveals to you your patterns of behavior and coping mechanisms that are sinful and harmful to other persons. We can pray along with the psalmist, "Lord, there are hidden sins in me that I don't even know about. What do I do about them?" The psalmist prayed that God would hold him innocent until he became aware of his presumptuous sins and could fix them. He asked God to keep him from these sins committed in ignorance. He ends the psalm by saying,

Let the words of my mouth and the meditation of my heart
Be acceptable in Thy sight,
O Lord, my rock and my Redeemer.

Psalm 19:14 NASB

to be in his presence

psalm 84

Better is one day in your courts
than a thousand elsewhere;
I would rather be a doorkeeper in the house of my God
than dwell in the tents of the wicked.
Psalm 84:10

Meeting God profoundly affects our confidence and our expectations. When we find him, it is always a shock to realize how much he cares about us. Instead of confronting a vindictive judge who waits for a chance to deal with us about our shortcomings, we find a God of grace who looks for the chance to forgive our sins, establish us in his favor, and pour on us his blessings. To our surprise, we learn that he will withhold nothing good from those who walk in sincerity and uprightness before him. He is the source of all good, and his will toward us is loving concern. He is our sun who gives us light and our shield who surrounds us with protection.

The most important consequence of meeting God is what it does to our sense of priorities. We come to realize that we need him more than anything else. In fact, we need him even more than we need his gifts. It is for God himself that our soul cries out. The association with God will leave in us the hallowing impact of place and people and seasons, but our hearts will hunger for his presence. He is the source of all good, but he is better than all good. There is no justification needed for our searching for him. Although some do not know it, to be near God is the deepest desire of every human heart.

october 6

water in the wilderness

psalm 84

> *As they pass through the Valley of Baca,*
> *they make it a place of springs;*
> *the autumn rains also cover it with pools.*
> *They go from strength to strength.*
> Psalm 84:6–7

Psalm 84 is a beautiful and liberating psalm. One of the glorious themes of this psalm is that the negatives of human life do not have to be victorious over us because there is a power that can break their depressing hold. The psalmist speaks about passing through the Valley of Baca, and although no one knows exactly what this refers to, it seems to speak of a place of great dryness. The writer alludes to an experience of extreme difficulty that the presence of sufficient water would solve. We find that the Lord provides refreshing streams and pools of water.

Have you found yourself in a place of great dryness spiritually, emotionally, or even mentally? Do you know that there is One who can break through the dryness in your heart and produce streams in the desert? The resources of another world can be made available to enable you and me to face the dryness in our lives just as waters were provided to help the psalmist through the Valley of Baca. We can find comfort in the fact that the psalmist remembered God's provision of food and water to the Israelites as they passed through the wilderness. God did not desert the Israelites, and he will not forsake us. The knowledge that there is another world, that there is One in that world who cares about us and is able to provide for us, enables us to see our situation in a new light.

to know him by name

psalm 146

Praise the LORD!
Praise the LORD, O my soul!
Psalm 146:1

The last five of the 150 psalms begin and end with the same expression, *Hallelu-Yah.* These five psalms are called a *hallel,* a section for which the theme is praise. The Hebrew word *hallelu* means "praise," and the Hebrew word *Yah* is the personal name for God, revealed to Moses. Since these praise psalms conclude the end of the book of worship, it is fair to say that worship should always end in adoration and praise. Is this the way your quiet time ends? It should be.

Psalm 146 suggests that worship should end in praise because Christians have the privilege of knowing God personally; the personal name for God occurs eleven times in the ten verses of this psalm. The psalmist exults almost to the point of monotony in his repetitive use of God's personal name, Yahweh. The composer knows the God of all gods by his personal name, and finding himself full of praise, he speaks that name again and again.

Do you have a love affair with the name of the Lord Jesus? Do you find his name tumbling out of your mouth without even your conscious thought? Our lives should be lives of worship in which we cannot keep ourselves from speaking the name of Jesus.

october 8

wickedness and trust

matthew 6:19 – 34

Many are the woes of the wicked
but the Lord's unfailing love
surrounds the man who trusts in him.
Psalm 32:10

What do you believe is the opposite of wickedness? Until recently, I would have said righteousness. But according to Psalm 32, the opposite of wickedness is trust. Scripture contrasts the people without God—the wicked—with the people who trust in God. On occasion these trusting ones are called righteous, but their righteousness does not come from anything they have done; it comes from God himself.

This theme runs throughout the Old Testament. Salvation comes to those who trust God. We do not have to wait until the New Testament to find the doctrine of justification by faith.

Are you trusting God to provide for your every need? For your loved ones, your future, your finances? In order to be surrounded by God's unfailing love, you must trust him in all areas of life, all the days of your life. The opposite of trust is not simply anxiety; it is wickedness.

trust

john 15:1–8

Remain in me, and I will remain in you.
No branch can bear fruit by itself; it must remain in the vine.
Neither can you bear fruit unless you remain in me.
John 15:4

My wife and I used to make the arduous trip from Kentucky, where I went to school, to Schenectady, New York, where my wife's family lived. We would travel by rail, and our train was pulled by two large steam engines. The colder the weather, the more beautiful those great iron horses were; they were symbols of tremendous power. On the return trip the train would stop in a little nondescript hamlet outside New York City called Harmon, New York. One day I asked the conductor why the train stopped in such a little town outside the huge metropolis of New York City.

"Well," the conductor said, "we change engines here. We go down underneath the city, and we can't take these steam engines with their smoke and cinders down there, so we use an electric engine."

I went out to see that electric engine. To my dismay, it was the dumpiest, most unromantic thing I had ever seen! It was small, and it did not shake or smoke at all. It just sat there. So I asked the conductor where that puny engine got its power.

"Do you notice that third rail over there?" he asked me. "That third rail is hooked to Niagara Falls, and all the electrical power that Niagara Falls produces is available to this train through that extra rail."

That is the biblical picture of trust. When Christ takes the sin out of your heart, you can jam yourself up against him and hook onto his life, and into your life will flow the very power of God. That power will enable you through the Holy Spirit to resemble the Lord Jesus, who is the source of all righteousness. This third rail enables people like you and me—dumpy, grimy, and unromantic though we may be—to become new creatures, vibrant, radiant, and effective in the power of the Holy Spirit.

worship and litany

mark 10:32–45

"We are going up to Jerusalem," he said, "and the Son of Man will be betrayed to the chief priests and teachers of the law. They will condemn him to death and will hand him over to the Gentiles, who will mock him and spit on him, flog him and kill him. Three days later he will rise."
Then James and John ... came to him. "Teacher," they said, "we want you to do for us whatever we ask."
Mark 10:33–35

Mark records three instances in which Jesus tries to prepare his disciples for his suffering and death. In each of the three stories, the disciples miss Christ's message. In the first, Peter declares it to be a blasphemous impossibility; in the second, the disciples just do not understand. The third time Jesus tries to prepare them, they immediately change the subject, and John and James ask to sit at his right and left in the kingdom. Jesus' carefully worded warnings to help them face the most traumatic event in human history became to them a religious litany. They must have thought to themselves, *You know, Jesus always makes that funny little speech about a cross. I don't know what it means, but he seems to feel obligated to make it.*

That is exactly how much of our worship is. We do not understand it, but we feel obligated to do it. For years when I took communion, it was about words and action instead of grace. I was baptized. Water was poured on my head and the right words were said over me, but there was no regeneration. We turn the realities of the gospel into a litany that we do not even attempt to comprehend.

Never think for an instant that because you go through the motions of religion you have a saving relationship with Jesus Christ. It is only by coming to know him in his reality and coming to understand his words because of that relationship that we find salvation. Then the ritual becomes reality, and meaning transforms boring traditions into eternal truth.

you must have a center

colossians 1:15 – 19

He is before all things, and in him all things hold together . . . so that in
everything he might have the supremacy. For God was pleased to have all his
fullness dwell in him.
Colossians 1:17–19

Recently I found myself in conversation with a young man who was a senior at a Christian university. He said to me, "I have come to believe that there is a unity to all knowledge, which is reflected in the fact that if you take any discipline—history, literature, science, math—and push it far enough, you will find yourself in philosophy."

Then I said, "Yes, that is right. This is the reason that the terminal degree in every discipline has been the Ph.D. To be a master in any discipline, one needs to be a philosopher, knowing the theory behind one's subject."

"If you push philosophy far enough," he asked, "you will find yourself in theology, won't you?"

I grinned to myself and said, "Right! Philosophy raises questions that only theology can answer."

"If you push theology far enough," he continued, "you find you have to have a center, don't you?"

"Yes," I agreed.

"Well, that is where I would like to dedicate my life. I would like to locate that center, know it, and give myself totally to it."

Are you searching for the center of reality? Do you know that the center is the Lord Jesus? He is the center of all knowledge and all truth. If you give yourself totally to him, you will find yourself in the middle of all that is good and significant.

a sense of destiny

genesis 15

The LORD had said to Abram, "Leave your country, your people and your
father's household and go to the land I will show you.
I will make you into a great nation
and I will bless you;
I will make your name great,
and you will be a blessing."
Genesis 12:1–2

One of the things that happens when we become a Christian is that we pick up a sense of destiny and a sense of mission. After God placed his hand on Abraham (Gen. 12), Abraham never viewed his life in the same way again. He said, "I am special, and I am here for a purpose. All the nations of the earth are going to bless themselves in me." This was not pride, but a sense of purpose.

The moment you become a Christian, you begin to realize that God has a work for you to do, and that work is important. Not only that, but if you are not faithful to complete God's purpose for you, you will be held accountable in the Judgment.

God does not call us to a work for our personal fulfillment. We are called for the sake of the world. And we will be held accountable for what we do with the truth that is given to us. From the first day that God called Abraham, he had the whole world in mind. God's plan for you and me includes no narrow provincialism. God took Abraham into kings' courts, to the center of political power, so God's witness could extend into those pagan places. God never intended you and me to be off on the eddies of society and on the margin of history. It is his gospel, his redemptive work, and it will be in the center of all that is valuable. Important things are going on in the world today, but there is nothing more important than fulfilling God's destiny for our life—becoming a witness to the world for him.

authority of scripture

matthew 7:24 – 27

*Therefore everyone who hears these words of mine and puts them into practice
is like a wise man who built his house on the rock. The rain came down,
the streams rose, and the winds blew and beat against that house;
yet it did not fall, because it had its foundation on the rock.*
Matthew 7:24–25

Biblical religion says that God completely transcends the grasp of human
senses; we cannot find him, contain him, or exhaust him. Human reason
does not have the capacity by itself to locate and explain God. We need a
revelation from God himself if we ever are to know who God is. Our own
searching merely produces sterility and illusion. The initiative must come
from God's side; the Creator must reveal himself to his creation. If he does
reveal himself, we know he is a giving God who discloses himself not only
to our hearts but to our intellects as well. This is the reason that Scripture
is so crucial to our faith. The Bible is the record of God's revelation of himself to humanity. Without it, we have neither religious certainty nor any
other security, for if we are not sure about our foundation, then we will wob-
ble on everything else.

Wherever the Scriptures have been seen as the Word of God, there has
come into the hearts of many people an assurance that one can not only
know what God is like, but also personally know him. Scripture must be
absolutely authoritative for Christians as we begin the third millennium
from the time of Christ's birth. The Bible is the record of God's personal
revelation of himself to us.

a world beyond my grasp

acts 2

When the day of Pentecost came, they were all together in one place.
Suddenly a sound like the blowing of a violent wind came from heaven
and filled the whole house ... All of them were filled with the
Holy Spirit and began to speak in other tongues as the Spirit enabled them.
Acts 2:1–2, 4

The day of Pentecost made clear that there is a reality beyond human reality who is personal and is anxious to be in relationship with human beings. On that day the sound of a mighty rushing wind suddenly descended on those who were gathered together. But that sound was simply a symbol because the greatest thing that happened was neither the sound of a mighty wind nor the shaking of the room in which they met. The unbelievable event occurred when the Spirit came from beyond time and space and filled their hearts with his empowering presence. They went out of that room transformed and transforming. It was here that the church began.

The church is the body of people who know Someone who exists beyond themselves, who know that Person to be the Holy Spirit. It is a wonderful thing to understand that a world exists beyond my grasp even though I cannot see, touch, measure, or control it. In fact, I was made for it to control me. The marvelous reality is that the Ruler of that other world cares more about you and about me than he does about himself, and if we open ourselves to his presence, he can transform our routine daily existence so that it becomes a window looking into heaven.

confidence in yahweh

psalm 146

Do not put your trust in princes,
in mortal men, who cannot save . . .
Blessed is he whose help is the God of Jacob.
Psalm 146:3, 5

The psalmist commands people to put their full trust in God and not in other people. What is the essence of a relationship of trust? The Hebrew word *batah*, meaning "trust," signifies the type of relationship that exists between two people who know each other well enough that each can predict the other's actions on the basis of that one's character. It is the word used of the confidence a person has in a friend. It means that one person can depend on the word of another person.

The psalmist has come to know that there is no salvation anywhere except in Yahweh, and for this reason, he chooses to wholly trust God. Yahweh alone is the Savior. The psalmist has tried trusting in other people, even in the noblest of other people, and yet he has found that there is no salvation outside of God.

The answer to the human dilemma will not be found in ourselves, nor will it be found in other persons. God and God alone is the answer to every human question. When we trust him completely, he is free to trust us with his name, his message, and his character. Do you trust him totally? Perhaps the more pertinently, can he trust you?

october 16

christian perfection

ezekiel 36:25 – 29

Now a man came up to Jesus and asked,
"Teacher, what good thing must I do to get eternal life?" . . .
Jesus answered, "If you want to be perfect . . ."
Matthew 19:16, 21

How can we become blameless? How is perfection possible? Perfection simply means completeness, living so there is nothing in me to deflect my attention from Christ, and being fully concentrated on him. It takes the Spirit of God to do that for you and for me, but he is able. If today my attention is not completely centered on Christ, it is because I have failed to let him place me in himself. When I am centered on Christ, I am free to live. I must allow the Holy Spirit to rid my life of anything and everything that turns my focus from Christ.

If the Lord Jesus is not in control of our lives, we carry in our breast something that has the capacity to crucify him. We may simply break his heart, but our disloyalty to him will ultimately separate us from him and destroy us. He has the power to perfect the love in our hearts so that he is in control and he is our Lord. Does he have a rival inside of you, or are you complete in him?

october 17

he shall overcome

revelation 21 – 22

I am the Alpha and the Omega, the First and the Last,
the Beginning and the End.
Revelation 22:13

The first two chapters of Genesis and the last two chapters of Revelation contain no reference to evil or to the devil. Satan does not appear at the beginning, and he will not appear at the end of human history. God reigns alone without rival; it is he who brackets human existence with his sovereignty and greatness. The master Artist designed our world to begin in a garden, and a garden is a place of order and beauty—a place of aesthetic and physical nurture. He designed the world to find its fulfillment in a city, not one like our cities, but the Holy City in which there will be no suffering, no pain, no sorrow, and no heartache. It will be clean, beautiful, and full of life.

Ultimate reality, the beginning of all things and the end of all things, is not evil; goodness and beauty fill the beginning and the end because of the presence of God. With all the evil in our world, we are sometimes seduced into thinking that evil is more powerful than God himself. But it is simply not so. "In this world you will have trouble. But take heart! I have overcome the world" (John 16:33). Let us fix our eyes on Jesus, who is leading us to his holy and beautiful city.

exploding truth

john 8:31 – 32

*In reply Jesus declared, "I tell you the truth, no one can see
the kingdom of God unless he is born again."*
John 3:3

Christianity must maintain its objective intellectual foundation. The day we
depart from orthodox Christian truth, we will find the seeds of death already
in our midst to sterilize us spiritually. We must have some basic common
beliefs in order to win people to Christ. But there is more than an intellectual component in the Christian faith; there is also a subjective element in
receiving the gospel. Some people think intellectual assent is all that is necessary to be a Christian, but this is not true. Christian belief must become
authenticated in one's life.

Truth comes first, and then personal experience. John Wesley preached
the gospel a long time before his heart was transformed. In fact, one of Wesley's most powerful sermons, "The Almost Christian," he wrote before he
was even born again. Wesley's beliefs did not change after his conversion;
those beliefs exploded into his life, becoming a burning passion within him
instead of intellectual baggage. The result of his conversion could be seen in
his preaching. He preached the same sermons, but they bore fruit and people
found Christ. It is not enough only to have intellectual truth. The truth
must break into our lives in a deeply penetrating and intimately personal
way. Then we can say, "He is not only *the* Savior; he is *my* Savior." Then the
gospel message becomes authenticated by our witness. Has the truth you
are proclaiming exploded into your heart? Is the truth you are proclaiming
authenticated by your life?

the future element in our faith

exodus 3:11 – 12; 19:3 – 6

And God said, "I will be with you. And this will be the sign to you
that it is I who have sent you: When you have brought the people
out of Egypt, you will worship God on this mountain."
Exodus 3:12

A number of years ago I began to sense something in the Old Testament that I think may be clearer there than it is in the New, where it is only assumed. Biblical faith contains not just intellectual, historical, and subjective elements, but also a future element, and if that future outlook is lost from our faith, we will falter. Remember the story of Moses when he stood by the burning bush and God said, "I am going to send you to deliver my people."

Moses looked up and said, "God, would you just give me a sign? I want to believe you, but I need a sign."

God said, "All right, I will give a sign. When you get the people out of Egypt, all Israel will worship me on this mountain, right at the place where you are standing."

My heart responds like I think Moses' did: "Lord, that is not the kind of sign I am asking for. I want a sign before you send me to deliver the people."

God replied, "No, I will give you a sign after I have delivered them so you know it has happened. At this moment, you must trust me that it will take place."

Moses went forward with that future element in his faith.

Is there a future element in your faith? Do you believe Christ is going to give you victory in your situation? Do you believe the people to whom he has called you are going to be delivered by his marvelous power? Are you trusting that he is going to demonstrate his hand and move redemptively in your situation? Moses may have gone in fear and trembling, but he believed God enough to obey. And do you know what? God kept his promise.

god the provider

exodus 16:1 – 8

*Moses said, "This is what the LORD has commanded: 'Take an omer
of manna and keep it for the generations to come, so they can see the
bread I gave you to eat in the desert when I brought you out of Egypt.'"*
Exodus 16:32

Inside the ark of the covenant in the Most Holy Place in the temple of Israel,
there was a pot of manna. Every time the chief priest came in to meet with
God, he stood not only in God's presence, but also in the presence of the pot
of manna that was placed there to remind him that God does provide for his
people.

When the Israelites were hungry in the wilderness, they began to grum-
ble against God, wishing they were back in captivity. Moses commanded
them to trust God to provide for their needs. In the morning when they
awoke, the Israelites discovered white stuff covering the ground. The word
manna comes from the Hebrew phrase *man-hu,* which means, "What is it?"
All the people of Israel initially wondered what the manna was, and then
they realized that it was their food, God's provision to sustain them.

One of the truths that each person must believe is illustrated by that
pot of manna. The God who revealed himself in Jesus Christ is the Creator
of the universe. Not only did he create all things, he also sustains all things.
Even beyond that, this Creator and Sustainer is also the Provider, the one
who sees our every need and takes care of those needs. He is in sovereign
control, and we must recognize that he will provide for our needs in every
situation, no matter how small or how desperate.

god, the ultimate other

isaiah 40:12 – 31

To whom, then, will you compare God?
What image will you compare him to?...
Do you not know?
Have you not heard?...
He sits enthroned above the circle of the earth.
Isaiah 40:18, 21–22

God is different from you and me. He is really the Other in your life and mine. There is a sense in which other people are not truly other, because we are all remarkably similar. It is our similarity that enables us to know and understand one another. I am either where you are or where you have been or where you will be. Our lives are intertwined in many ways. But when we approach God, we find the One we can truly call Other. He is completely different from us; the uncreated One, beyond our reality; the One whom we cannot trap in our life or our world. He transcends it all.

In this sense he is ultimately the One you and I have to face. I can run away from you, and it is possible for us to live without impinging upon each other. But there is no way for God, the ultimate Other, ever to be excluded from my life. He is the first and the last, the beginning and the end. He is the last authority in your life, whether you acknowledge him or not, and he will have the last word. God is the One you will have to face. Let us not run from him like Jonah, but allow our lives to be given over to fellowship with the transcendent One.

god is the source of light

1 john 1:5 – 7; 2:7 – 11

The LORD is my light and my salvation—
whom shall I fear?
The LORD is the stronghold of my life—
of whom shall I be afraid?
Psalm 27:1

Scripture says that God is the Source of all light. He is "my light and my salvation." Fire is a symbol of God, and fire produces light. In the wilderness God led his people with a cloud by day and with fire by night. The fire was given so they could see their way. When Moses came down from the mountain after his encounter with Yahweh, his face was shining so brightly that he had to cover it with a veil. When one is in the presence of God, one is in the Source of light.

I remember one hard-nosed businessman who told me, "I came to a point of total surrender where I died to myself and became alive to God. I went into my study and shut the door and locked it. I fell face down in the dark, and all of a sudden I could have sworn that there was a light in that room."

God's presence brings illumination and brilliance. He is the Source of light, and when we turn away from the Source of light, we should not be shocked if shadows begin to fall across our pathway. If we continue to walk in the shadows, we will eventually find ourselves in the dark. Jesus described hell as "outer darkness"—a deliberate walking away from the light.

Are there shadows across your path? If so, do whatever it takes to come into the light of God's presence.

nothing held back

genesis 22:1 – 19

"Take your son, your only son, Isaac, whom you love . . . Sacrifice him there as a burnt offering . . ." Early the next morning Abraham got up and . . . set out for the place God had told him about.
Genesis 22:2–3

There is something intriguing about Abraham's faith. He held nothing back from God. We can choose to walk with God while holding back with a considerable amount of foot-dragging, but Abraham lifted up his life to God and offered it to him freely. He was willing to give to God the two most precious things he had: his son and his future.

We have never really been filled with the Spirit until we have reached this place. The Spirit is not going to fill us until Christ is absolutely first. God asked Abraham for more than his son; Isaac represented Abraham's future. Abraham had lived in the light of God's promise, and now God was asking him to give up the promise for which he had lived.

We are never free until we are detached. Holy detachment comes when we live not for our wishes or for another human or for our future, but only for God. He is our life. It is even possible for a person to peacefully watch the crumbling of a life ministry or the ending of a life relationship because neither is the person's life. If my first allegiance is to Jesus, then I can have a holy detachment from other people and other things that enables me to obey Jesus and therefore keep those other relationships clean.

God does not want people who are grabbing for what they can get. God wants people who can hold everything—their profession, their wealth, their status, their family—on an open palm. The only thing we are to clutch to our hearts is God himself. God wants us to allow him to give and to take away. We can only allow him this freedom if our security is not in our Isaac but in Christ. This is the job of the sanctifying Spirit. When our security is Christ, we can never be destroyed.

he bore me in himself

isaiah 53:1 – 9

Surely he took up our infirmities
and carried our sorrows,
yet we considered him stricken by God,
smitten by him, and afflicted.
But he was pierced for our transgressions,
he was crushed for our iniquities;
the punishment that brought us peace was upon him,
and by his wounds we are healed.
Isaiah 53:4–5

In about 1950 I ran across an article in *Time* magazine that told an astounding medical story. In those days doctors were just beginning to experiment with new kinds of treatments, and there was a young boy on the West Coast who had a kidney infection. The infection became so bad that his kidneys were contaminating his blood rather than cleansing it. His situation reached a crisis point, and the doctor told the parents that unless something radical was done he would die.

The boy's doctors had a conference with the best medical people in California, and one of them suggested a radical experiment. The idea was to hook the boy's body up to another person with healthy kidneys and let the good kidneys clean the boy's blood and give his kidneys a chance to recuperate. The doctors agreed that it might be possible, so they talked to the parents about it. The parents immediately agreed to the procedure.

The father's blood type matched his son's, so they took the father into the hospital, put him on a bed right beside his son in the operating room, and linked the blood systems together. The blood from the boy began to flow into the body of the father, and the blood from the father began to flow into the body of the son. The boy had maintained a very high temperature. As they lay there together, the boy's temperature began to drop and the father's temperature began to rise until they reached the same level. Then both temperatures slowly dropped until they were normal.

The experiment appeared to be a success. They kept the boy in the hospital for nine days, and he was fine. After nine days they let him go home, but they kept the father for observation. On the eleventh day the father' temperature suddenly skyrocketed, and he quickly died.

This is perhaps the best illustration of the Cross that I have ever heard. The heavenly Father has caused his holiness to meet the fatal disease of ou sin—all our crookedness and twistedness—in his Son. Jesus took our sir and disease in his body, bore our punishment, and died in our place.

october 25

i love you for you

luke 15:11 – 24

We all, like sheep, have gone astray,
each of us has turned to his own way;
and the LORD has laid on him
the iniquity of us all.
Isaiah 53:6

Jesus came into our broken world to provide a way to get the prodigals back home. He wanted to purge the rebellion from our hearts so we would not only come home, but also enjoy being home, so we would rejoice in the privilege of being a part of the family we had abandoned. Jesus paid the price for our return and our healing.

As the years have passed, a conviction has deepened in my soul that Jesus wants to do far more for us than most of us imagine. So often we think in quite selfish terms about what Christ came to do. Yet in fact Christ died to do more for human beings than we have ever dreamed. If we do not dream a little bigger, we are never going to experience the deeper reality of his presence.

The reality is that Christ came to do more than just keep us out of hell. He wants to develop a personal relationship with each human being for whom he died. He died to save me not just from my sins, but also from myself. "We all, like sheep, have gone astray, each of us has turned to his own way" (Isa. 53:6).

Self-interest is the ultimate definition of sin, and the Cross holds the power to set each person free from self-interest. A French Catholic priest in the court of King Louis the XIV one day said, "Oh, God, isn't there anybody left anywhere who loves you just for who you are? Can't you find one such person? And if you can't find one, couldn't you make one?" That is why Jesus went to the Cross: to bring me to the place where I love him simply because of who he is and not because of what he can do for me.

The ending of the story of the Prodigal Son would have been terribly disappointing if the son had merely returned for more of his inheritance without an interest in his father. Once the father saw his son coming home, the relationship between father and son became the thing of paramount importance, and the reader forgets that the son ever needed anything except his father.

god the source of truth

psalm 1

He is like a tree planted by streams of water.
Psalm 1:3

The Scriptures say that God is the source of all truth. If we turn away from truth, we will end in illusion or delusion because only truth is reality. When we walk away from truth, we lose reality and are destroyed by delusion.

I was in my sixties before I ever wondered where the word *true* comes from. I pulled down my dictionary and found that the word *true* comes from an old Indo-European word for *tree*. I was intrigued by the idea that the word *truth* comes from the word for *tree*. The more I thought about it, the more it seemed to make perfect sense. Trees do not move. We can count on them to be there every morning when we wake up. Truth is the same way. We can count on it. It will not deceive us. It will not give us one face today and another tomorrow. The best news of all is that Jesus Christ is true. He is absolutely, totally reliable and faithful. And when our lives are ordered by him, we stay in reality, and we walk in truth.

He is like a tree planted by streams of water,
which yields its fruit in season,
and whose leaf does not wither.
Whatever he does prospers.

Psalm 1:3

holiness and love

matthew 22:36 – 40

And he has given us this command:
Whoever loves God must also love his brother.
1 John 4:21

In Scripture, God says two things about his essence: he is holy, and he is love. All holiness comes from God, and no one is holy apart from his presence. Yet even in our sin, humans cry out for that which is sacred, moral, and right. Human beings cannot cease from moralizing, and they will become irate if injustice is done to them. Personally they may be immoral, but they will retain their standards of morality for other people to live up to. No one should steal *their* car or kidnap *their* child, even though if you quiz them about the inconsistency, they will justify their own immorality. All people come from the holy One, and he has stamped us with his own image.

However, God is not simply holy; he is holy love. Because we came from his hand, we also cry out for a true and pure love. We long to find our fulfillment, not in our isolated desires and ambitions, but in something bigger than ourselves. I have come to wonder whether the emphasis on love in our generation, even in all its perversity, is a symbol that our hearts are desperately hungry for a love that truly satisfies.

In God holiness and love are inseparable. His moral purity is combined with his personal loving presence, and his love is a pure and burning one.

in his image

psalm 17

Then God said, "Let us make man in our image, in our likeness."
Genesis 1:26

We speak sometimes of a God-shaped vacuum within us. We say that God made us for himself, and that we are incomplete without his presence in our lives. Many Christians have given thanks for that inner emptiness because without it they would never have turned to God. We rejoice in God's design that made his creatures incomplete so they would need him.

However, the reality is not that God made us different from himself, but that he made us like himself. He made us in his own image and likeness, the very likeness of the Son. He made us as persons just as the Son is a person, and as the Son is not complete in himself, neither are we. Persons, divine or human, cannot live without relationship. The divine persons live in Trinitarian relationship, and human persons are also incomplete without relationship. We must be connected to God—the source of our lives—and we must be connected with other people whom he brings to us.

This is why the Bible places such an emphasis on holy love. We are made for love, not a love that uses persons for its own satisfaction, but a holy love that finds its fulfillment in giving itself to and for another.

"if you are . . . i am grateful."

luke 17:11 – 19

*One of them, when he saw he was healed, came back, praising God
in a loud voice. He threw himself at Jesus' feet and thanked him.*
Luke 17:15–16

I was sitting on an airplane next to a man who claimed to be an atheist and who told me a story I have never forgotten. It was the story of why he believed in prayer. He said, "I used to have vicious migraine headaches that I thought were going to drive me crazy, and medicine could do nothing for me. One day, I thought, *Religious people pray.* I didn't know anything about religion, didn't even believe in God, but I thought it surely couldn't hurt to try; so I prayed.

"I said, 'Lord, I don't know if you are or not, and if you are, I don't know whether you can help me or not, and if you are and you can, I don't know whether you would or not, but if you are, and if you could, and if you would take away these headaches, I would be very grateful.' Do you know what? The headaches went away, and I thought to myself that it was a very happy coincidence.

"Then I had a second thought, *That is a cheap way out. What if God is, and what if he did? If I attribute my healing to chance, it would be extremely ungracious.*

"So I prayed again, 'Lord, I don't know whether you are or not, and I don't know whether you did or not, but if you are and if you did, I want you to know that I am grateful.'

"Then I had another thought, *There have been many good things that have happened in my life that I assumed were accidents. I wonder if those are blessings from God too. And if they are, I have never even told him thanks.*"

So he said, "I prayed again. 'I don't know whether you exist or not, and I don't know whether you are responsible for the good things in my life, but if you had anything to do with them, I want you to know my gratitude.'"

Are you as grateful to God as that atheist was?

the way

isaiah 30:18 – 21

I know, O LORD, that a man's way is not in himself;
Nor is it in a man who walks to direct his steps.
Jeremiah 10:23 NASB

There is no guidance system within the human psyche. I realized this one day as I sat in a small plane with a friend of mine. He had been a missionary pilot in Africa, and a small plane had been his life. It was my first experience of one.

Before takeoff, while he checked his instruments, I noticed the panel in front of me with its strange faces. I asked him what the instruments were. He told me that two instruments are essential in every plane, no matter how big or how small: a compass and a horizon. I understood what a compass was, but I inquired about the horizon.

He pointed to a dial with a black line across it. The tips of that line were orange and larger than the rest of the line. He said, "That instrument tells me which way is up and which way is down." When I asked if he was so dumb that he needed an instrument to tell him which was up and which was down, he informed me that he was not the dumb one.

Then he explained to me that when a plane is in heavy cloud cover and the pilot can see nothing but the clouds around him, there is nothing inside his body to tell him which way is up and which is down. To know where the plane is, the pilot needs a point of reference outside of himself or herself, so a compass indicates the lateral direction and a horizon shows the vertical direction. Without the two there is no survival.

Our way is not found in us. That is why Jesus said, "I am the way" (John 14:6). That is why we need the Spirit and the Word to guide us. Without them we wander or we crash.

ready for an adventure

exodus 3:1 – 4:20

*So now, go. I am sending you to Pharaoh to bring my people
the Israelites out of Egypt.*
Exodus 3:10

God puts his people and his witness right in the center of all that is important. We expect that when we follow him, we are doomed to a life of significant smallness, but the truth is that he is waiting to explode our smallness
and put us in places of which we have only dreamed. God put the baby
Moses right in the middle of the most powerful family in all the world, to
be trained with the best educators anywhere in order to understand leadership and responsibility. God also put Israel in the center of the military world
of that day. If you wanted to go from Rome to Egypt or from Egypt to Babylon or from the Hittite empire to Egypt, you had to go within a few miles
of Jerusalem.

We must understand that we are not in partnership with a human
being. On our own we will amount to little, but we are in partnership with
the Triune One who is the Sovereign God, and he is out to redeem a world.
The amazing thing is that he has entrusted a large part of that job to you and
me, and the more amazing thing is that with his empowerment, we can be
used in his redemptive plan for the world.

Do not settle for smallness, even significant smallness. God is waiting
to take you into places and open you up to opportunities that exist only in
your wildest dreams. The key is that you must let him give you the opportunities and move you into new places. Are you ready for an adventure?

nothing wasted (part 1)

romans 12:1–2

*And he died for all, that those who live should no longer
live for themselves but for him.*
2 Corinthians 5:15

I was in Macao, a tiny colony off the China coast. I was there for a pastors'
conference and was staying in the home of an American missionary couple.
Toward the end of my stay, my host asked if I was interested in seeing the
missionary Robert Morrison's grave. I was, so he took me to a Roman
Catholic cemetery. I stood beside that grave, now weather-beaten and mossy,
barely able to make out the name, date, and inscription, and I found myself
uncharacteristically moved with emotion.

Robert Morrison had been a young British man studying accounting
when God saved him and called him to the mission field. When he arrived
in China and the Chinese learned what his mission was, they booted him
out. In those days people who went to the mission field went for life; there
was no such thing as a furlough. So Robert went to Macao, a Portuguese
colony. He stayed there a little while and then returned to China, but again
was deported, so he found a job with the East India Company as an account-
ant. Periodically he would travel into China, only to be expelled each time.
Morrison worked all day for the East India Company, which hated missionaries, and at night he translated the Bible into Chinese. Eventually he
finished translating the Bible, and later he died in Macao. For days after his
death, there was no agreement on where to bury his body. The Chinese certainly did not want a Christian to be buried in their cemetery, and the
Roman Catholics were not about to have a Protestant buried in their cemetery. Finally someone negotiated with the Roman Catholic archbishop, who
sold one cemetery plot so they could bury Robert Morrison. He was rejected
all his life and even rejected in death.

Rarely do we recognize the cost that other people have paid to be faithful to the Lord Jesus. In our society, we focus so much on our own personal
needs that few people will stand up and say, "Whatever God asks, I will do."
Are you willing to do that?

nothing wasted (part 2)

1 peter 3:13 – 18

*For Christ died for sins once for all, the righteous for the unrighteous, to bring
you to God. He was put to death in the body but made alive by the Spirit.*
1 Peter 3:18

As I stood there by Robert Morrison's grave, an astounding memory scrolled
through my head. I had been on another trip to China back in 1982. Right
at that time the government permitted four churches to open in Canton.
So we attended the services in one of these new churches. On Wednesday
night we went to prayer meeting, and there were nearly three hundred
people in a church that had just been opened.

While the Bible study was taking place, I looked around and received
the shock of my life. Sixty percent of that audience was under thirty years of
age, which meant that all but the smallest of those had been born under Mao.
They were born under a government so hostile to Christianity that Christian parents hesitated to talk to their children about Christ lest the police
hear the children speak about him and the whole family be imprisoned.

After the service I had tea with the old pastor. "Sir," I said, "I have a
question. Am I right that at least 60 percent of this audience is under thirty
years of age?"

He smiled and said, "Yes."

"Let me ask you another question," I said. "If they're under thirty years
of age, weren't they born under Mao?"

"Yes." (There were volumes of suffering in that one word.)

"How under the sun did they become believers?"

He smiled as if he had a secret and didn't know whether he could trust
me with it. Then he simply said, "They're children of believers, or else they're
friends of children of believers, or else they're friends of friends of children
of believers."

At that moment all I could think about was a Chinese mother and father
who were willing to risk their lives so their children could know about Christ.
At night they would close all their shutters and pull a stone from the floor and
take out an old Chinese Bible and read it to their children. The salvation of

those children came from reading the Bible that Robert Morrison gave his life to translate.

No devotion to Christ is ever wasted. No lover of Christ is ultimately rejected. Everybody's redemption begins in somebody else. What is he calling you to do?

i'd rather have jesus

luke 14:25 – 34

Any of you who does not give up everything he has cannot be my disciple.
Luke 14:33

The design and structure of the tabernacle of the Jews was filled with sign-posts that pointed the way to eternal reality. Even the furniture pointed to God. The first item in the outer court of the tabernacle was a brazen altar where the animal sacrifices were made. God dwelt in the Holy of Holies in the middle of the tabernacle, and in order to approach his dwelling place, each worshiper had to stop at the brass altar and make a sacrifice. That sacrifice was an atonement for sin, and it had to be a sacrifice of life, the shedding of blood.

Intimacy with God costs; we can never enter his presence without being willing to pay the price. Knowing the triune God personally never comes cheaply. The Bible says nothing about cheap grace. Grace became available at an enormous cost to the Lord Jesus. There is a price for us as well if we are to know God in an intimate way.

Nothing of value in life comes effortlessly. God has so ordered our world that the things we desire most are the things for which we must sacrifice in order to find. Loving someone, either God or another person, means putting that one ahead of our own self-interest. It is infinitely better to live in intimacy with Jesus Christ than to have all the comfort and luxuries in the world.

joseph's faith

hebrews 11

All these people were still living by faith when they died. They did not receive the things promised; they only saw them and welcomed them from a distance. And they admitted that they were aliens and strangers on earth . . . Therefore God is not ashamed to be called their God, for he has prepared a city for them.
Hebrews 11:13, 16

Remember when Joseph was dying? He called his sons Ephraim and Manasseh and instructed them not to bury him when he died, but to embalm him. He wanted to be preserved until the Israelites traveled out of Egypt to the land of God's promise. Joseph was confident that God would fulfill his promise to his family, and he wanted to join in death the family from which he had been separated in life.

Can you imagine the family that kept Grandpa Joseph's body throughout the years? Every generation of grandchildren would come in and say, "Grandma, what is in that box in the living room?"

"Why, honey, that is Grandpa Joseph," she would calmly respond.

"Grandma, the Egyptians and other people put their dead people in pyramids or bury them in the ground. No one keeps dead people in their living room!"

"We are different from the Egyptians. You see, we have a future, and in that future we are going somewhere. God has a land for us, and he has promised to take us there. We cannot leave Grandpa Joseph here in Egypt. We must bury him in the Promised Land."

This is biblical faith: believing and not doubting. Believing that God has a future for you and for your people.

joy, delight, fulfillment

john 14:19 – 31

Then will I go to the altar of God,
to God, my joy and my delight.
I will praise you with the harp,
O God, my God.
Psalm 43:4

I wish I could adequately illustrate the interdependence of the different persons of the Trinity. Let me say this. The love between the Father, Son, and Spirit is the kind of love in which their chief delight and fulfillment is found in each other. That is the essence of their relationship. They so co-inhere within each other that if you know one person of God, you know all three persons and have found all that God is. Co-inherence is their essence. Love is their character.

The Christian God is not like Allah, who loves only on occasion. The Lord God is love. What to Allah is an action, to Yahweh is his essence and nature. It would be impossible for God to be love if it were not for the Trinity. For before the creation, whom could he have loved? Love is when we find our joy in another, our fulfillment in another, and our delight in another. This tri-unity of persons existed before the beginning of all time and space; before there was any creation, God was, he is, and he ever shall be love.

This personal character of God and the personal character of Christianity, along with its emphasis on faith, means that God does not desire primarily obedience from us. If he wanted servile obedience, he could force it. What he really desires from us is that we should love him so much that he is our joy, our delight, and our fulfillment.

knowing and knowledge

romans 2:25 – 29

*Therefore let all Israel be assured of this: God has made this Jesus,
whom you crucified, both Lord and Christ.*
Acts 2:36

The people responsible for crucifying Jesus had more knowledge about ultimate reality than any other people group that had ever lived. They were the
only true monotheists around. They had entered into a covenant with the
one God, and they were living by the commandments he had given them.
These people were the most knowledgeable and ethical people alive. And
yet that very knowledge kept them from acknowledging the One who was
the reality behind all their intellectual knowledge. The ethics of the Jews
kept them from recognizing the Creator of all human existence, including
human relationships. It was these people, remarkably similar to you and me,
who killed Jesus.

Knowledge about God is deadly. It is only when his presence enters our
lives and minds so that our knowledge of him becomes personal that we are
protected from crucifying the very One for whom we wait.

We read in Numbers 9:15–23 that the people of Israel were led by Yahweh's presence. He guided them in a pillar of fire by night, and in a cloud
by day. When he wanted the people to stop, the cloud settled down over
the tabernacle. The Israelite's knowledge of God was personal. His presence,
gloriously dwelling in their midst, was the supreme reality of their lives. Do
you know him in the same personal way? Or is your knowledge merely
about him?

learning the joy of work

proverbs 6:6 – 11

Let us make man in our image . . . and let them rule over . . . all the earth.
Genesis 1:26

Following Jesus is not possible without hard work. It takes an intellectual shaping of our minds as well as a surrender of our will in order for us to be like Jesus. Christianity is not a matter of sitting around and waiting for inspiration; it is a matter of using what God has given us in order to know him better. There is not a realm of intellectual, moral, or spiritual activity that is not open to us and that is not the believer's responsibility to master and know. And one of the delightful things is that some of us can be masters of the esoteric theories of nuclear physics or of Sumerian grammar with confidence, knowing that we are doing the will of God, if that particular discipline is God's call for us. It is God's will that someone somewhere master every one of these domains of human knowledge and experience.

What does it take to really know Jesus? It takes hard work in every area of life, and strenuous labor is what we shy away from. There is no magic in knowing Christ, and there is no shortcut. Believers must roll up their spiritual sleeves and tackle the task he has assigned them to do. We certainly have divine help, but God will never do for us what it is our responsibility to do. We do not have the privilege of leisure; rather, work is our responsibility and calling. The joy of work is something that has to be learned, and this is the reason a structure is built into society that enables people to work. The things that are most redemptive in this life, we would never do without pressure.

man's way is not in himself

Jeremiah 10

I know, O LORD, that a man's life is not his own;
it is not for man to direct his steps.
Jeremiah 10:23

At the end of Jeremiah 10 the prophet comes to a conclusion about humankind. In a priceless passage, he writes about the nature of God and the human tendency to force an alternative to God, to fill the hole in life created by God's absence. He says, "I know, O LORD, that a man's life is not his own; it is not for man to direct his steps" (Jer. 10:23). One characteristic of human beings is that our way is not found inside ourselves. Our society's love affair with self-help resources and self-fulfillment ventures will never ultimately produce happiness or satisfaction. The end for which humans exist, collectively and individually, must be located beyond ourselves. We were made for Someone outside our own reality. Therefore, we are free not to have all the answers.

The amazing thing is that this truth applies not only to human personhood, but also to divine personhood. Jesus' way was not determined by himself. His course was set by his Father. He lived for his Father and looked to him for direction, answers, and fulfillment.

If the Lord Jesus could not find his way in himself, but had to look to the Father, then our way must be outside of ourselves and also in the Father. We are certainly no more capable of making autonomous decisions than Jesus was. Christians who are walking in intimate fellowship with the triune God find the freedom that comes from looking to the Father for every decision, every answer, and every need. It is a glorious revelation to realize that we are not big enough to find our own way or to meet our own needs, but there is One who is.

more christian

matthew 5:1 – 16

You are the salt of the earth. But if the salt loses its saltiness,
how can it be made salty again? It is no longer good for anything,
except to be thrown out and trampled by men.
Matthew 5:13

What Western Christianity needs first and foremost is not more Christians, but for Christians to be much more Christian than they are. I have thought about Jesus' words directing his followers to be the salt of the earth. Christians are to be a positive influence in society, driving back corruption, and bringing cleanliness where pollution exists. Christians are to add the flavor and zest to life for which all society seeks diligently and fruitlessly.

Saltiness is not a quality that you and I can control, keep, and dispense; rather, it is a direct result of living in intimacy with God. I have never met a person whose life was a rebuke to me who was walking at a distance from God. The people whose lives have challenged, excited, and rebuked me have been those who have dwelt in intimate fellowship with God.

Our world does not need to hear more people talk about God or even about Jesus if those people do not have a lifestyle that reinforces every word they utter. The interesting thing is that the closer we walk in intimacy with God, the less we have to say. Our very lives become a bold and beautiful testimony to the purity, the freedom, and the beauty of the Lord Jesus.

the otherness of god

john 1

In the beginning was the Word, and the Word was with God, and the Word was God. He was with God in the beginning. Through him all things were made; without him nothing was made that has been made. In him was life.
John 1:1–4

Genesis 1–2 presents a vastly different worldview from that reflected in all other ancient creation stories. In those creation myths, the humans and the gods are mixed together, so that if one could trace the lineage of a person back far enough, one would find a god. All those religions blurred the line between the finite and the infinite, thus creating cultures of idolatry in which the creation was worshiped rather than the Creator. These stories appeal to the human imagination, as do many other worldviews that confine all reality to time and space. It is a captivating but illusory thought that nothing exists outside of ourselves and our situation.

I once listened to a theologian who said that the Incarnation is proof that God loves humanity and identifies with human beings. But when that speaker was questioned about the Resurrection, he admitted that he did not believe it had taken place. That man's theology could be summed up in three statements: (1) Life is tragic. Look at Jesus' suffering. (2) Life is absurd. Look at Jesus: the worthy suffer injustice. (3) God is in the same mess that human beings are in. Look at Jesus.

As I listened to the speaker's morbid theology, I realized that once you wipe out the biblical view of the otherness of God, there is neither hope nor help for humanity.

Genesis 1–2 says something radically different. The God of creation is not caught in the flux and flow of human life. He is not limited by our limitations. He enters our existence and brings order where there is chaos, life where there is death. Where there is ambiguity, God brings certainty, and where there is ignorance, he brings knowledge and truth. These qualities—order, life, certainty, knowledge, and truth—can come only out of the biblical view of God.

november 11

presence as the basis of ethics

isaiah 42:5 – 9

I, the LORD, have called you in righteousness;
I will take hold of your hand.
I will keep you and will make you
to be a covenant for the people
and a light for the Gentiles,
Isaiah 42:6

The basis of Christian ethics is not a universal consciousness or general moral laws; it is a personal relationship with the Creator of the universe. Out of that relationship comes a concern for others, insisting that each human is made in the image of the triune Creator and is therefore worthy of respect and honor. I remember what a shock it was to me to realize that the word *righteousness* in Scripture does not mean the keeping of an abstract law. Instead, *righteousness* means being in relationships that are right and true and clean. We are to be in right relationship with God and with other people. That is the meaning of righteousness.

God's nature is the basis of our treatment of other people, and his nature is unfailing truthfulness, unending loving-kindness, and unchanging righteousness. Because God is true, loving, and right, we are to treat other people with truthfulness, loving-kindness, and righteousness. Each individual person is made in God's image, and therefore we are designed to honor other people as being made in his image.

This destroys the concept of relativity in ethics. God's presence is the standard of right and wrong. Our ethical foundation is neither a set of rigid, old-fashioned regulations, nor a spectrum of ever-changing rules that we can manipulate to suit our needs. The triune God should be the basis of all human treatment of other persons and of the world in which we live. Are we living in right relationships, the way we were designed to live? Are we treating other people as persons made in the image of the One who is all truth, love, and righteousness?

where your treasure is

matthew 6:19 – 23

*But store up for yourselves treasures in heaven, where moth
and rust do not destroy, and where thieves do not break in and steal.
For where your treasure is, there your heart will be also.*
Matthew 6:20–21

Jesus, priceless treasure,
Fount of purest pleasure,
Truest friend to me:
Ah, how long in anguish
Shall my spirit languish,
Yearning, Lord, for thee?
Thine I am, O spotless Lamb!
I will suffer naught to hide thee,
Naught I ask beside Thee.

In thine arms I rest me;
Foes who would molest me
Cannot reach me here.
Though the earth be shaking,
Every heart be quaking,
Jesus calms my fear.
Lightnings flash and thunders crash;
Yet, though sin and hell assail me.
Jesus will not fail me.

Hence, all fear and sadness!
For the Lord of gladness,
Jesus, enters in.
Those who love the Father,
Though the storms may gather,
Still have peace within.
Yea, whate'er I here must bear,
Thou art still my purest pleasure,
*Jesus, priceless treasure.**

Is Jesus your treasure today?

---

*Johann Franck, "Jesus, Priceless Treasure," *Trinity Hymnal* (Suwanee, Ga.: Great Commission
Publications, 1990), no. 550.

doubting versus questioning

2 timothy 2:11 – 13

What if some did not have faith? Will their lack of faith nullify God's faithfulness? Not at all! Let God be true, and every man a liar.
Romans 3:3–4

What is the difference between doubting and having questions? I used to think that if I had any question I was a doubter. And there was a time in my life when I thought God had cursed me. He had put into my head a little black box that spewed out questions at a phenomenal rate; it did not seem that anyone else had the number of questions I did. But as the years have passed, I have been extremely grateful for that box of questions. God has used it to save me from illusion and self-deception.

So if questions are distinguished from doubting, what is the difference? In Genesis 3, the serpent says, "Did God tell you not to eat the fruit of every tree of the garden?"

And Eve says, "Yes. There is one tree, and we're not supposed to eat of it or even touch it."

"He is a nasty old man, isn't he?" the serpent hisses. "Look at that tree. Its fruit is beautiful and tasty. It will make you a much richer person if you eat it. He is holding out on you. He is depriving you."

Thus Eve is faced with a dilemma. The tree looks very good, and the serpent sounds as if he knows what he is talking about. But every indication has shown that God wants the best for her.

So far, there is no sin. But now comes the doubt. Is God holding out on me? Is he keeping something from me that would be for my good? And as soon as Eve assents to this idea, she has sinned.

Have you ever accused God of holding out on you? Have you ever grown angry with him for not giving you everything you wanted? As soon as I accuse God of not being good, I have sinned and stand aloof from God. As soon as I allow myself to be detached from God, sin has entered my life.

november 14

subtle calls to sin

luke 4:1 – 13

"You will not surely die," the serpent said to the woman.
"For God knows that when you eat of it your eyes will be opened,
and you will be like God, knowing good and evil."
Genesis 3:4–5

The devil is always subtle and tricky in his temptation. First of all, he always tempts us through something good. Eve's story illustrates this for us. Where did the tempter come from? We are told that the Lord God made him. He was a creature of God. What did he use to tempt her? It was fruit, and it was good because God had created it. Where did the temptation happen? In Eden. It did not happen on the outskirts of hell. There is temptation even in Paradise. Who was targeted for the temptation? It was a person made in the very image of God—the noblest, the highest, and the best of all God's creation.

Temptation always comes through something good and valuable. Significantly, a person can be in the center of God's will and endure grave temptation. Adam and Eve were who they were supposed to be and where they were supposed to be, and yet temptation still came.

Second, Satan disguises submission to himself under the ruse of personal autonomy. He never asks us to become his servants. Never once did the serpent say to Eve, "I want to be your master." The shift in commitment is never from Christ to evil; it is always from Christ to self. And instead of his will, self-interest now rules and what I want reigns. And that is the essence of sin.

Third, the devil always says, "This isn't very serious. You can always say 'I'm sorry.'" But the interesting thing is that the story ends with Eve on the outside and with something so lost that though she finds forgiveness, she never regains Paradise.

When temptations come, don't be bamboozled by the appearance of good. Don't hunger for personal autonomy, which really is slavery, and don't believe that forgiveness removes the consequences of sin. Set your will on the fact that you belong to Christ and to Christ alone. Fly his banner and stand under it. March with him, keeping yourself inwardly and outwardly attached to him. The beautiful thing is that overcoming your temptation will become what defeats the enemy because the experience will draw you closer to Jesus. God uses temptation to conquer the kingdom of evil and bring his children through victoriously.

temptation

james 1:2 – 18

Blessed is the man who perseveres under trial,
because when he has stood the test, he will receive the crown of life
that God has promised to those who love him.
James 1:12

Temptation is not sin. There is as much confusion about this matter as about anything else in our experience of the grace of God. James says that each of us is tempted by our own desire, and that desire gives birth to sin and brings forth death. This progression can be clearly seen in Eve's story. She desired what was placed before her, that which God had forbidden. When she looked at it, she wanted it; and yet, she did not sin by wanting it. Sin came when she reached out, took the fruit, and ate it. When her will consented to do what God had forbidden her to do, then defilement and sin entered her experience.

This is important because many people find within themselves a desire for something they know to be wrong. Then they hear a condemning voice that already accuses them of guilt and says, "You might as well go ahead and sin." But only when your will has consented does the break in your relationship with God occur. God is looking for warriors who will come out victorious, and there is no victory without a fight.

november 16

the problem of evil

joel 2:12 – 13

When the woman saw that the fruit of the tree was good for food and pleasing
to the eye, and also desirable for gaining wisdom, she took some and ate it.
She also gave some to her husband, who was with her, and he ate it.
Genesis 3:6

How can Christians intellectually handle and emotionally face the evil in
our world? How did life become so corrupt if God is so wholly good and if
he is in sovereign control? It would be easy to say that there must have been
some enormous and tragic event that cast its curse across all of time and into
every corner of space. Interestingly enough, Scripture reports that the source
of the curse did not seem to be a monumental act. Two people simply looked
in the wrong direction, turned their faces from the source of their lives, and
looked to a tree that could bring them knowledge of evil and of the good
that they then lost.

There is no indication that Adam and Eve wanted to get rid of God.
They were perfectly content to keep God around as long as they could have
the fruit of that one tree. Sin is simply turning your eyes away from God
and reaching for what you want.

Alarming and disastrous consequences resulted from that simple choice
to look away. The effects of sin, even of what appears to be the smallest sin,
ripple through hundreds of generations. Once a sin is committed, there is
absolutely no way to ever undo it. Adam and Eve gained only the knowledge
of evil through their choice; they had already known the good. Their sin
separated them from the One who is himself goodness. The question for
Adam and Eve and for us is, "Is it really worth it?"

not self-fulfilling

mark 8:34 – 38

For whoever wants to save his life will lose it, but whoever loses his life
for me and for the gospel will save it.
Mark 8:35

One of the keys for understanding not only the problem of human evil but also its solution is understanding the basic nature of human beings. Because we are made in the image of God, we never come alone. We always are part of a web of relationships. Therefore, our decisions affect other people. We are not self-originating. We begin our life in another person, ideally the fruit of a married couple's love. Neither are we self-sustaining. We draw our life from the world around us, through food and water and air. We are not even self-explanatory. There is no typical human person because we come in male and female editions. It takes two to explain one. So our whole life and identity is built upon the lives of other people.

What this means is that although we try to fight it, we are not self-fulfilling. Our fulfillment is always in another person. This is why Jesus said, "For whoever wants to save his life will lose it, but whoever loses his life for me and for the gospel will save it" (Mark 8:35).

So how does this affect the problem of evil? People come in webs of relationships that help establish their existence, identity, and fulfillment. If those relationships are broken, people suffer. In addition, our decisions affect a wide circle of people. So if we make choices for good, other people have the opportunity to grow and excel. If we make choices for evil, then the doors are slammed on other people's opportunity for growth.

Therefore, the problem of evil will be solved for us only when we recognize our need for our primary relationship to be in proper order—our relationship with God. Having come from the hand of God, we are made for relationship with him; similarly, since we have come from a love relationship between two humans, we need a relationship with one we call Mother and another we call Father. To be deprived of either of these two relationships—

with God or with our parents—can be destructive. To be deprived of our relationship with God is ultimate death for us and for others.

When we find our joy and fulfillment in our relationship with God, then we gain a new freedom to make choices that will open doors of grace for other people. As we make consistent choices based on self-giving love, then the evil diminishes and begins to lose its iron grip on those in our circle.

salvation in the heart of another

isaiah 53

We all, like sheep, have gone astray,
each of us has turned to his own way;
and the LORD has laid on him
the iniquity of us all.
Isaiah 53:6

Salvation never begins with the person who is saved. When I was a young pastor and looked at the problems in my congregation and in my community, I'd say, "If that rascal would just straighten up and fly right, things would be much better. Why doesn't he do it?"

Nobody ever decides on his own to get better. Not a soul alive wakes up one morning and says on his own, "I believe I'll become a Christian," or "I believe I'll get my life right with God today." The key to every person's change rests in somebody other than himself. That is the way God designed human beings. We are persons. I dare you to sit down and read the gospel of John and try to explain Jesus on his own. Jesus insisted that he could not be explained on his own. He was not on earth to do his own business.

I read the gospel of John for decades before it dawned on me that the main character in John's gospel is not Jesus. The main character in the gospel of John is the Father. Forty times the word *sent* is used in the gospel of John. Jesus speaks about his Father, and in the Greek the word order is literally "the sending-me Father." You'll never understand Jesus until you know he came from his Father. What he has for his guidance is not his own will, but his Father's.

None of us, not even Jesus, is self-explanatory. We are all interrelated, and the key to every person is in somebody else. Your physical life started in somebody else's womb. Your salvation began in somebody else's heart. Everyone of us is the result of somebody else's caring. God became a human person for us, taking all of our sins into himself.

Are we willing to carry other people in our heart?

free to receive

john 14:15 – 18

He came to that which was his own, but his own did not receive him.
Yet to all who received him, to those who believed in his name,
he gave the right to become children of God.
John 1:11–12

One of the effects of our fallen nature is that we do not like to receive from other people. If I receive, then I'm dependent, and I do not want to be dependent on you. I came from one of those sections in North Carolina where a good Scottish family did its own farmwork. The motto was, "Do your own. Stand on your own feet. Be your own man." And I find myself resisting dependence on others.

If I am dependent on you, then you have some control over me. I do not want to be controlled. So I resent my dependence. I resent that matter of receiving. The interesting thing is that when I refuse to receive or when I receive resentfully, I deprive you of a chief reason for existence, because you find fulfillment only in giving.

Has someone you loved ever given you back what you gave to them? Has your son or daughter or wife or husband ever used a gift as a manipulative weapon? The pain that it causes us is an indication that we were made to give, not for selfish reasons, but for the good of other people. When we quit receiving or others quit receiving our gifts, we have shut each other out. In graciously receiving, you give another person the best thing you can give.

Are you willing to receive the gifts of love that others are waiting to give you? Is your heart open and willing to be dependent upon other people? This is the essence of salvation—receiving the gift of God's love.

free to give

ecclesiastes 11:1–2

Freely you have received, freely give.
Matthew 10:8

Another effect of the Fall (cf. Genesis 3) is that we do not want to give. We like to keep for ourselves, amassing wealth instead of spending ourselves. If we do give, we give with hooks in our gifts. Let me ask you, Do you know anything that corrupts human relationships more than the hooks that we keep in what we give? A father gives to his child and then says, "After all I've done for him . . ." and the minute he says it, the gift is defiled. He did not give graciously; he gave one thing in order to get or keep something else.

What if we could freely give without hooks? That would be perfect love. I am convinced that this is the way Adam and Eve lived together before the Fall, and that this is God's intention for you and me. The Lord Jesus gives to me and I give to you, then you give to me and he gives back to you. We find ourselves drawing our life out of each other, and we come to the realization that I couldn't make it without you and you couldn't make it without me. We are bound together in that bond of love. I believe that's what eternal life is going to be like.

Give yourself away today as freely as the Lord Jesus gave himself to us. Do not give a thought to yourself or to the effect of your giving on yourself. Give with all your heart.

the arm of the lord (part 1)

isaiah 63:5

The LORD looked and was displeased
that there was no justice.
He saw that there was no one,
he was appalled that there was no one to intervene;
so his own arm worked salvation for him,
and his own righteousness sustained him.
Isaiah 59:15–16

When I imagined the arm of the Lord as discussed in Isaiah 59, I always thought about Zeus on Mount Olympus with a lightning bolt in his fist. God straightens things out with a zap of his power. What a shock when I read the first verses of Isaiah 53, which describe the "arm of the LORD" (v. 1):

He grew up before him like a tender shoot,
and like a root out of dry ground.
He had no beauty or majesty to attract us to him,
nothing in his appearance that we should desire him.
He was despised and rejected by men,
a man of sorrows, and familiar with suffering.
Like one from whom men hide their faces
he was despised, and we esteemed him not.

Surely he took up our infirmities
and carried our sorrows,
yet we considered him stricken by God,
smitten by him, and afflicted.
But he was pierced for our transgressions,
he was crushed for our iniquities;
the punishment that brought us peace was upon him,
and by his wounds we are healed. . . .
He was oppressed and afflicted,
yet he did not open his mouth;
he was led like a lamb to the slaughter.

Isaiah 53:2–5, 7

Now a lamb being led to the slaughter is completely unlike Zeus with his lightning bolt. This passage has transformed my understanding of the power of God. When I realized what it was saying, I found myself thinking that God had looked at the world in its sin and declared, "If I cannot find one person to bring salvation, then the only thing I can do is become one of them."

Consequently, there was a baby conceived in a virgin's womb, there was an infant born in a stable, and there was a boy raised in a carpenter's shop. And eventually, there was a Savior for all the world.

the arm of the lord (part 2)

psalm 98:1 – 3

But when this priest had offered for all time one sacrifice for sins,
he sat down at the right hand of God ... because by one sacrifice
he has made perfect forever those who are being made holy.
Hebrews 10:12, 14

There are moments when, in the presence of the truth of God, I become speechless. The implications of truly understanding the "arm of the LORD" are astounding. Was it not possible for salvation to have taken place unilaterally in heaven? No. God had to come down here in the middle of our mess, to experience what we experience and be one of us in order to redeem us.

Do you know that Jesus didn't have to die on a cross to cleanse a leper? He didn't have to die on a cross to make a blind man see. He created that leper and those eyes in the beginning. Every miracle Jesus performed, he could have done without ever going to the Cross. There was only one thing he couldn't do without the Cross. Jesus could not turn around the selfishness inside me. And God knew that if he did not turn me around, I would damn myself by living for myself. The only way for salvation to come was for God himself to come down here and become a human being.

Salvation had to occur here, in history, if it was to deal with the problems that exist in the human heart. Now we can go to the exact spot in time and space where Christ died so we could live. Heaven is on its face in adoration and praise for a God who loves like this, and we should be as well.

He became one of us. When you see Jesus face-to-face, he will look like you look. When you see Jesus, you're going to be able to touch him and feel him. In order to make our redemption possible, God assumed our nature for the rest of eternity.

the intellectual component of faith

mark 8:27 – 9:13

Now faith is being sure of what we hope for and certain of what we do not see
Hebrews 11:1

Christian faith must contain an intellectual component. When we believe in Christ, we must not throw our mind away. If we have a biblical faith, there will be a close relationship between what we know and what we believe. It is my conviction that there ought to be a steady progression in a believer's life from faith to knowledge. What is faith one day, the next day becomes knowledge. These two things build upon one another rather than fight each other. For example, what was faith in Peter when he declared that Jesus was the Christ in Caesarea Philippi became firm knowledge after the Transfiguration, when he saw Jesus talking with Moses and Elijah. We live perpetually believing, then finding that what we believe works in actual practice, and knowing that it is true.

God has given us a revelation of truth, and it is our business to reach out to the men and women who live in intellectual darkness and let the light of the gospel in our lives shine into their minds and lives. All Christians began their walk with Christ after receiving some intellectual information about who Jesus is and why they should believe. We have a serious obligation to know the gospel well enough so that when we share it, the winsomeness of its truth is evident and compelling.

Are you continuing to train your mind so God can use it to reach a world in darkness? Let us not become lazy in our salvation. We will have to give an account of the way we have used our intellectual resources.

the joy of exclusivity

song of songs 2:2 – 3

I will sing for the one I love.
Isaiah 5:1

Is your relationship to the Lord Jesus an exclusive relationship? He wants us to be in an intimate and healthy relationship with him. This is the stumbling block that has forbidden me across the years to forsake the Wesleyan teaching on entire sanctification. The one thing I know about my wife is that she wants my exclusive commitment. I can be nice to a billion other women, but she wants my devotion. That kind of relationship is not restricting; it is liberating. Jesus wants that same kind of relationship with us. And when we are in love with him, it is not a sacrifice but a total joy.

There is something in the Cross of Christ that can so capture my heart that no rival to the Lord Jesus can tolerate living inside me and with me. Jesus stands supreme. He is first, and he is Lord alone. The funny thing is, when Jesus becomes first, I love everybody and everything else better. But when he is not my first love, I am alienated from everyone else, and my resources and ability to give myself to others diminishes drastically. The world is waiting to see people who are in an exclusive love relationship with the Lord Jesus, a loving relationship that overflows to all other persons.

Are you in a relationship like that?

the least of these

luke 23:39 – 43

Thinking he was the gardener, she said, "Sir, if you have carried him away,
tell me where you have put him, and I will get him."
Jesus said to her, "Mary."
John 20:15–16

There are some people who say that it is not possible to have a clean and pure heart, especially for people with fewer privileges. Their theory is that all the days of life one will yearn, hope, pray, and seek but never find a completely clean heart. However, there are passages in Scripture indicating that it is possible in this life to have a heart made clean by the blood of Christ Jesus. This may well mean that the heart yearning for freedom from sin longs for the very thing for which that heart was created.

I once heard a sermon by Henry Clay Morrison in which he took his audience on an elevator ride down to hell and then up to heaven. When we reached heaven, we saw a creature more beautiful than anything we had ever seen. Because if its grandeur, we assumed it was the archangel Michael or one of the great saints such as Moses or Paul. When we asked, the creature laughed almost gleefully and said, "No, I am Mary Magdalene. I am the woman of sin made clean by the blood of the Cross."

The most beautiful people in heaven may be the ones in whom the Holy Spirit has wrought the greatest transformation. We do not glorify God by lessening the standards for those we determine could never meet them. We glorify God by recognizing all of his holiness and recognizing that somehow, in the miracle of redemption, Jesus can make any person compatible for fellowship with the Father, the Son, and the Spirit—holy, clean, and beautiful.

the love challenge

1 corinthians 13

If I speak in the tongues of men and of angels, but have not love,
I am only a resounding gong or a clanging cymbal.
1 Corinthians 13:1

I was at a conference with about 180 missionaries, and we spent four days in retreat together. In that group was an elderly lady who was one of the matriarchs of that mission. Her husband had been one of the mission's founders. I remember that as the days passed she listened intently to the Word as it was preached. One day she encountered me at a luncheon and said, "You are not really going to tell me that you believe a person can live by 1 Corinthians 13, are you?"

And I said, "Yes, I am. Here it is in the Word of God. The Scriptures say that if we have everything and do not have this kind of love, we have failed in everything."

In our own strength we can never attain to the love that is described in this great chapter. Yet the question is not whether we can love like that but whether God can love through us like that. The power behind that love rests in the shed blood of the redeeming Savior and in the Holy Spirit, who can come and cleanse, fill, and renew our hearts in perfect love.

The missionary lady at this conference looked at me and said, "I never felt it was really possible to live that way." But the next afternoon she opened her heart to let the Holy Spirit love through her. Is your life marked by the love of God? If it is not, you are failing in everything else.

Love through me, love of God.
There is no love in me.
O fire of love, light thou the love
That burns perpetually. *

---

*Amy W. Carmichael, "Love Through Me," *Toward Jerusalem* (London: SPCK, 1950).

the rod of witness

exodus 4:1 – 5

*Raise your staff and stretch out your hand over the sea to divide the water so
that the Israelites can go through the sea on dry ground.*
Exodus 14:16

Inside the ark of the covenant was the rod used by Moses and Aaron when
they led the Israelites out of Egypt. That rod symbolized God's power. Moses
had lifted it to challenge Pharaoh, to bring the plagues, and to part the Red
Sea. It declared the absolute superiority of Yahweh over all the other gods,
the reality that Yahweh alone is God.

The latter chapters of Isaiah continue to witness to God's preeminence.
God refers to himself by saying, "I am the LORD, and there is no other" (Isa.
45:5–6, 18). Yahweh is the sovereign Lord, and his rod indicated that he is
the most powerful and also that he is the Savior. God was the deliverer of
the people of Israel, and if he had delivered the people once, he could do it
again. Therefore, the chief priest was required to make the sacrifice for the
Day of Atonement in the presence of the rod of God, which witnessed to
Yahweh's delivering and redemptive power.

When you and I come before God, we need to be reminded that he is
our Savior and our Deliverer. He is greater than any problem we have, and
he is more powerful than any foe we face. It doesn't matter whether that foe
is external or internal; God is big enough to save us from it. It is through his
power and our obedience that Jesus Christ can be Lord in your life and in
mine.

trinity and family

malachi 2:13–16

Let us rejoice and be glad and give him glory!
For the wedding of the Lamb has come, and his bride has made herself ready.
Revelation 19:7

The doctrine of the Trinity not only explains the Godhead to the human mind; it also explains how interpersonal relationships among humans are to be. No longer can we think of the parent-child relationship as something social scientists imagined and instituted. Now we must think of it as something taken out of the eternal nature of God. No longer are we left with the question of what kind of pattern to follow; we have a model. I am to be to my child as the first person of the Trinity is to the second person, and the child is to be to me as the second person of the Trinity is to the first person. We are entwined in very serious and sacred relationships patterned after the very nature of God.

The Trinity also explains my marriage relationship. No longer is it a social convenience, a mere transient institution. The one-husband-for-one-wife relationship was born in the very heart of God—it was his idea from the very beginning of time. All of history began with a wedding between Adam and Eve, and all history will end with a wedding between Christ and his bride, the church. The engagement between Jesus and his bride has already taken place. Now Christians are to look to the future as a young woman who has just accepted a proposal from her beloved; a gleam of adoration should shine in every Christian's eye.

truly human

philippians 2:5 – 11

*Christ suffered for you, leaving you an example, that you should
follow in his steps. "He committed no sin, and no deceit was found
in his mouth." When they hurled their insults at him ... he
entrusted himself to him who judges justly.*
1 Peter 2:21–23

In Genesis 1–2 we discover the reality about the connection between God
and human beings. The key to humanity is found in Paradise, not in the
world as we know it. In fact, you may never have seen a real person—a complete person. True persons are rare, and you must search to find one. When
you do find a true person, you will discover that he or she is free from inten-
tional sin. Christ can set us free from sin, and then we become bit by bit the
person we were designed to be.

Are you aware that a person can be fully human without sin? You do
not have to sin to be human. Sometimes when people have done wrong,
they say, "Well, I am only human." The reality is that although human
nature gives you the capacity to do wrong, you are not any more human
after you have done it. In fact, there are strong indications that you may not
be quite as human after the sin as you were before the sin occurred. It is our
sin that causes us to live at a subhuman level.

This is the key to the Incarnation. God could wed himself to our
humanity because our humanity in its essence is not sinful. Sin is a historical accident that came to human beings, and it is possible to be free from it
again through the blood of Jesus. Totally free.

we were made for love

song of songs 8:6 – 7

*May they be brought to complete unity to let the world know that you
sent me and have loved them even as you have loved me.*
John 17:23

If I were the devil and wanted to disrupt the work of God, there is no question about what I would do. I would attempt to keep all human beings from discovering that self-giving love for which they were made. It is this self-giving love with which Christ desires to surround us and in which he desires to include us. Our fallen nature hinders us from realizing his purpose for us, and our sinfulness makes us easy prey for the devil's blinding and deafening lies.

If I were the devil, I would do my best to corrupt every loving human relationship that I could find because love relationships point to the eternal love of God. If I could get people to the place where they have never known what love looks like, I could keep them from knowing that for which they were made. Then each of them would dwell in a loveless cocoon; they would never know the wealth of reality outside their immediate conscious existence.

The enemy of our souls knows from whence we came, and he knows what our future will be if we participate in the fellowship and self-giving love of the triune Godhead. He will do everything he can to keep us from glimpsing the depths of love the Father has for us. This is why Jesus said, "My prayer is not for them alone. I pray also for those who will believe in me through their message, that all of them may be one" (John 17:20–21). The only way the people in the world will ever break out of their isolated shells is if they can see other humans living in love of such quality that it bursts their sinful understanding of love and gives them something they can dream about. That dream of a soul-satisfying and never-ending love will be the road that leads them to Jesus.

prepared hearts

psalm 46:10 – 11

Be still before the LORD and wait patiently for him;
Psalm 37:7

The Christmas season is approaching, and we must prepare our hearts for Christ's coming. So often we come into his presence hurriedly, anxiously, and unprepared. We would do well to pay attention to the old Scottish Church's communion service, which regarded spiritual preparation as paramount. The believers who desired to take communion on Sunday were to go to a special midweek service ahead of time so they would not come rushing pell-mell into God's presence. The leaders instituted this preparation service so people would come to communion ready to receive from God the grace that is needed for life's circumstances.

The next few weeks should be a time of preparation for us. In the midst of all the Christmas activity, there should be in our lives a dimension of spiritual hunger and thirst, a seeking of God.

Our prayer should be, "God, what do you want to say to me during this season? I want my heart, my mind, and my whole being to be open to your Spirit during your birthday celebration."

This is the time when we must be extremely careful about the priorities in our lives. There is no question that the gift-buying, the family times, and the church activities are quite important, but these days the primary thing in your life and mine should be our relationship to Immanuel—the One who came to dwell with us.

december 2

the name of jesus

psalm 99:1 – 5

*Therefore God exalted him to the highest place and gave him the name
that is above every name, that at the name of Jesus every knee should bow,
in heaven and on earth and under the earth.*
Philippians 2:9–10

In a few days the world will pause to acknowledge the birth of Jesus. How many world leaders will see a relation between the One whose birth is celebrated and the events that take place in our world? Most of the Western world will again hear Handel's *Messiah,* but few will think that the "Hallelujah Chorus" has anything to do with actual world events and history. The reality is that those lines "King of kings and Lord of lords, and he shall reign forever and ever" are not just music. They are truth. Jesus will reign. Better still, he does reign. It is he who presides over world history, even though the media and the politicians do not know it. Jesus is Lord.

Sam Kamaleson was preaching in an evangelistic crusade in Romania just as the Communist world of Eastern Europe was collapsing. His audience, so long deprived of God and his Word, was large and attentive. One night as he preached, Sam became conscious of an unexpected sound that swept across his audience. Slowly he recognized that the wave of sound came every time he used the name of Jesus. Then he realized that it was the women in the audience weeping. The sound increased, and he realized that the men were weeping as well. Sam said that by that time he found himself weeping every time he used the name of Jesus. Sam explained, "You know, when the last alternative option to Jesus has been exhausted and shown for its true bankruptcy, the name of Jesus takes on great power and allure."

Sam's statement is the best expression of the biblical philosophy of history that I have ever heard. When we choose to go our own way, God does not stop us. He lets us go until our lives collapse around us. Then in the chaos and hurt we become open again to the One from whom we have turned, and we find hope in his name. This is true for institutions, movements, countries, and cultures as well as for individuals like you and me. We may reject him for a long time, but the end of every road will be the ultimately inescapable Christ. Ezekiel has a word for this, recurrent through his prophecy: "You will know that I am the LORD" (Ezek. 13:23).

december 3

the anointing of the spirit

john 1:29 – 36

I am going to send you what my Father has promised;
but stay in the city until you have been clothed with power from on high.
Luke 24:49

One of the most significant aspects of the baptism of Jesus is found in the descent of the Holy Spirit upon the Messiah. Here the Holy Spirit assumed a new relationship with the Son. In Old Testament times kings and high priests were anointed with oil as a sign that God had chosen them for their specific leadership roles. When Saul and David were anointed, Scripture records, the Holy Spirit came upon them. It was promised in the Old Testament that the Messiah would be marked by the presence of the Spirit in him. In fact, the meaning of *Messiah* is "the anointed one."

The Spirit's anointing on Jesus preceded his public ministry. Similarly, the early church was not released for or prepared to witness until the Holy Spirit came upon them (Acts 2). Saul of Tarsus received the Spirit when he regained his sight, before he began his ministry.

We can never accomplish effective and enduring work for Christ unless we have experienced the anointing of the Holy Spirit. If this anointing was necessary for Jesus and the apostles, surely it is necessary for us as well. Has there come into your life an anointing that prepares you for his witness and his work? If not, you are not equipped to minister to other people.

his grace, my power

2 corinthians 12:7–10

*He said to me, "My grace is sufficient for you, for my power
is made perfect in weakness." Therefore I will boast all the more gladly
about my weaknesses, so that Christ's power may rest on me. That is why,
for Christ's sake, I delight in weaknesses, in insults, in hardships,
in persecutions, in difficulties. For when I am weak, then I am strong.*
2 Corinthians 12:9–10

Grace, for Paul, is simply the presence of God at work redemptively in a person's life. This means that the important thing is not what we do for our salvation but whether we free the Spirit to work unhindered in our lives. If we release the Spirit, then we can even rejoice in what we do not have to offer. We can rejoice in our very weaknesses, because our lack clears the way for the Spirit to be glorified in our lives. He is enough. Paul tells us that God is able to make his grace abound in us so we can abound in every good work (2 Cor. 9:8). Because of this, our weaknesses can be a source of joy because they give Jesus the opening to show himself at work in us.

Years ago, when I was an immature and inexperienced first-year seminary student, I found myself invited to conduct revival services in an Eastern port city. It was during World War II, and the city was filled with sailors from all over the Western world. When I arrived, I learned that I was scheduled to speak twenty-six times. I had only rough notes on a half-dozen talks that could in no way be called sermons. You can imagine my terror. For the next seven days, when I was not in the pulpit, I lived on my knees before my open Bible. There was only one evening service out of fourteen where there were no seekers after Christ. My weakness proved his strength.

On the last night I sat exhausted on the platform and looked at the crowd. Two faces captured my attention. One was that of a bald, tough-looking naval officer who looked threateningly at me. The other was that of a lovely young coed, stylishly dressed, sitting on the front row. Neither seemed to belong. I knew I had nothing to say that would mean anything to either of them.

I have no idea what I preached, but when I finished, the tough-looking naval officer burst from his seat. I still remember his prayer: "O Lord, is there anything you can do for the likes of me?" Then I noticed the young coed. She was looking up at an older lady from the church and was speaking. I could read her lips. She was saying, "What am I supposed to do?" That night she found Christ.

That was when I began to learn that the greatest gift we have to offer to God is our weakness. When we know that we cannot provide what is needed, then he is free to occupy center stage. We just step out of the way and let him work. And he does!

holy moments

2 chronicles 30

*The LORD said to Moses, "Speak to the Israelites and say to them:
'These are my appointed feasts, the appointed feasts of the LORD,
which you are to proclaim as sacred assemblies.'"*
Leviticus 23:1–2

Some moments have more significance than others. These are times that the Scriptures call holy moments, holy days, and holy seasons. All of Scripture is concerned with those holy times that are worth more than other moments. Can two hours make a difference in someone's life so the person is never the same? It is not hard to realize that there are a lot of biblical stories that fit this pattern. A bush burned, and Moses was never the same. Isaiah had a vision in the temple, and Israel heard the word from God. Saul had a vision on the Damascus road, and the Gentile world heard about the Savior. One moment with God changed the course of their lives. Obviously these holy times did not last long, but all of human history was different because God came and made ordinary moments into holy moments.

There ought to be holy moments in everyone's life, and some of them ought to come on a predictable basis. They ought to come like the feast days for Israel, days that were set apart to be holy days. We need to set some time apart and allow the Spirit to sanctify it so that we are available and open to anything to which he wants to call us.

holy places

exodus 40

*The cloud covered the Tent of Meeting,
and the glory of the LORD filled the tabernacle.
Exodus 40:34*

One of the most misunderstood terms in the English language is the word *holiness*. In Scripture, *holiness* means the presence of God. He is the only Holy One, and therefore anyone who is holy is merely someone who is filled with the presence of God. In the Old Testament we read about the Holy Land, a Holy City, holy places, holy things, and holy seasons, but none of these was holy in and of itself. Each was made holy by the presence of God.

Canaan was not a holy land when it was controlled by the Canaanites; it became the Holy Land when Yahweh came and dwelt there. The city of Jerusalem was not holy when it was a Jebusite stronghold; it became holy after it was captured by the people of God. Even the Holy of Holies in the temple was not holy until the presence of God came and filled it.

An ordinary land, a common city, and a small space became holy only when the presence of God descended upon them. He can take the regular, the secular, and the profane and make them holy and sacred. The holiness that came to these places was not a possession of the places themselves. The holiness only stayed as long as Yahweh was there. When he left, the sacredness was lost. Holiness is the presence of God. The Holy One can take the ordinary, the common, and the simple, and then sanctify, beautify, and hallow it by his personal presence. The Holy One can take you and me in all our ordinariness and sanctify us so that we are like him.

mutually exclusive worlds

matthew 10

A student is not above his teacher, nor a servant above his master.
It is enough for the student to be like his teacher, and the servant like his
master. If the head of the house has been called Beelzebub, how much more
the members of his household! So do not be afraid of them. There is nothing
concealed that will not be disclosed, or hidden that will not be made known.
Matthew 10:24–26

When Jesus sent the twelve disciples out to preach, he spoke pointedly about
the radical difference between the kingdom of God and the kingdom of this
world. It was necessary for Jesus to disillusion his disciples about the likeli-
hood that those to whom they would minister would readily accept them
and their message. Normally the disciples of Jesus could expect to be rejected
and shunned. They would be like sheep among wolves and therefore must
be wise as serpents and harmless as doves (Matt. 10:16). The disciples had
to understand the radical demands that the King and Savior made on all
those who would follow him. They had to be ready to stand firm when
people refused the message. The disciples had to know that identification
with Christ would not make them popular with the world.

The kingdom of this world and God's kingdom involve diametrically
opposed loyalties. There can be no mixing of devotions. One cannot be in
both kingdoms at the same time; they are mutually exclusive. It is little wonder that when people realize the full claims of Christ and rebel against him,
they heap their wrath upon his ambassadors. Diplomats cannot be thought
of apart from the country they represent. They will be treated with as much
respect and affection as the country they represent receives. The disciple of
Christ will receive treatment similar to that which the Master himself
received.

These words must have comforted the hearts of martyrs and persecuted
Christians throughout the ages. The opposition today may not be as bitter
or seem as deadly, but Christians must ever remember that the way of Christ
and the way of the world are opposed to each other. The center of one is
ego while the center of the other is Christ. Two persons may do many things

alike, but the basic motivation must be different. Basic loyalty will ultimately lead clearly to a life conformed to one image or the other. We need to recognize the opposition when we agree to follow Christ. There is a price to be paid, and those who take their hand from the plow and turn back are not worthy of the kingdom of Christ.

Let us pray that he will keep us faithful.

the missing presence

1 samuel 4

Let us bring the ark of the LORD's covenant from Shiloh,
so that it may . . . save us.
1 Samuel 4:3

The devil was a participant in the first conversation ever held about God. It was Eve's conversation with the serpent. Biblically, up to that point the conversations had been directly with God. Throughout Scripture we find passages in which people who have lost God talk about him.

In the Old Testament, the Philistines were giving Israel difficulty, so the sons of Eli decided that the Israelites should carry the ark of the covenant into battle. They reasoned that the ark was where God dwelt, so if his throne accompanied them, he would too. Unfortunately, when they carried the ark into battle, they were soundly defeated. They had failed to realize that when they carried his throne it did not mean that they carried him. They had broken God's Law and had been heedless of his ways, and his Spirit had long since departed from them, even though they continued to talk about him. The reality of his presence was gone.

It is always dangerous to think of God as an abstraction. I am convinced that Joseph and Mary were talking about Jesus that day when all of a sudden they looked around and discovered that he was not with them. They had left him in the temple and had traveled a whole day without his presence among them, and they had to retrace their steps in order to find him (Luke 2:41–52).

We must have a personal relationship with God in which we know he is a vital, living person to whom we can relate every moment of every day. Are you like the Israelites who carried the relics of his presence without the reality of his Person? Are you like Mary and Joseph, who traveled awhile without Jesus before they missed him? During this Christmas season, as we celebrate the Lord of lords, let us not be without his immediate presence. The symbols and celebrations can never replace Jesus Christ himself.

a treasured possession

Exodus 19:4 – 5

If you obey me fully and keep my covenant, then out of all nations
you will be my treasured possession.
Exodus 19:5

Exodus 19:5 is one of the most beautiful verses in the Old Testament. It was spoken to the people whom God had just redeemed and called his own. The word was not given to tell them how to find God; it was given to people who already knew him. God had brought his people not only to a journey toward a new land but also to himself. They were not to think first of the Promised Land but were to find their identity in a personal communion with him. That relationship with God was to be very intimate and special, as indicated by the word *segullah*, which is translated "treasured possession."

This Hebrew word occurs only eight times in the Old Testament. On each occasion it is used of a special and highly prized possession. Once it refers to David's special sacrificial gift for building the temple. Another time it is used by the wise man to describe the things that delight a person's heart. The other six times Yahweh uses the word to describe his chosen one, Israel. When this term was translated from Hebrew into Greek, it meant "one's own" in the way that a bridegroom claims his bride at the altar. The context of God's Law is not a courtroom but a wedding celebration.

The personal character of the relationship between Yahweh and his people in this passage is more obvious in the Hebrew than in the English. The expression, "If you obey me fully," literally says in the Hebrew, "If, listening, you will listen to my voice." Yahweh's people are not to have a relationship with an abstract law, but a fellowship with the One who has loved and chosen his people.

Do you realize that the almighty God, Creator of all that exists, treasures you? He takes more pleasure in you than you will ever find in him.

december 10

the allure of legalism

matthew 15:8–9

You will be for me a kingdom of priests and a holy nation.
Exodus 19:6

Several metaphors in Scripture describe God's relationship to his people. One of these is a corporate metaphor that comes from the establishment of Israel as a political entity in the Middle East. When God called Moses to lead Israel out of Egypt, it was that they might become a separate nation. Israel was no longer to be a subgroup within another national entity; God's people were to be a "holy nation" and a "kingdom of priests."

A nation must have order, and to maintain that order, it must have a legal system. The fact that Israel's legal system was religious meant that it had a priesthood and a national system of worship. The pentateuchal books of Exodus, Leviticus, and Numbers give us the account of the establishment of that legal and religious system. The Old Testament sums up all of this legislation in the word *Torah,* which is translated "Law."

This Torah had its authority in the fact that it was revelation given by Israel's God, Yahweh, to Israel's leader, Moses. To question any part of the Law was a direct challenge to Yahweh. The Law was given not to be a troublesome burden for the Israelites, but to protect them and to further God's redemptive purposes in the world by maintaining their integrity and unity as a nation.

A subtle danger arose at this point in Israel's history. They knew what offended the Holy One, and they could easily turn their attention away from the Giver of the Law to the Law itself, just as Adam and Eve turned their eyes from the Creator to one tiny aspect of creation. As Adam and Eve thought their fulfillment lay in the fruit, so also many people in Israel came to believe that their salvation lay in the Law instead of in Yahweh, who gave the Law. In idolatry one gains the thing made but loses the Maker. In legalism one becomes self-righteous and loses the righteous One.

The slip into legalism happens quickly and subtly. Are you devoted to the righteous One or to his Law? It is possible for Christians to even become idolaters of Scripture. We are to worship the One whom Scripture reveals to us. To what or to whom are you devoted?

anticipating god's action

hebrews 11

Asa cried out to the LORD his God, and said, "LORD, it is nothing for You to help, whether with many or with those who have no power; help us, O LORD our God, for we rest on You, and in Your name we go."
2 Chronicles 14:11 NKJV

The author of Chronicles portrays God as an actor on the human scene and in individual lives. The book is a history of the kings of Judah. In describing these kings' lives, the writer occasionally indicates God's involvement in human life. Sometimes that involvement is in the form of natural forces and sometimes God acts supernaturally; either way, the chronicler wants to affirm that God is alive, present, and active in the nation of Israel. We also need to think in terms of God being present with his activity, and we should expect him to work in our lives.

My mistake in too much of my life has been to simply look back and give God thanks for what I can see he has done instead of living in anticipation of what he is going to do. I tend to see the dark clouds and not see the One who is behind and above those looming clouds. However, if we take Scripture seriously, there ought to be an anticipation in our hearts that says, "I wonder what he is going to do today. I have this massive problem; I wonder how he is going to work it out." We need to expect his action and presence in our lives.

We live in a most significant moment in human history. Every barrier to the gospel either has been broken down or is permeable. The great missionaries such as David Livingstone would have loved to have the opportunities and the open doors that we have. Unfortunately, the Western church is spiritually bankrupt and largely apostate, so all we see is the death around us. But God is at work in the world, and the opportunities are everywhere. The devil wants us to be blind so we won't take part in the greatest move of the gospel ever.

God is at work in the world, and he wants to use you and me to accomplish his purposes. Are you anticipating him today?

making a way (part 1)

psalm 107

This is what the LORD says—
he who made a way through the sea,
a path through the mighty waters.
Isaiah 43:16

In 1991 I received a letter from a young woman in China. She said, "I have become a Christian, and I believe God is calling me to be an evangelist. Could I come to Asbury College and get training?" She was admitted, so she went to the American embassy, but they refused her visa because she already had a bachelor's degree. We then got her accepted at Asbury Theological Seminary for graduate work, but the American embassy put all sorts of obstacles in her path. For two years they blocked her from coming to the United States for training. I became discouraged. Then on June 10, 1993, I received a communication from her that said if she could be readmitted and guaranteed financial help, she could get a visa, so we went through the whole process again. In July I received another letter: "I will be arriving in Houston, Texas, in September. Could someone pick me up?"

When the young woman arrived, she told us the rest of her story. The embassy official who had given her more than two years of hassle finally looked at her and said, "Okay, one final question." Joy knew that her future would be determined by her answer to that question. He said, "Would you please explain to me the theological significance of the Song of Songs in the Old Testament?" Joy looked at him in horror, wondering how in her broken English she would ever be able to explain it to him. Then the answer came to her as if Jesus had whispered it in her ear: "'Oh, that you would kiss me with the kisses of your mouth. For your love is better than wine.' Sir, that is the second verse of the first chapter of the Song of Songs, and it speaks of my love for the Lord Jesus and his love for me."

The American embassy official stared at Joy, shrugged his shoulders, and said, "Let her go. She is for real." So Joy came to America for school.

Sometimes we strain in frustration and anger at the delays that seem to lie in our way, delays that seem to be keeping us from going where we could be of most service to God. But the reality is that he uses every delay, and when his timing is right, he will open the doors, and we will walk through them with confidence. That confidence comes from knowing that we allowed God to make a way instead of pushing ourselves ahead of his time schedule. Are you waiting on him today? Are you bearing the delays he allows with grace and patience?

making a way (part 2)

psalm 107

As for God, his way is perfect;
the word of the LORD is flawless.
He is a shield for all who take refuge in him.
2 Samuel 22:31

Joy valiantly struggled through three years of school in a second language, and as the end of her program drew near, she began preparing to return to China. But she was afraid. She didn't know what would happen to her when she went back to China: imprisonment, persecution, rejection? She fought that battle and came out victorious, saying, "God will take care of me. I will go with him."

A week before she was to fly to China, a knock came at my door, and when I opened it, I was confronted by a total stranger. "You don't know who I am, but I am the principal of the International School in China, and I am in Wilmore looking for staff." As I stared at him in disbelief, all of a sudden Joy popped around the doorpost into full view and said, "My miracle!" This man had started a school for internationals in order to have a Christian presence in China. The school was successful, and he had three positions open. Joy could take her pick. I have had enough communication with Joy to know that she is back in China in her home church, bearing witness to Jesus in her city, her school, and her home.

God will take care of his children. He is at work. He will not intervene if the natural processes will take care of his children. But if they will not, God moves in to ensure that his eternal purposes are accomplished. God is an actor in our lives, and we can count on him working for us if we are living in the center of his will.

salt of the earth

matthew 5:13

Salt is good, but if it loses its saltiness, how can you make it salty again?
Have salt in yourselves, and be at peace with each other.
Mark 9:50

Some jobs in life are hateful and yet necessary. I remember one of those from my teenage years. In those Depression days, there was no such thing as a refrigerator. If meat was to be kept, it had to be salted heavily. Every fall I knew that one day I would come home from school in the afternoon and find a gutted pig lying on the back porch. I knew there would be no playing ball that afternoon. My job was to rub salt into the pieces of that pork as my mother cut them up. The only thing that brightened that unpleasant task was imagining the smell of bacon frying for breakfast or the taste of ham when company came.

One day we were having some special company for supper, so mother took me out to the smokehouse and pointed to the largest ham hanging from the rafters. I pulled it down, opened the sack, and laid the beautiful ham out for my mother to cut. The big butcher knife penetrated the best portion of that ham, and I waited with anticipation to see the meat. Then I had two simultaneous and shocking perceptions. One was of the frown on my mother's face and the other was of the most offensive odor I have ever smelled. The ham was full of maggots. My mother looked at me with dismay and said, "Son, not enough salt."

I have never heard Jesus' words "You are the salt of the earth" (Matt. 5:13) without remembering that ham. We live in a day in which our society is loaded with corruption. The problem is not that evil is so powerful; in fact, evil only works in the absence of that which is holy. Where the Holy One reigns, evil can no more exist than maggots can live in salt. This is the reason we must be filled with the Holy Spirit. Then we can find freedom from the corruption that surrounds us. Even more important, the Spirit in us can be a check on the evil around us.

december 15

save me from me (part 1)

jeremiah 24:7

As Solomon grew old, his wives turned his heart after other gods,
and his heart was not fully devoted to the LORD his God,
as the heart of David his father had been.
1 Kings 11:4

What does God want me to be like? If you go through the books of
Chronicles and Kings in the Hebrew, you will find an expression that is
not used anywhere else in the Old Testament. I believe that the writers
used the phrase as a technical term—similar to our word *conversion*. It is
usually translated in these books as "wholly committed" or "fully dedi-
cated" to God. The literal translation from Hebrew is "a heart of peace."
God is looking for people who have a heart of peace. We like that phrase
because we like peace, but we understand peace as a result, not a cause.

What is peace? It means simply that the war has stopped. Has the war
stopped in your heart? Has the strife ended? God's eyes run to and fro
throughout the whole earth, looking for people in whom the war has ended,
for whom the peace has come. The one who has peace is the one who is
wholly committed to the Lord. Peace is the test by which the writers of Kings
and Chronicles measure the kings of Judah and Israel. David told Solomon
that he must have a heart that is united and in which the commitment to
serve the Lord is complete. The last word said about Solomon is that he did
not have a heart that was wholly committed. His heart was led astray by his
foreign wives. He was God's chosen man for the people of Israel, but he was
not wholly committed.

The writers go through every king's reign with this standard. Some meet
the standard and some do not. As you read through Chronicles, you realize
that this singleness of heart is not easy to attain, and if one attains it, it is
even harder to keep. Solomon started out well, but fell away at the end.
Occasionally a king would start out lousy and end up with a single heart, and
many of the kings never had singleness of heart at all.

In a heart that is undivided, the war is over; Jesus has won permanent possession of that life. There will still be temptation, but the choice to follow Jesus will have already been made. There will be other battles, but they will not be over the territory that has already been won—the resolve to do the will of God. Christ can bring me to the place where that choice is made, and even more gloriously, he can bring me to the place where that choice is maintained.

save me from me (part 2)

jeremiah 24:7

Commit your way to the LORD;
trust in him and he will do this:
He will make your righteousness shine like the dawn,
the justice of your cause like the noonday sun.
Psalm 37:5–6

Entropy is the disintegration and disorientation at work in an organization or an institution. I have decided that this is a magnificent word for original sin. There is a principle of disintegration within us. Before we know God, it is entropy that creates problems within us, and after we meet him, entropy is still at work.

A heart at peace will not be found through human effort. All of us try to get there by our own effort. We crank up our devotional life, deciding that we are going to do more, give more, and be more. To our dismay, we find that our effort is a dead-end street. As hard as we try, we cannot release control of our own lives. The "I" inside of us will not kill itself. It is subtle and clever, and it will always find a way out through religious sentiment or with religious methodology.

There is One, however, who can bring peace to us, and there is a grace that will come if we will trust him for an undivided heart. That One died on the cross to get the battle outside of us, and it is his sacrifice that enables us to be set free. There is something in the Cross of Jesus Christ that can save me from me.

When you come to the end of yourself, cry out to God, "Can you help me?" He can and he will if you will trust him. Then wait in hope, and you will find that when you are not looking, he will begin to set you free. If God makes your heart single, you will be part of the answer to the world's problem because of the grace of God flowing through you.

the source of life

1 john 5:11 – 13

For with you is the fountain of life;
in your light we see light.
Psalm 36:9

God is the source of life. The alternative to communion with him is death. Genesis 2:7 tells us that when God had formed the first man from the dust of the earth, he breathed into him the breath of life, and the man lived. John says of Jesus, "In him was life, and that life was the light of men" (John 1:4). Peter, in speaking to the Jews of Jerusalem in the temple says, "You killed the author of life, but God raised him from the dead" (Acts 3:15). Jesus himself said, "I am the resurrection and the life . . . and whoever lives and believes in me will never die" (John 11:25–26). To his enemies, Jesus said, "You refuse to come to me to have life" (John 5:40).

Yes, God is the source of life. There is something in fellowship with him that overcomes death. Enoch is the prime example. Imagine the fellowship between God and Enoch; it was so intimate and precious that they would rather be together than apart, and so one day God simply took Enoch into his eternal presence. In a startling contrast to the sweetness of communion between Enoch and God, we find this verse in Ezekiel: "The soul who sins is the one who will die" (18:20). The sin is not the agent of destruction; death comes because the sin has caused separation from Life itself.

In our delusion we think that things have value in themselves—and that life has value in itself. The gifts of God are good, so we seek them. But the choice to seek his gifts rather than his presence is the addictive power of idolatry. Our earthly life is not more important than the One who is the source of life, and it should not rival him for importance in our attention or affection. When we separate life and time from Christ, even those good things become destructive and meaningless. When we turn from the Creator of life, we lose Life.

december 18

turn toward love

1 john 4:17 – 21

Dear friends, let us love one another, for love comes from God.
Everyone who loves has been born of God and knows God.
Whoever does not love does not know God, because God is love.
1 John 4:7–8

When we turn from God, we turn away from the ultimate source of all love. Among the religions of the world, Christianity alone says that love is not just something God does. It is what he is. God is love (1 John 4:8), and to turn from him is to turn away from the One who holds together all things. As a society becomes more secular, it inevitably becomes more violent and more alienated from itself. This may not be easy for many to see, but there is massive data to support it. The gel that binds things together is gone.

Biblically, love is caring more for another than we do for ourselves. It is love that continues even when it is not reciprocated. It is sacrificial love, extended even to enemies. And that love comes only from God. I am not speaking here about religion; religion can be as disruptive as any other force in life. I am speaking about God, who revealed himself in Jesus Christ and enabled Christ to love in such a way that he could pray for the men who crucified him: "Father, forgive them, for they do not know what they are doing" (Luke 23:34). When we turn our face from God, we turn our face from love.

Today when you hear the voice of love, turn toward him.

liquid gratitude

luke 15:11 – 32

*I tell you that in the same way there will be more rejoicing in heaven
over one sinner who repents than over ninety-nine
righteous persons who do not need to repent.*
Luke 15:7

I had the opportunity one day to hear my son Denny give his testimony. I'd never heard Denny make a speech in his life. I'll never forget how hesitant his opening words were. His head was down, almost as if he were embarrassed about it: "As most of you know, I grew up in a Christian home, a fairly good Christian home. It was in Wilmore, Kentucky. I learned about Christ very early in my life. When I was seven years of age, my mother prayed with me to receive Christ and I found him. I have very precious memories of the next two or three years of the presence of Christ in my life."

But he said, "As I began to approach that great chasm of inferiority, which we call adolescence, when my Adam's apple was entirely too big and my muscles not big enough, I began to put my thoughts on me instead of on Christ, and I found that he moved to the margin of my life. By the time I reached college, I was convinced that Christianity was simply one of the religions of the world. By the time I went to the university, I was priding myself on the fact that secretly I was an atheist."

He continued, "You see, I believed that when I entered the university, I would be with people who were free and open, but the disillusioning thing was to find that they were neither open nor free. I sat in a class one day when a professor ridiculed and made fun of a student who suggested that there might have been something more than the natural in the creation of the universe. I found that they had their own agendas and their own prejudices as well, and what they were trying to impart to me was a view of reality that fit neither what my family had taught me nor what I had myself already learned about the nature of life.

"So I began to move back to Christ, and Christ began to come back to me. Finally, I finished medical school and began my residency. I found that I could work thirty-six hours at a stretch without sleep, but I also found that when I didn't talk to Christ, he didn't talk to me. And he moved to the margin of my life again, and it left a big vacuum in the middle of my life, but vacuums are temporary. Before I knew it, appetites and desires moved in to take Christ's place in my life. And slowly it began to dawn on me that I didn't control them; they controlled me. I began to realize that unless God did a miracle in my life, I was done and done forever. So I had a day off, and I gave myself to fasting and prayer. I wouldn't recommend that to you unless you're ready for some changes."

He said, "It was just six weeks later that one of my partners slipped in surgery, his instrument penetrated my glove, and I found myself out of residency and sick in bed with a fatal form of hepatitis. I had plenty of time to read my Bible and pray. In fact, I didn't have anything else to do. I knew great pain, great discomfort, and great depression, but the strange thing is that, as I look back now, I don't remember any of that. All I remember is that in that time Jesus Christ came back to be the living reality at the center of my life, and the memory of his presence has erased all other memories.

"Then miraculously the Lord Jesus touched me and healed me. And when he healed me I thought he would give me a guarantee on tomorrow. But to my surprise he didn't, and that troubled me. So I asked him about it and he said to me, 'I didn't give the apostle Paul a guarantee on tomorrow, so why should I give you one?' I have come to believe that he does not give a personal guarantee to anybody on tomorrow, and that changed my way of living.

"I don't take anything for granted anymore. I don't take my wife for granted; I don't take my children for granted; I don't take my work for granted; I don't take a new day for granted. I don't take anything for granted anymore. Some mornings on the way to work, I find myself facing a morning sun just breaking over the horizon, and I discover that my cheeks are wet with liquid gratitude to God for a new day that he's given to me. It is his special gift of love for me to enjoy and to use for his glory.

"And you know, that's not a bad way to live."

Do you know the place where eternity meshes with time, and the two fuse into one? Living at this place gives life a richness that is only possible when we live with no guarantees but Jesus.

free to be sent

isaiah 6

"Woe to me!" I cried. "I am ruined! For I am a man of unclean lips,
and I live among a people of unclean lips,
and my eyes have seen the King, the LORD Almighty."
Isaiah 6:5

One of the great lessons of Scripture is in Isaiah 6, where Isaiah comes into the presence of God and is immediately overcome by his own sinfulness. Always when we are brought into the presence of God, we are made conscious of our sin. Our sin must be known if we are to know God. When we recognize our sin, God is free to cleanse our hearts. True fellowship with him is possible after this cleansing.

When Isaiah made his confession, a seraph took a live coal from the altar and placed it on Isaiah's lips to purge them. The word *seraphim* in Hebrew means "the burning ones." A burning coal held by a burning one was touched to Isaiah's lips. Fire is the necessary purifying agent in Scripture and in life. It speaks of God's holiness and of his cleansing power.

It is after that cleansing that Isaiah heard a voice saying, "Whom shall I send, and who will go for us?" (Isa. 6:8). The timing here is significant. Isaiah was not ready to hear a call from God before his cleansing took place. The moment he was cleansed, he heard God's voice speaking. Because Isaiah was clean, he could hear, and he could respond, "Here am I! Send me!" (Isa. 6:8).

If we have trouble hearing God's voice, his direction, and his call, it may be because our lives have not yet been touched by his fire.

december 21

a consuming fire

isaiah 6

Since we are receiving a kingdom that cannot be shaken,
let us be thankful, and so worship God acceptably with reverence
and awe, for our "God is a consuming fire."
Hebrews 12:28–29

What does the consuming fire symbolize? As we saw in yesterday's meditation, it can represent cleansing. Fire also symbolizes judgment. Remember Sodom and Gomorrah. When those cities turned their backs on God and lived in lasciviousness and sin of every type, fire came down from heaven to consume them. In Revelation we read that the end of those who reject God is a lake of fire that burns forever.

So fire can be seen in opposing ways by different people. To one it means death; to another it means life and purpose. To one it means separation from God; to another it means fellowship with God. To one it means eternal judgment; to another it means eternal bliss. What is this fire? It is God himself who is the consuming fire. If we are wedded to impurity, when we come face-to-face with him, he will consume us along with the corruption. But if we allow him to purify us, then when we meet him, we will experience incredibly sweet fellowship with him. His very fieriness is what gives us the promise of cleansing and freedom from sin.

To one, his presence destroys; to another, it cleanses. To both, it is an awesome and a fearful thing. God is the Holy One, and when we meet him, our sin must go. If it is more important to us to keep our sin than to let God purge us, the result is judgment. If we are willing to be purged, the end is redemptive.

december 22

is faithfulness possible?

hosea 2:19–20

I will betroth you in faithfulness, and you will acknowledge the LORD.
Hosea 2:20

I was in a serious conversation with a lovely young college student. "Dr. Kinlaw," she asked, "is it possible for a man to love one woman so much that he will be faithful to her all of his life?" The soberness with which she spoke gave evidence of the battle that was taking place in her soul with a precious dream. Was what she so desperately hoped for impossible to find? Was it unrealistic for her to dream of a lover who would choose her and give her his undivided heart until death would part them?

I was glad I could tell her that in Christ it really was possible for two human lovers to give themselves to each other in a commitment so deep that with his help it could be kept inviolate as long as they lived.

And then I thought of Jesus and his bride. Dare I think that he does not long for the same thing in us? Or dare I suppose that the sacrifice of Christ on Calvary and the gift of his divine Spirit are not adequate to unite my heart in devotion to him and to keep it united in that commitment? No! If my heart is not pure, nor my eye single, it is not because he cannot make it pure. It is because I will not let him even when he longs for my faithful devotion. Apparently this was what Charles Wesley was thinking about when he wrote

> *O for a heart to praise my God, a heart from sin set free,*
> *A heart that always feels Thy blood, so freely shed for me!*
> *A heart resigned, submissive, meek, my great Redeemer's throne;*
> *Where only Christ is heard to speak, where Jesus reigns alone;*
>
> *A heart in every thought renewed, and full of love divine;*
> *Perfect, and right, and pure, and good, a copy, Lord, of Thine!*

---

*Charles Wesley, "O for a Heart to Praise My God," *Hymns for Praise and Worship*, no. 350.

angel visits

matthew 1:18–25; 2:13–23

When Joseph woke up, he did what the angel of the Lord had commanded
him and took Mary home as his wife. But he had no union with her
until she gave birth to a son. And he gave him the name Jesus.
Matthew 1:24–25

I love the story of Joseph of Nazareth. All he wanted to know was the right thing to do. His girlfriend was pregnant, and it was not his baby. She said that an angel had appeared to her and told her that her child was from God. That explanation did not seem plausible, but she had never lied to him before; she had always been a model of purity. Now she was telling him that she was pregnant, and he faced a dilemma. If he believed her story, he might be cooperating in her evil. But if he denied her story and it was true, then he would be guilty of evil. What should he do?

At this point, an angel appeared with directions for Joseph. The angel told him to believe Mary and take her to be his wife. Angels do not usually visit humans, but at this crucial moment in history they entered our world in order to help righteous people differentiate the truth from a lie. We must be in communication with the One from outside of our world if we are ever to know what is right and what is wrong. It is no accident that modern America has nothing to say about ethics and truth because true ethics come from outside our space-time universe.

At two other times in Joseph's life, he received supernatural guidance when his only concern was the protection of his wife and her child. Could it be that the purpose of these stories is to let us know that there is no way we can be responsible for our family unless that we are in communication with heaven? At crucial points in each family's existence, divine counsel and guidance are needed to protect each member of the family. God provided direction to Joseph, and he will do the same for you.

the seekers of truth

matthew 2:1 – 12

After Jesus was born in Bethlehem in Judea, during the time of
King Herod, Magi from the east came to Jerusalem and asked,
"Where is the one who has been born king of the Jews?
We saw his star in the east and have come to worship him."
Matthew 2:1–2

I am glad that the wise men are included in the story of Jesus' birth. They legitimize for all ages those souls who seek for the truth. Those few who are looking for truth are actually seeking the True One. There is something within each heart that cries out for the key to all reality.

One day, a great musician sat down at the organ, weary and ill at ease. His fingers wandered idly over the keys, and as he played he hit a chord, a chord so wonderful that for him all of the perplexity of life was bound together and understood in one complete moment. He later said, "I have spent the rest of my life trying to find that chord again!"

The human heart longs for the key, and somehow or other we know that the key cannot be found in ourselves. Christ must be the center. He is the Truth. When hungry hearts come to Jesus, they will not simply find truth, they will find the Truth for all existence. He is the one chord that makes sense out of all the music of reality. He brings all the notes together and causes life to make sense and even to be beautiful.

When the wise men found the One for whom they sought, they worshiped him, falling on their knees and presenting him with gifts. The response of all seekers of truth who find him will be worship and adoration.

the most and
the least significant

Luke 2:8 – 21

The shepherds returned, glorifying and praising God for all the things they
had heard and seen, which were just as they had been told.
Luke 2:20

I have come to appreciate the story of the shepherds. I can hear those guys around their fire on that hillside after they had gathered all their sheep together for the night. They may have been saying, "Boy, this is a boring way to live. We will spend the rest of our lives out here instead of down in Jerusalem where things are happening. All we have out here are smelly sheep and shining stars."

All of a sudden a heavenly being breaks into their world of monotony with the best news that the world has ever heard. The angel declares that if they will run quickly into the city, they will see the One on whom all of history will depend. They will experience personally the greatest event of all time. Those shepherds turn in wonder to look at each other, and then suddenly a whole host of angels appears, singing. Before their song has ended, those shepherds are racing to a stable to see the One about whom prophets prophesied and saints dreamed.

There are moments for all believers when the eternal breaks into the normal routines of daily life—when God himself comes to visit us. On this holy day, are we anticipating his divine presence to break into our lives?

able to keep you

matthew 14:22–34

*To him who is able to keep you from falling and to present you before
his glorious presence without fault and with great joy—to the only God
our Savior be glory, majesty, power and authority, through Jesus Christ
our Lord, before all ages, now and forevermore! Amen.*
Jude 24–25

Do you believe that God is able to keep you as you begin a new year with
him? Do you believe that he is powerful enough not only to create the universe, but also to keep you from falling as you turn from the Christmas season to all that lies beyond in the next year? This year, perhaps this month,
you have made some headway with Jesus. You are walking closer with him
than you have at other times, and now you face a new year. Will you be the
kind of witness, blameless and winsome, that he has called you to be?

I remember attending camp meeting in my thirteenth summer and
committing my life to Christ. I will never forget saying to God as I got
ready to go back home, "I will gladly go to China in the morning instead
of North Carolina." It is infinitely easier to share Christ with people who
do not know you than it is to share him with those with whom you live
and work. Taking a stand and being obedient to Christ in places where
people know us and are watching us is so much more difficult. When I
returned home, it was marvelous for a while, and then I found myself dry-
ing up inside for lack of Christian nurture and fellowship. As the next
summer drew near, I found that I was dreading camp meeting because I
had become immersed in my own sin, pride, and self-will, and I didn't
know how to come back to Christ.

The promise from Scripture is, "Greater is He who is in you than he
who is in the world" (1 John 4:4 NASB). It is only our sinfulness that causes
us to fear, and when we fear we begin to sink and look at ourselves instead
of God. When we do that, we immediately know that there is no hope for
us; there is no way we can stand for Christ in our circumstances. The envi-
ronment is too difficult, the enemy too strong, the problems too great, the
obstacles too mountainous. When we have reached this point, we sink. But

if we can keep our eyes on Jesus, he is able to keep us from falling into sin or from sinking into despair.

Sixty-six years after that first camp meeting, I want to witness to the fact that God is able to keep us. We can walk into any circumstances joyously and courageously because the God whom we worship has the capacity to care for us.

there is no "no" in my heart

1 corinthians 1:18–31

All the promises of God find their Yes in him.
2 Corinthians 1:20 RSV

Have you ever stopped to think that God is smarter than you are? Now, I know you will tell me quickly that you know God is smarter than you are. But if you are honest with yourself, do you believe it? That has been a difficult lesson for me to learn. I struggled to believe not only that God was smarter than I was, but even that he was as smart as I was. Let me tell you the crux of the matter.

God looks at you and says, "I want you to take your hand off your life and let me put my hand on it. I want you to let me lead you, guide you, and direct you so you live your life the way I want you to instead of living it for yourself." And something inside of you wants to ask two questions. First of all, "God, where are you going to take me?" And second, "Do you know what will make me happy and fulfilled?"

Unless you are totally, fully, and completely yielded to God so that all that says no inside of you has been exchanged for one big yes to him and his will, you will begin to wonder if he is as smart as he claims to be. That nagging doubt in your mind about his goodness will prevent you from taking your hands off your life, and you will ruin your life by your own contaminating touch.

The truth is that God is smarter than I am, and he is smarter than you are. When he instructs us to go a certain way, it is because he sees the whole picture, and he knows what is best for us. We must come to the place where we look up into his face and say, "I cannot see as well as you can see. Will you lead me and guide me so that I do not hurt you, myself, or those whom I love? I will trust that you are wiser than I am, and I will obey even if the way you lead looks wrong to me."

Why don't you ask God today to exchange the "no" that still exists in your heart for the "yes" that exists in him? You will never be sorry if you trade all of you for all of God.

my best interest

Acts 16:6–10

Don't be deceived, my dear brothers. Every good and perfect gift is from above,
coming down from the Father of the heavenly lights,
who does not change like shifting shadows.
James 1:16–17

I have great sympathy for young people today. How well I understand the questions that come to their minds and hearts!

I can remember when God told me to break up with a young lady with whom I believed myself to be madly in love. And the devil said to me, "Well, that is what you should expect. If she is good-looking, and if she appeals to you, and if she is the kind that will really make you happy, you can count on it that God will not give her to you. He will give you some old religious girl in whom you have no interest."

I found myself wondering if that was true. Was God really good, and would he really give what would be best for me? It was a difficult area in which to trust him, but finally I said, "Lord, I know this is a very personal decision, and my happiness is intimately bound up in it. I also know that you love me and will not lead me in any way that will not be fully pleasant and joyous. I know that when you tell me no, it is not because you do not want me to be happy, but it is because you do not want me to regret any choices that I make. You are protecting me for my own well-being and my own happiness." Time has confirmed that his way was the best way.

Why is it so hard to trust him with our future, with our personal decisions, and with our lives? We usually submit to his will with tears of sorrow and remorse as if we offer some enormous sacrifice, but his will for us is good for us, and it is good for those we love. It usually takes a little time, but inevitably when we obey his direction, we look up and say, "Thank you, Father, for not letting me make a mistake."

Do you believe that he is good and that he has your well-being at heart?

a change of plans (part 1)

Acts 10

So if God gave them the same gift as he gave us, who believed
in the Lord Jesus Christ, who was I to think that I could oppose God?"
Acts 11:17

Recently a man who has had a great impact on my life was in the hospital, and I went to visit him. He told me about how he became a missionary. His mother was a very godly woman, and his father was a successful business-man. His father had every intention of turning his business over to his son, and he trained his son to take his place. The son had every intention of fol-lowing in his father's footsteps, and he was confident that he would have a successful start in life because he was building on his father's reputation and success.

After this man became a Christian, his mother went to a holiness prayer meeting, and God brought her to a place of full surrender. The Holy Spirit filled her, and she began to live with the mind of Christ. At this point she began to earnestly pray for her son, and the Lord began to say to her, "If your son becomes wholly mine, I may change the direction of his life, and he may not fulfill the family's plans for him in business." Finally, she sur-rendered to his will, and she continued to pray.

One night the son had to go and pick up his mother from the prayer meeting. He slid into the back of the church at the end of the service just as the leader said, "I believe there is someone here who knows Christ but has never fully surrendered, and God wants him to do it tonight. So I am going to take two chairs and use them for an altar. If you want to come and sur-render to him, you are welcome at this altar." The son hesitated, fearful of what full surrender would mean to his plans. But then the leader looked right at him and said, "Son, you are the one." So the young man went for-ward and surrendered all he was to the Lord Jesus.

During college, he traveled overseas with a singing group. He said, "When I reached Japan, I knew that I was to be a missionary; when I arrived in Korea, I knew that I was to serve in the Orient; and when I entered China, I knew that God had called me to China." The life of that man has blessed the world. He had no idea of what God wanted to do with his life, and he shrank from the uncertainty, but God has made him a missionary statesman because of his choice to surrender to the will of God.

Are you willing to do whatever God asks of you as you begin the new year? Or are you living in a state of continual frustration because of your own stubborn grip on life? Remember: God knows the job for which you were made. You can trust him.

a change of plans (part 2)

ephesians 3:14–21

*To know this love that surpasses knowledge—that you may be filled
to the measure of all the fullness of God.
Ephesians 3:19*

When a certain young man from Texas found Christ, God told him that he should get more education because he had something difficult for him to do. So he went to college, and there God talked to him about full surrender of his life to Christ. He accepted all that God had to offer, and God said to him, "I want you to serve me." So this man began doing evangelistic work. Eventually he went to seminary. He planned to go into Christian education, but one day God said to him, "I do not want you in this kind of Christian service."

He asked, "God, what do you want to do with my life then?"

"I want you in the business world," God said. And so God called him straight out of seminary and into the world of business. He and his wife founded an insurance company, and he became a pioneer in something that has been a source of security and blessing for many of us. Multitudes of people would be in great trouble if it were not for the fruit of that couple's labor. This man's life has been one of untold blessing to all the world.

God looked at a man headed for full-time Christian service and saw his genius for business, and he used those gifts in the arena where they would be most fruitful.

Would it not have been a tragedy if the would-be businessman who became a missionary had entered business and had spent his life embittered and cynical because he knew that he was made for something different? And what a tragedy it would have been if the would-be Christian worker had become a flop of a preacher because God had made him to use his gifts in the business world.

It is only our graspiness and groveling smallness that keeps us from looking up at a holy God who knows all things and saying, "God, you pull the strings in my life. When I put my hand back on my life, you rap my knuckles until I once again surrender to you so that you are in full control of my life and can make me what you want me to be and what I am destined to be."

hallelujah! praise god forever!

habakkuk 3:17 – 19

Yet I will rejoice in the LORD, I will be joyful in God my Savior.
Habakkuk 3:18

Once I had the privilege of taking an afternoon walk in the Helderberg Mountains with Norman Grubb, the son-in-law of C. T. Studd, a well-known missionary to Africa. Grubb had spent many years in the heart of Africa, working with his father-in-law. I had been deeply impressed with the biography of C. T. Studd, so I quizzed Grubb about him. One of his stories was unforgettable.

Studd and his missionary team lived deep enough in the interior of Africa that their mail only came every two weeks. Their existence depended on the money that was in that mail, so its arrival was always an event. C. T. Studd was master of ceremonies at the opening of the mail. He made it quite a ritual.

One fortnight there was a pleasing amount of money in the mail. Studd's comment was, "Bless God forever! He knows what a bunch of grumblers we are. He has sent us enough to keep us quiet." Another fortnight the amount was quite small. Studd's comment was, "Hallelujah! We must be growing in grace. He thinks we are learning to trust him." One fortnight there was nothing. Grubb said that the missionaries gathered around Studd waited, wondering what he would say. They were not disappointed. He lifted his voice in a shout, "Hallelujah! Praise God forever! We are in the kingdom already, for in the kingdom there is neither eating nor drinking, but righteousness, joy, and peace in the Holy Ghost."

Some would think Studd's faith was reckless. I suspect, though, that he had a special place in the heart of God because he dared to expect God to be faithful to his promises.

As you look back, can you see in your life the undeserved goodness of God? As you look forward, do you look with joyous anticipation? You should. His track record is very good!

Scripture Index